GEORGIAN CRAFTSMEN

AND THEIR WORK

Castle Howard, Yorks., Great Hall; scagliola niche. *c.* 1710.

GEORGIAN CRAFTSMEN

AND THEIR WORK

Geoffrey Beard

COUNTRY LIFE LIMITED LONDON

First published in 1966
by Country Life Limited
Tower House, Southampton Street, London W.C.2
Printed in Great Britain by
Billing & Sons Limited
Guildford and London

For

GEORGE HOWARD

who cares about it all

Castle Howard. York

'*Nobody . . . had informed me that I should at once see a palace, a town, a fortified city, temples in high places, woods being worthy of each a metropolis of the Druids, vales connected to other hills by other woods, the noblest lawn in the world fenced by half the horizon, and a mausoleum that would tempt one to be buried alive.*'

Horace Walpole to George Selwyn, 12th August, 1772.

Contents

List of Plates

ACKNOWLEDGMENTS FOR PHOTOGRAPHS

The following have kindly provided photographs, or given permission to reproduce them.

The Dowager Lady Aberconway, 60; G. W. Beard, 71–2; Bedale Rural District Council, 57; *Country Life*, 1, 2, 4, 5–7, 10, 12–14, 16, 19, 20–7, 30–8, 41–4, 46–8, 59, 61–3, 65–6, 73–5, 77–8, 81–6, 88–90, 94–104, 106, 108, 111, 114–17, 120–1, 122; Marquess of Exeter, 110; A. F. Kersting, 40, 49–53, 87, 91–3, 105, 107, 109, 118–19, 123; London County Council, Iveagh Bequest, 112–13; Paul Mellon Collection, 11; National Monuments Record, 3, 8–9, 17, 39, 45, 54–6, 64, 67–8, 76, 79–80; Royal Institute of British Architects, 68; E. H. Sargeant, 15; *The Yorkshire Post*, 67. Lord Cholmondeley gave permission for the National Monuments Record photographs of Houghton (39, 58) to be reproduced. The drawing of Castle Howard on p. 5 is by Felix Kelly.

Acknowledgments

Iᴛ has become fashionable of recent years to say that one is indebted to so many people that a list of their names is too long to print. Much of my work has been possible only through the kindness and long-suffering of others. I hope that they will feel this formal acknowledgment is backed by a full sense of my gratitude. They are, of course, not responsible for the use I have made of their researches. Firstly, four friends, Mr Howard Colvin, Mr Edward Croft-Murray, Mr John Harris and the late Rupert Gunnis, always provided me with references relevant to my work. I was also allowed to see the typescript of the second part of Mr Croft-Murray's definitive two-volume work, *Decorative Painting in England*. The few comments I have included, for completeness, on this subject owe much to his knowledge. I am also much indebted to the Leverhulme Trustees and the British Academy for travelling grants, and for certain leave of absence in 1959 to the Leeds Corporation Art Gallery and Temple Newsam House Committee, and the Director, Mr R. S. Rowe.

My further obligation divides neatly into two groups – to those owners who allowed me to see their houses and examine family documents, and to everyone who provided references and services of many kinds. In the first category I am indebted to the Duke of Devonshire; the Duke of Northumberland; the Marquess of Bath; the Marquess of Exeter; the Marquess of Lansdowne; the Earl of Aylesford; the late Earl of Bradford; the Earl of Coventry; the late Earl of Halifax; Viscount Cobham; Viscount Scarsdale; Sir Gyles Isham, Bt; Sir Richard Sykes, Bt; Sir William Worsley, Bt; Lord Brownlow; Lord Leigh; Lord Sandys; the late Sir Walter and Lady Blount; the Dowager Lady Aberconway; Lady Trevelyan; the Hon. Mrs Elizabeth Hervey-Bathurst; Colonel F. Lane-Fox; Mr Henry Vyner and Mr John Wyndham. Mr George and Lady Cecilia Howard and Miss E. M. Lawson-Tancred were most helpful on many visits to Castle Howard. Lady Trevelyan, Mrs Pauline Dower and Mr and Mrs Simon Towneley took me to houses I otherwise may not have known of, and Mrs E. Bissell helped to sort documents on many occasions at Enville.

In checking references, moving boxes, climbing ladders, taking photographs and providing clues my friends were all very diligent. The staffs of the Birmingham and Leeds Reference Libraries and the Barber Institute of the University of Birmingham gave willing and varied service over many years, for part of which time I was colleague as well as reader. In this connection I would thank Professor Ellis Waterhouse, Dr Kerry Downes; Mr Frank Simpson; Mr P. N. Allen; Mr A. Andrews, Miss D. McCulla; Miss D. M. Norris; Mr J. C. Sharp; Miss I. A. Wilson; Mr D. Wright; Mr M. Collinson; Mr A. Craven; Mr F. G. B. Hutchings and Mr H.

Nicholls. The staffs at the Brotherton Library, University of Leeds, the Guildhall Library, and in the Reading Room and Departments of Manuscripts and Prints and Drawings at the British Museum were similarly helpful. The senior officials and archivists of the London banks mentioned in the Bibliography allowed me to make many visits. Mr J. R. Cuthbertson (Drummonds); Mr S. W. Shelton (Glyn Mills); and Mr R. W. Winder (Hoare's) were ever helpful and knowledgeable.

This same attitude characterised the assistance given by many County Archivists and Record Office staffs, especially Mrs E. Berry (Shakespeare's Birthplace Trust); Miss M. Jancey (Herefordshire); Mr P. I. King (Northamptonshire); Mr E. H. Sargeant and Miss M. Henderson (Worcestershire); Mrs Joan Varley (Lincolnshire) and Mr Anthony Wood (Warwickshire). Mr F. S. Stych provided Italian translations and bibliographical references and Mr Miles Hadfield and Mr Michael Felmingham placed their specialist knowledge of many country houses and gardens at my disposal, a service which was provided by all members of the editorial and book production staff of *Country Life*. More especially this includes Mr John Adams, Mr Gordon Fairley, Mr Webster Evans, Mr F. Harden, Mr Christopher Hussey, Mr Arthur Oswald, Dr Mark Girouard and Mr John Cornforth. The late Gordon Nares, the late Miss Margaret Jourdain and the late Mrs M. I. Webb also gave me valuable references to manuscript materials.

For help of various kinds I wish to thank my wife, Margaret; Mr G. R. Batho; Miss G. M. A. Beck; Miss Elizabeth Brunskill; Mr J. Kenworthy Browne; Lady Dorothy Corry; Miss A. W. Cutler; Mr Richard Dell; Miss Jean English; Mr John Fleming; Mr J. Homery Folkes; Miss A. G. Foster; Mr Christopher Gilbert; Mr David Green; Mr S. A. Harris; Mr Hugh Honour; Mr Arthur Illes; Mr Edward Ingram; Mr Francis Johnson; Mr G. H. Kenyon; Dr Arnold Noach; Mr Derek Sherborn; Mr Damie Stillman; Miss Barbara Thompson; the Hon. Mrs F. Uhlmann; Miss M. Wight; Dr Peter Willis; Mr R. B. Wragg; and Mr Tom Wragg (Chatsworth). The Estate Office staffs at Alnwick, Belton, Bowood, Burghley, Harewood, Melbourne, Studley Royal and Wilton gave much practical assistance, and in particular Mr D. Bush and Mr C. Ford at the Compton Place Estate Office, Eastbourne cheerfully produced boxes of documents in difficult circumstances on three occasions.

My friends Mr Cecil Farthing (National Monuments Record) and Mr A. F. Kersting, F.R.P.S., provided many photographs for publication and research purposes. Dr Patrick Nuttgens, Dr Lindsay Boynton and Miss Mary Mauchline allowed me to lecture to specialist groups of their students at the Universities of York and Leeds, and The College, Ripon. I learned a great deal in their company. The same invaluable assistance in letter and conversation was always cheerfully given by Dr Eric Gee and Mr J. D. Williams of the York office of the Royal Commission on Historical Monuments. For my own part I found that the many visits I made with them to York houses and churches at all seasons of the year gave to me not only a little of their knowledge but a visual experience I shall long value.

G.W.B.

Introduction

IN writing this book I have many times been conscious of some words of Dr Samuel Johnson. 'It is impossible', he said, 'for an expositor not to write too little for some, and too much for others. He can judge what is necessary for his own experience, and how long soever he may deliberate will at last explain many lines which the learned will think impossible to be mistaken, and omit many for which the ignorant will want his help. These are censures merely relative and must be quietly endured.'

My aim is to give details about the life and work of eighteenth-century craftsmen, and in particular those who decorated in various ways the large country houses. I have said little about the decorative painters and sculptors – already, as the Bibliography indicates, the subject of learned study – but considerable attention is paid to plasterers, wood-carvers and workers in metal. I have tried to solve many problems and in a few cases have succeeded. In other instances there was, for lack of information, a miserable failure. It has not always been possible to weigh and assay every detail and evaluate it in the text – the patience of the reader would be sorely tested. I have tried to choose only what appears to me, from the evidence, to be close to the truth. Where there is need for care in attribution I have said so.

In the early years of the eighteenth century patrons were, for the most part, still breaking away from the pattern of Jacobean times. This was to work with a builder and books of instruction, and with the advice of knowledgeable friends.

'First resolve', said Sir Roger Pratt in 1660, 'with yourself what house will be answerable to your purse and estate, and after you have pitched upon the number of rooms and the dimensions of each, and desire in some measure to make use of whatsoever you have either observed, or heard to be excellent elsewhere, then if you are not able to handsomely contrive it yourself, get some ingenious gentleman who has seen much of that kind abroad and been somewhat versed in the best authors of architecture: viz. Palladio, Scamozzi, Serlio, etc., to do it for you . . .'[1] Towards the end of the seventeenth century this period of amateur competence had played itself in, but the splendours of interior decoration had changed little since the days of Inigo Jones.

In building a large country house in these years there came a time when a talented army of craftsmen, many of them foreign, were assembled by the patron and his advisors. Grinling Gibbons, Jonathan Maine and Edward Pearce were hard at wood and stone carving. Antonio Verrio, Louis Laguerre and Sir James Thornhill were embellishing almost every ceiling of

---

[1] R. T. Gunther, *The Architecture of Sir Roger Pratt*, 1928, pp. 60-1.

note, and the skilled decorative smith, Jean Tijou, was creating filigree patterns in wrought-iron. George London and Henry Wise were transforming or making gardens and bringing order and pattern with parterres and long vistas of fountains and canals. Leonard Knyff and Johannes Kip busied themselves with their perspective engravings, fulsome dedications and elevations of the 'great fine houses'. John Vanderbank inherited the traditions of the long-established tapestry manufacturers, and soon his exciting and colourful Soho chinoiseries were hanging over Thornton or Etty's sombre wainscoting. Dufresnoy and Francis Lapierre stretched their damasks and velvets over skilfully wrought wood and papier-mâché and erected the great 'State Beds' which still adorn houses like Belton and Chatsworth. Edward Goudge was the leading plasterer and, as the architect Captain William Winde told his cousin Lady Mary Bridgeman, 'is looked on as the beste master in England in his profession'. John Wilkes provided delicately wrought locks with elaborate mechanisms, and Thomas Tompion's clocks stood on ornate overmantels, surmounted by portraits of arrogant patrons by Kneller, Closterman, Riley and Van Dyck.

Craftsmen travelled extensively: out from York plasterers went north to Scotland and south to London in search of work and ideas. London craftsmen such as Edward Pearce the carver and Robert Bradbury and James Pettifer the plasterers came north to Sudbury in Derbyshire in 1676. Pearce carved the staircase and 'ye carved work in ye p'lour and ye 2 dore cases on ye top of ye great staires and the panel in ye staire head chamber'. Domination over the craftsman by a trade guild, while showing signs of decline, was yet strong in centres like London, York, Bristol and Chester.

The patron himself was often very discerning and knowledgeable. Robert Benson, Lord Bingley, who was to build at Bramham, Yorkshire, at the turn of the eighteenth century had made his Grand Tour and, full of ability, advised many owners, Lord Strafford and Lord Chandos among them, about their buildings. The third Earl of Carlisle, who was to employ Sir John Vanbrugh at Castle Howard in 1699, was a member of the fashionable Kit-Cat Club and had also been on a Grand Tour, probably meeting the great sculptor Bernini in Italy, and filling notebooks with comments on pictures, statues, books and curiosities he had seen. Thomas Osborne, first Duke of Leeds, was beginning to ponder over the building of Kiveton, which was being erected from 1694 to 1704, but regrettably was demolished, apart from the staircase, in 1812. He employed Thomas Young, the master joiner, who also worked at Burghley and Chatsworth, and the London joiner John Chaplin, a London plasterer, Henry Margetts, the Oxford carver, Jonathan Maine, the eminent French smith, Jean Tijou and his Derbyshire follower from Baslow, John Gardom. The French decorative painter Louis Laguerre contracted to provide 'four pannells' as by 'choice and approbation of the Duke of Leeds' and decorated the staircase and ceiling with scenes from the story of Cupid and Psyche.

While many of these craftsmen prepared their own designs it was the usual custom for the work to be measured, and then the costs agreed by the architect. William Winde was punctilious in this respect for, as he wrote in November, 1693, 'I finde without a dilligen inquiery & viewing of ye worke they will not finish their worke soe neatly as they ought to doe'. This concern by architect and patron was common throughout the eighteenth century, especially in commissions supervised by Robert Adam. It did not always produce good work, but craftsmen were forced to be competent and many improved their skills to the point of virtuosity. There was a general understanding (as Reynolds was to write of Vanbrugh) of light and shadow, 'of the conduct of the background, by which the design and invention is set off to the greatest advantage'. And if, halfway through a century typified by great learning and fine craftsmanship, but also by nauseating smells and bugs in bed or chair, a scribe in *The Connoisseur* could write that 'in this amazing super-abundancy of taste few can say what it really is . . . ' there were always those few who knew unerringly when it was absent. In the main these were the architects, and a few discerning patrons like the Duke of Northumberland (p. 82).

Work in the early years was dominated by the architects, and the families of mason-contractors such as the Ettys of York and the Patys of Bristol. Sir John Vanbrugh, Nicholas Hawksmoor, James Gibbs, Colin Campbell, Lord Burlington and William Kent were followed by hosts of active figures who grouped around Robert Adam, James Paine, Sir William Chambers, the Wyatt brothers and John Carr. Of recent years the careers of these architects and builders have been well studied. We know much about the careers of Vanbrugh and Hawksmoor, for example, and the part they played in creating houses such as Castle Howard and Blenheim.

The early work of the Scottish-born architect Colin Campbell, like that of Vanbrugh, was for influential patrons in Yorkshire, and, in London, for an important Yorkshire land-owner, the architect Earl of Burlington. Campbell came south in about 1712 and within three years published the first volume of his important source-book, *Vitruvius Britannicus*, which incorporated designs – as the title-page states – provided to him by other architects as well as those worked up by himself with parts drawn from Palladio originals. His own designs show a remarkable acquaintance at first hand with Palladio and there seems little reason to doubt that he was the 'Colinus Campbell, Scoticus' who passed through Padua on an Italian tour in the late years of the seventeenth century.

The relationships between Campbell and Lord Burlington, or his 'master' William Benson, Wren's successor as Surveyor of the King's Works, are not easy to define. Surviving accounts at Chatsworth show the help he gave to Lord Burlington with the building of Burlington House, Piccadilly. What emerges throughout this period is the pre-eminence of Campbell and the Palladian style of architecture. His great mansion, Wanstead in Essex, erected in 1715 for the banker Richard Child, was being copied twenty years later at Wentworth Woodhouse, Nostell Priory, and Prior Park, Bath. The three volumes of his book were widely subscribed for, and Dr Lindsay Boyton and I have recently traced many of the original drawings.

It is easy in writing of the erection of a great country house to forget the part played in its creation by the owner and the craftsmen, and also factors such as the amenities of the site and the accessibility of materials. There is a natural inclination to say that it was 'built' by, for example, Vanbrugh or Robert Adam. These phrases, however, need to be modified to 'style of Vanbrugh or Adam' if we know little of the architect or craftsmen. This is true of the career of the 'gentleman-architect, William Wakefield of Huby Hall, Easingwold, Yorkshire'. It is not known when or where he was born, and, together with his wife and son, he comes mainly to our notice by the record of his burial.[1] The York historian Francis Drake, writing in *Eboracum* in 1736, says that at St Michael-le-Belfry, York, 'lies also, as yet without any memorial, that worthy gentleman, William Wakefield, Esquire, whose great skill in architecture will always be commended, as long as the houses of Duncombe Park and Gilling Castle shall stand'. Despite the fact that he was a Vanbrugh follower, and had the assistance of the Etty family (who worked for Vanbrugh, Hawksmoor, Campbell, and on their own account) he could still be considered old-fashioned if contrasted against Lord Burlington and his protégés, or Robert Adam and his 'regiment of artificers'. He is an example of one of whom we would wish to know much more.

Burlington and his life-long friend William Kent had met in Italy and returned to England together for the Christmas of 1719. Kent was given apartments at Burlington House, worked for his friend on the decoration of his house at Chiswick and after an eventful and varied career – he was architect, decorative painter and landscape gardener – was laid to rest in the Burlington family vault at Chiswick. He worked alongside the Italian stuccoists at houses such as Ditchley, but it has not been possible to find much about his relationships with craftsmen working under him, although we know many of their names. There is nothing so 'anonymous' as a well-carved lime-wood festoon or doorcase in a Kent-style house with no surviving documentation to show its precise date and price.

Their 'styles' were to characterise most of the decoration until the advent of Robert Adam in 1760. The Adam brothers enveloped everything with the cloying mantle of neo-classicism fashionable to the end of the century. Horace Walpole protested that he did not mean 'to make (his) house so Gothic as to exclude convenience and modern refinements in luxury', but modern observers, while admiring, may well have cause to think that he and others fell into the trap of doing just that. I hope, however, it may be felt that an epitaph, bereft of laudatory Latin, has been written for the craftsmen who created these whims, or altered to fancy and to satisfy the Great Goddess, Taste. In Horace Walpole's words on Grinling Gibbons, 'if these encomiums are exaggerated, the works are extant to contradict me'.

[1] St Michael-le-Belfry, York, 28th April, 1730 (Yorks. Parish Register Soc., Vol. XI).

PART ONE

The Age of Orders

1700—1760

'By the time your Lordship returns I hope my little building will be advanc'd so far as for one to be able to make a guess what appearance it will have; & if it shou'd be such an one as is displeasing to your Lordship I shall pull it down with more satisfaction than I carry it up. . . '.

James Brydges, first Duke of Chandos, to Robert Benson, Lord Bingley, 3rd September, 1719.

I

The Virtuosi of York

THE eighteenth century has in recent years given rise to many epithets when its architecture, decoration or literature are discussed. The Age of Reason, Elegance, Enlightenment, the Golden Age and the Augustan Age are a few of the familiar phrases. They are used in an attempt, however unsuccessful, to give credit to a period and a system of patronage which allowed architects and craftsmen to create for their clients buildings and decorations which have rarely been surpassed. Groups of artisans, such as those centred on York, worked hard to satisfy the urges to build – 'all the world is running Mad after building as far as they can reach . . .' Sir John Vanbrugh wrote in 1708 to the first Duke of Manchester. Twelve or so years later he was still able to write from Yorkshire to Brigadier Watkins that 'here are several gentlemen in these parts of the world that are possess'd with the Spirit of Building'.

The activities of York craftsmen divide fairly readily into three or four chronological divisions. A steady trend of artisan work from the 1670s to the turn of the eighteenth century, a vast reaching out in the Vanbrugh period to the late 1730s, a continuance of interior decoration in particular in the Palladian and rococo styles to the late 1750s, and then the domination at houses like Harewood, Newby, Sledmere, and Everingham of the style of neo-classicism imposed by Robert Adam, and to a greater degree in the north by John Carr, the York architect. York itself relied for its supplies on the East Riding ports and in particular Hull. Prior to the eighteenth century the needs of economy and the difficulty of transporting heavy materials led all but the very wealthy to use local materials. But by the time Sir Robert Walpole was having Houghton built in the 1720s Aislaby stone from Whitby was being sent by ship down the coast. It was this same water transport which made it feasible to obtain building materials from abroad – bricks from the Netherlands and timber from North Germany and the Baltic countries came in huge quantities to the port.

The Hull Port records at the Public Record Office date from 1706 onwards, and the inwards and outwards schedules of goods are useful in tracing this trade. For example, the Christmas 1705–6 schedules show oak planks, spruce deals, paving stones, linen, flax, iron, deals, pitch, coming in, and the outwards trade – mainly to Norway, Rotterdam, Amsterdam, Bremen, Gothenberg – consisted of malt, lead, woollen goods, red lead, leather and wine. In addition the coastal trade was extensive and King's Lynn and Newcastle were served. In 1722 china, looking-glasses, upholstery, marble, perfumes, oilmen's colours, wine, iron and copper wares, clock cases, glass, pewter, and chairs were coming in. At Bristol[1] it was a similar story with

[1] W. E. Minchinton, 'The Trade of Bristol in the XVIIIth Century, *Bristol Record Society*, Vol. XX, 1957.

240 ships arriving there from ports outside Britain in 1700 alone. By 1787 the number had risen to 485. Cedar planking was coming from South Carolina[1] and in 1754 one ship of fifty-five tons brought in 20,000 feet of mahogany. In 1723 Isaac Hobhouse reported that 'we have on board seventy three thousand feet of pine boards at 3.10.0 a thousand'. The building fever was at its peak, even if the South Sea Bubble disasters had slowed matters in certain directions and for certain people.

York had always been an important building centre with a Company and Fellowship of Carpenters which started in York in the reign of Edward IV. In the 1573–1688 *Register of Apprentices*[2] there were fifty-two Carpenters and seventy-five Joyners, and in the eighteenth century among the comb-makers, translators, saddlers, pewterers, silk weavers and brass founders some 358 joiners were admitted to the freedom together with twenty-three carvers, fourteen upholsterers and sixty-five cabinet-makers. Contrast this with the fact that only about seven plasterers appear in the same period and one has reason to think their activities merited examination as a monopoly. The vigorous hold of the plasterers guild had relaxed from the strictness of the Elizabethan ordinances[3] which asked them 'not to talk disorderly in any place' and 'to leave apprentices and not to take them from their masters'. Principally activities revolved around the Etty family and in the first few years of the century – until his death in 1721 – around the talented joiner William Thornton.

James Etty provides a convenient start to a confused genealogical muddle; he was a carpenter, free by 1629 and dying in 1664. His son John was born in 1634 and by the time of his death on 28th January, 1708–9, had earned enough fame for it to be stated on his monument at All Saints Church, North Street, York, that he had 'acquired great knowledge of mathematics, especially geometry and architecture in all its parts far beyond any of his contemporaries in this City'. He would be the Etty building for the Duke of Buckingham at Helmsley in 1665–6,[4] and the one to show the young Grinling Gibbons around York in about 1667 when he first came to England. Seven years later he was rebuilding the west wing at Temple Newsam House, Leeds, for Sir Arthur Ingram and some idea of the importance of his connections is given by Sir Christopher Wren writing to him[5] in April, 1688, to thank him for his 'description of the palace at Berwick which is very full and satisfactory'. His best known piece of carving is in St Michael-le-Belfry, York (Figs 8–9).

John Etty's son William had an even more successful patronage and before his death in 1734 was to be Vanbrugh's clerk of works at Seaton Delaval and Castle Howard, to be associated with the gentleman architect William Wakefield,[6] and with Colin Campbell at Baldersby

[1] Timber imports, P.R.O., C.O. 390/5, 27, 38.

[2] York Reference Library. *Registers of Apprentice Indentures* commence in 1461. D12 is for 1573–1688, D13–15 cover the eighteenth century, but there is a gap from 1688 to 1721.

[3] York Minster Library MS, BB/5.

[4] East Riding Record Office, Beverley. Forbes Adam MSS (DD/FA/2/39), letter of 9th January, 1665–6, from Brian Fairfax to Sir Henry Thompson.

[5] *Wren Society*, Vol. XVIII, p. 68.

[6] Mr Derek Sherborn has drawn my attention to letters from Lord Langdale's agent, William Martin,

Park. When he died the architect Hawksmoor wrote on 6th July, 1734, to Lord Carlisle to recommend 'young Mr. Etty' – another William – 'for he is sober, carefull, ingenious and industrious, I hope he is honest, and as he was bread up in ye way of Building under his father, he may be of use to you'. It cannot be emphasised too strongly that, while documentation may often be lacking, the names most likely to appear in connection with the building and decoration of Vanbrugh type houses near to York are of various members of the Etty family[1]. The successful York plasterer, Thomas Perritt (1710–59) was thinking of more than love when he married Ann Etty at York Minster on 8th December, 1739.

A glimpse of William Etty's busy life is afforded in the Harford letters referred to below. William Martin writes on 23rd November, 1724: 'I was then with Mr. Etty to get a draught for the Beuvel which I have been duning him for betimes. . . . He had Drawn a Draught but being in London in Easter weeke where he was in Hopes to see something that might be newer fashoned and better desired me to defarr writeing to yr Lordshipp till his returne.' And again on 24th April, 1727, Martin writes: 'Sam Sidall [p. 55] left Mr Etty about two yeares agoe and falne into verry good Bussiness as Master Builder, if he be in or about York, I believe I Cann get him to draw the Planns according to your Lordshipps directions, for a Giney & one half. . . . If he be not verry full in Buseness perhaps I may Bargin with him for less; however when I have Lordshipp's further orders I shall gett it drawn as cheap as posable I Can . . . I doubt Mr Etty would expect more . . . and besides he is verry Apt to delay . . .'

But despite the delay and expense, Etty's business thrived as befitted Sir John Vanbrugh's clerk of works. Apart from Marmaduke Woolbran, he also took John Seppington as an apprentice in 1724 and saw to it, as a subscriber, that James Gibbs's *A Book of Architecture*, 1728, found its way to his and presumably many other York work-tables.

In 1724 he was working at the Mansion House in York, the design of which from time to time has been credited to Lord Burlington. If, however, we bear in mind that Francis Drake, the York historian, in his *Eboracum* (1736) mentions only one house (the Assembly Rooms[2]) in his dedication to Lord Burlington and that there is no mention of him in the House Books, Chamberlain's Accounts,[3] or in Drake's fuller description in the text of his book, it is difficult to believe the ascription. Whatever the truth, Etty helped the joiner John

---

in which the collaboration of Wakefield and William Etty is recorded at a house at Holme-on-Spalding Moor, Yorkshire, and Wakefield's 'goeing into Lincolneshire' is noted (East Riding Record Office, Beverley, Harford Holme MSS, DDHA 14/25, 26).

[1] Leeds Reference Library, Temple Newsam, Correspondence 1719. William Etty writing to Arthur Ingram, 2nd February, 1719, details his work at Barrowby Hall, 2m. N.E. of Temple Newsam, and describes halls he had designed for 'Mr Tankred and another for Mr Pelham.' The correspondence is useful for detailing Etty's methods.

[2] Rudolf Wittkower, 'Burlington and his Work in York' in *Studies in Architectural History*, ed. W. A. Singleton, 1954, pp. 47–61.

[3] York Reference Library. It is also significant to note that Lord Burlington was made a freeman of York in September, 1732, one month after the opening of the Assembly Rooms.

Terry, the painter-stainer William Midgley, the plasterer Richard Nelthorne, the carver Henry Thrisk and the carpenter Matthew Rayson in enriching the house which was complete enough by 31st August, 1726, for the first celebration, a 'Lady's Feast', to be held. Throughout their lives John and William Etty had lived up to the maxim of T.N., who in his *The City and Country Purchase and Builder's Dictionary . . .* (1703) had said: 'the drawing of Draughts is most commonly the work of a Surveyor, tho' there be many Master workmen that will contrive a Building, and draw a Draught, or Design thereof, as well as most (and better than some) Surveyors.' Indeed Etty was very capable of doing this as we shall see in his work for the Robinson family.

One useful art he practised was estate layout, and in 1710 he was to start the arrangement of the East Avenue ponds and bridge at Temple Newsam, Leeds, surveying, preparing plans and visiting the site – indeed anticipating the landscaping movements soon to be so active under Charles Bridgeman,[1] William Kent, and later Brown and Repton. The Studley Royal archives[2] also indicate his presence as clerk of works to Colin Campbell when he was building Baldersby Park for the Robinson family. When he died, in 1734, Nicholas Hawksmoor, attending as best he could to the progress of the Castle Howard Mausoleum from distant London, wrote to Lord Carlisle: 'I am very much concerned to hear of the Death of Mr Etty, his loss will be felt by his family more than by anybody else, but as he was a usefull man to the World they will almost certainly miss him . . . ' Hawksmoor had cause to remember that Etty had proposed sixteen pillars for the colonnade of the Mausoleum, whereas he preferred and provided twenty.

The other bright luminary in the York circle at this time was William Thornton, the joiner. Recent research has established him as a very important figure in Georgian work in the north (p. 48). He was born in 1670, probably in or near York. No record of his apprenticeship survives. Suffice it to say that by the date of his will, made four days before he died in 1721, he had made sufficient name and fortune to have shares in Derbyshire lead mines and to be able to provide in good measure for his wife Ann and his seven children. He lived in 'St Marygate, without the walls of the City of York', within sight of St Olave's Church where he was buried.

The York historian Francis Drake describes him in *Eboracum* as a 'joyner and architect' and says that 'by the ablest judges in the former kind of work, he was look'd upon as the best artist in *England;* and for architecture, his reparation of Beverley Minster ought to give him a lasting memorial'. Geldart's engravings of 1730 show what a complicated job this 'reparation' was. The north gable of the Great Transept hung four feet beyond its base and was brought back into its place by means of a timber framing. The engraving, entitled *A Section of the Trusses and Building*, says: 'When the Trusses were fixed on both sides the wall was cut to ye Center at Q level with ye base of the S^d. Trusses, that it might give way upon ye raising ye whole Machinery & so come into its place & was in ye mean time supported by several wedges

---

[1] I found it very useful in studying houses of this period to read the text of Mr Peter Willis's Ph.D. thesis (University of Cambridge) on Charles Bridgeman.

[2] Leeds Reference Library. G. W. Beard, *Country Life*, 10th August 1961.

which were gradually taken out as ye Building came back into its place.' This was in 1716, the year in which a tread-mill crane was erected in the roof – probably of Thornton's invention. One wonders if, under the overall supervision of Nicholas Hawksmoor (who surveyed the Minster in 1713) and with City churches in mind, it was Thornton who was the author of the very elaborate font-cover, one of the finest in the country? The programme of Minster repair and restoration had unfortunate financial beginnings. 'One of the "undertakers" charged by the Trustees with the collection on the Royal brief absconded and the matter became the subject of special appeal in 1706 by John Moyser to Robert Harley.' John Moyser was Member of Parliament for Beverley at this time and a leading figure in organising the restoration scheme. He kept a keen eye on the proceedings and in 1720 found it necessary to state that he intended to give the Corporation 'some trouble' if, as he thought, they had misappropriated the specially raised funds. The accounts were prepared for examination by the Archbishop of York, but a satisfactory outcome seems to have emerged.[1]

Moyser, who was on friendly terms with Lord Burlington, seems to have counted architecture among his polite accomplishments and there is reason to think that he may have provided the plan for Nostell Priory, Yorkshire (1733), and that the youthful James Paine was working to his instructions. He died in 1738, but his son James, who also dabbled in architecture, survived him.

Work in Beverley among influential patrons brought Thornton to the notice of the architect Colin Campbell and to the Hotham family for whom Campbell was building a Beverley town house. But within a few years Campbell was to turn away from York men like Thornton and the plasterer John Bagnall and employ Italian plasterers, or *stuccatori*, and the Master Carver to the Crown, James Richards.

It has been fashionable in recent years to talk of regional 'schools' of plasterers centred in such cities as York, Bristol and Norwich. My reading of the *York Apprenticeship Registers* for the first eighty years of the eighteenth century suggests that there was no such organisation in the north; the structure was less rigid and dominated by a few names only. It is significant that the important London plasterer Isaac Mansfield (p. 168), who worked on occasion for James Gibbs, and for Vanbrugh at Blenheim and Castle Howard, settled at York in 1704 and was Mayor in 1728-9. He must surely have influenced the York plasterer Thomas Perritt (1710-59), who, after training under his father Jonathan, a well-known York bricklayer, developed an extensive patronage (p. 59) in Yorkshire. He took as his apprentice in 1738 Joseph Rose, senior (*c.* 1723-80), uncle of the better known Joseph Rose, junior (1745-99), who worked with his family extensively and almost exclusively for Robert Adam (p. 70). Joseph Cortese had a good northern connection in the 1740-70 period. He worked for the York architect John Carr and was perhaps the senior partner to Carr's favourite, James Henderson of York. Henderson acted as executor when Cortese died in 1778.

The available records suggest therefore that the majority of important plasterwork in

---

[1] *Beverley Corporation Minute Books*, 1707-1835, ed. K. A. Macmahon (Yorks. Arch. Soc., Record Series, CXXII, 1958), p. xiii.

Yorkshire up to the 1740s, if not given to Londoners, was entrusted to Mansfield, Perritt, or the Italian Cortese.

At Bristol, the second largest port in England in the early eighteenth century, the plastering at this time was probably largely in the hands of Joseph Thomas (*fl.* 1730–77), and John Griffin, who worked at the Exchange designed by John Wood the elder. The south-west, of course, had a strong naturalistic style, and in North Devon the Abbott family were still flourishing in the reign of George I, in the person of John Abbott (1639–1727).

A strong rococo feeling finds expression in the East Riding of Yorkshire in the vicinity of Hull, and while there are few plasterers listed in the Lists of Freemen, the early ordinances of trade guilds at Hull and York survive.

II

The Italian Plasterers

PLASTERWORK in early eighteenth-century England was, however, largely the work of Italians.

The two best-known names concerned with this form of decoration are those of Giovanni Bagutti and Giuseppe Artari, who worked principally for the architect James Gibbs. He used them, for example, at St Martin-in-the-Fields and the Senate House at Cambridge.

It has often been assumed that Gibbs was responsible for their introduction to England, but this seems to have little foundation in fact. Gibbs was certainly in Italy, and in particular Rome, from 1703 to 1708, but Artari was not born (at Arogno in Italian Switzerland) until 1697 and as far as we know Gibbs did not employ either stuccoist until the 1720s. Bagutti in any case was in England working at Castle Howard (p. 46) before 1710.

There seems little doubt that the Italian *stuccatori* in England worked on many occasions as partners. Indeed it may not be unreasonable to suggest that in the early years at least they were in partnership. Bagutti was certainly in the ascendancy over Artari. The evidence for this is available. When working at Moulsham Hall, Essex, for Lord Mildmay in 1731 it is noted, when a payment of £161 8s. was made, that 'my agreamt. was only with Mr Bagutti, & Mr Altari who did the Bustos & Figures assisted him'. In a list of the family assembled in James Brydges' house at Canons on New Year's Day, 1722, is 'Mr Bagutti, his Partner, Mr Artree'. They may have also worked at another Chandos house, The Mynde, near Hereford. As partners they seem to have stayed together until a little after 1730. I have traced no later work than their collaboration at Moulsham Hall.

This 'partnership' cannot, of course, have been an exclusive one, because among the receipts for the plastering at Ditchley, Oxfordshire, 1724–27, 'Francesco Vassally' and 'Giuseppe Artari' both sign for various sums of money for work done 'by me and my partners'. The Ditchley accounts,[1] which also list work done by the third 'partner', Francesco Serena, are most interesting. It is made clear that the payments to them were 'by the hand of Francis Smith' and that both Artari and his father, who worked at Sutton Scarsdale, were there in 1725. Payments are made to 'the two Mr Artares', Giovanni and his better known son Giuseppe.

After this important commission, which is well documented, the vexed question of the plasterwork at Stoneleigh Abbey must be carefully examined in discussing the craftsmen working for the Warwick architect, Francis Smith (1672–1738). After the fire of 1694 at Warwick, Smith found much work in the town including the rebuilding of the nave and tower

---

[1] Oxford County Record Office, Dillon MSS. See p. 188 for the plasterwork account of 1726.

of St Mary's Church to the designs of Sir William Wilson. In 1702 he married a local girl, Anne Lea, served as Mayor in 1713–14 and again in 1728–9. Smith probably designed Umberslade Hall, Warwickshire, for Andrew Archer and was employed by the Duke of Shrewsbury at Heythrop, Oxfordshire. But the first house he was certainly connected with was that started in 1714 at Stoneleigh, Warwickshire, for Edward, third Lord Leigh. Indeed Smith's activities were now to become so extensive that, as late as 1784, when the architect had been dead almost fifty years, the Hon. Daines Barrington wrote to the Rev. William Norris, Secretary of the Society of Antiquaries: 'there was a Smith of Warwick who between 60 and 70 years ago was employed by many gentlemen in this neighbourhood, in building their Mansion houses, several of which I have seen, and all of them convenient and handsome'.

At Stoneleigh Smith created the north wing which happily harmonises with the older parts of the house. A draft of his agreement survives, but we know little of the craftsmen he used for the interior decoration of this house of the 1720s. The Birmingham locksmith John Wilkes (?–1733) worked there as he did at Sutton Scarsdale. Regrettably, Lord Leigh's bank account is not one of the eight of various members of the family preserved at Child's Bank. The Saloon contains excellent plasterwork (fortunately hardly damaged by a fire in May, 1960) which Mrs K. A. Esdaile suggested[1] might be by the Anglo-Danish plasterer Charles Stanley (1703–61), but which, for various reasons, I believe is by the Italians.

There is no immediate evidence to suggest that Francis Smith ever used Stanley, and he had been dead six years when his son William Smith worked under Gibbs and with Stanley at the Radcliffe Camera, Oxford. Both Stanley and Artari submitted estimates in 1742 for the plasterwork at the Radcliffe Camera. Gibbs gave Artari the main commission. This I realise leaves the plasterwork at Stoneleigh without a definite attribution, although it is surely work by the Italians.

For tidiness the name of Giovanni Battista Cipriani (1727–85) as the 'plasterer' at Stoneleigh must be mentioned and dismissed in this context. Among the Leigh archives at Shakespeare's Birthplace Trust, Stratford-upon-Avon, is a record (No 53) in the Auditor's Accounts of a receipt dated 5th April, 1765, which reads:

Paid Mr Cipriani for eight designs for the

Hall at Stoneleigh.   £8. 8. –.

It is my belief that Cipriani, who became an important decorative painter (p. 85) in the Robert Adam period, submitted designs for paintings or bas-reliefs which were never executed. This receipt has not only acted as a deterrent to believing the Stoneleigh plasterwork to date from Smith's period, but has caused writers to credit the plasterwork to Cipriani. He did not come to this country until 1758 and was only a decorative painter with a long list of such work to his credit.

The Francis Smith house we could ill afford to lose was Sutton Scarsdale, Derbyshire. Lying only a mile or two from the dramatically sited Bolsover Castle and near to Chesterfield, it is surrounded by open-cast coal mines and survives only as ruin. Sacheverell Sitwell

---

[1] *Country Life*, 2nd October and 11th December, 1937.

has recorded how he visited the house in about 1920 and found the Venetian saloons deserted, with crumbling rococo plasterwork and cracked ceilings. Smith was employed by Nicholas, Lord Scarsdale, 'a dilettante of distinction' and an Ambassador to Venice.

An inscription on a lead plaque[1] recorded that 'this house was begun to be rebuilt in the year 1724 by the order of the Right Honourable Nicholas, Earl of Scarsdale. Francis Smith of Warwick, gentleman architect; Edward Poynton of Nottingham, gentleman carver; Thomas Broval of Warwick, gentleman joiner; Francis Butcher of Duckmanton, carpenter; Albert Artari, gentleman and Francis Vessali, gentleman, Italians, who did stuke work; Joshua Reading of Derby, gentleman painter; Joshua Needham of Derby, gentleman plasterer; John Wilks of Birmingham, gentleman locksmith; John Lillyman, gentleman steward; John Christian, gentleman gardener; John Nott, gentleman keeper'. No documents survive to tell us more. We are a little luckier with one of Vassalli's northern commissions for a letter from him and the bills survive.[2] It concerns his work at Towneley Hall near Burnley which was decorated for Richard Towneley in 1729–30. An assistant named Martino Quadry was in attendance The letter in Italian which is poor by modern standards (and linguistically may indicate a Neapolitan origin for Vassalli) reads, in translation:

> Most Respected Sir
>
> Having written a letter to you during the past month of July to which I have received no reply, I do not know to what I should attribute the reason for this &c. Perhaps you are dissatisfied with me for not having finished your hall before this time. Wherefore, if the reason lies here, I am very glad that it is within my power to win back your favour, in that, since I have been in Italy, it is in my power to satisfy you more than I could have done before I returned into Italy. I hope you have procured everything for the completion of the above-mentioned work, for, at the beginning of February I shall be at Towneley to finish all, and in everything which you may condescend to require of me you will find me ever ready to execute your most esteemed orders. At present I am at Aske near Richmond in Yorkshire, the hall of which I have decorated with 5 rooms, the hall *c.* 47 feet in length, and 30 broad, *c.* 30 high.
>
> I conclude by subscribing myself always
> Your most humble servant
> Fran: Vassalli
> Aske the 7th [?] day of December 1730

Presumably Vassalli was studying and obtaining engravings while in Italy which allowed him to think 'that since I have been in Italy it is in my power to satisfy you more than I could have done before I returned into Italy . . .'. His account shows that he charged £126 for the Hall (Fig. 54) and £21 for the 'ornaments on the stairs'. The letter was written from Aske Hall,

[1] The text is given by H. M. Colvin, *A Biographical Dictionary of British Architects, 1660–1840* (1954). I tried in 1959 to trace the plaque, without success.
[2] Lancashire County Record Office, Towneley MSS (DDTO/Q10).

near Richmond. Unfortunately Vassalli's work there has not survived, but his Towneley work suggests that he may also have worked at Knowsley in Lancaster at the Music Pavilion in Sun Street, and at Lumley Castle, near Durham[1] (Fig. 42). In 1736 he was working at Castle Howard where, against opposition from Artari, he was commissioned to do the stucco and scagliola decoration in the Temple of the Four Winds for which he received £141 15s. In later years (1758–63) he was at Hagley and Croome Court in Worcestershire, and Shugborough in Staffordshire. He was living near Shugborough in 1763, but I have not traced his death.

In these years of the seventeen-thirties the architect Giacomo Leoni, who had played so important a part in the literary aspects of the Palladian movement, fell on hard times. His bank account (at Drummonds) contained only £275 in 1739 and before his death in 1746 he was in part supported by Lord Fitzwalter. Many of his houses have been altered, rebuilt or demolished and it is perhaps at Clandon, Surrey, that we see his style most completely. In the Great Hall (Figs 50–52) he allowed the Italian *stuccatori* to take full command. The complexity of the Hall ceiling can surely only be the creation of Bagutti, if we ignore for a moment the unknown 'Germans' who worked at Compton Place, Eastbourne (p. 33), and the enigmatic Franchini brothers. As Leoni used Artari and Bagutti at Moulsham it is reasonable to think they were both at Clandon, Artari again doing the 'Bustos and figures'.

The Hall at Clandon is further enhanced by two fine chimney-pieces by the sculptor Rysbrack. It is assumed[2] they were in position by 1729 and were probably worked by Rysbrack himself. Both the reliefs are free copies of antiques, the small model for one of them being at Stourhead. Leoni's adherence to proportion – he had issued his edition of *Palladio* in 1715 – is commemorated in the Palladio room with its gilt mirrors, the full-length portrait of Elizabeth Knight (probably from Kneller's studio), and the French flock wall-paper. There is another elaborate ceiling (Fig. 53) surmounting splendid doors, but again no exact documentation.

At Knowsley, Lancashire, there was a Stucco Room which has largely disappeared. The wooden doorways are dated 1733, but the craftsmen are unknown, and the Derby bank account (at Drummonds) does not commence until 1736. The 'New Building' accounts at the Lancashire Record Office only extend from 1718 to 1729 and there is a break in the sequence from that time until 1754. The portion of Knowsley visible from the forecourt was probably complete by 1722 and it may well be that the tenth Earl of Derby did not employ an architect and that Edward Litherland, a Liverpool mason-contractor, built it to the Earl's designs. The double colonnaded south (garden) front dates from 1731 to 1737 and this appears to be by a skilled professional architect. Giacomo Leoni may have been involved as the front has similarities with two plates (III and XXXVIII) in the first volume of his edition of *Palladio*. There is only one plasterer, Robert Gill, mentioned in the 1718 to 1729 accounts, and wainscoting was done by Edward Guy, John Wattson and Henry Taylor, presumably all Liverpool men.

---

[1] W. Howitt, *Remarkable Places* (1842), Vol. 2, pp. 143, 197, says 'two Italians came over on purpose to do the room for Lord Richard Lumley'.

[2] M. I. Webb, *Michael Rysbrack*, 1954, pp. 130–1.

Any consideration of stucco decoration of this period must allow for the activities of the Franchini brothers, Paul and Philip, and for Charles Stanley. The two Franchinis are usually credited, with little foundation in fact, with the ceiling of St Mary's Chapel, Queen Square, Bath, which was demolished about 1875, and the staircase of No 15, Queen Square, the house John Wood the elder built for himself in about 1730. It has been suggested that they did the stucco-work at Moor Park, Hertfordshire (Figs 36–37), but this attribution allows no consideration of the drawing in the Gibbs collection at the Ashmolean Museum (iv, 24), endorsed 'For Mr Baguti at More Parke near Rickmansworth in Hertfordshire'.[1] Admittedly the house was probably designed by Giacomo Leoni, who is known to have used them (some say Sir James Thornhill, but the elevations are little to his 'style'), and not by Gibbs.[2] The Irish work of the brothers (the ceiling at Carton, for example) provides ample evidence of their skill.

The Franchini brothers were probably introduced to Ireland by Lord Burlington, and one of them was still at work there in 1759. It would, however, be true to say (even more so than in the case of the other Italian *stuccatori*) that exact details about the work of the Franchini brothers in England have still to be discovered.

We must now return to Colin Campbell and his employment of the Danish plasterer Charles Stanley. In these later years of his life he worked for Lord Wilmington at Compton Place, Eastbourne, and again used, as he had done at Burlington House, the master-carver in wood, James Richards, and foreign plasterers.

An account-book kept by Sir Spencer Compton is in existence and was quoted by H. Avray Tipping in the 1916 *Country Life* account of Compton Place. I have re-examined this account-book and many other documents at the Estate Office not previously available. Richards and his men were employed until 1731, when he received the balance of his bill for £290. The fine work in the Gallery, Dining Room, Library and Great Staircase are all presumably his and antedate his work by a year or so on the Royal Barge (1732), designed by William Kent for Frederick, Prince of Wales. Sir Spencer was incidentally a trusted adviser of George, Prince of Wales, and, on his accession in 1727, was pressed to replace Walpole as Prime Minister. As Campbell died in 1729 it may well be that Richards was engaged by Sir Spencer rather than Campbell. William Kent later used Richards for carving at the Horse Guards and at Lord Pelham's house at 17, Arlington Street, London.

English houses, as the illustrations here show, are rich in plaster decoration, but few can surpass Compton Place. The State Bedroom ceiling in particular is one of the most opulent examples in England. In a Danish biography of Charles Stanley, written by A. F. Busching in 1757, it is stated that he worked in England for almost twenty years (1727–46), 'and . . . with fame for My lord Willnington in Eastbourne, Sussex, and for My lord Maynard in Essex . . .'. In view of the fact that Stanley signed the monuments to Thomas Maynard at Hoxne, Suffolk,

---

[1] The drawing is for one of the small rooms and is, strictly speaking, for the four walls and the cove of the ceiling.

[2] There are small payments to the Franchinis in 1726 and 1731 in James Gibbs's bank account (Drummonds Bank).

and to the Maynard family at Little Easton, Essex, Mrs Esdaile assumed in 1937 that Stanley must have executed 'sculptures' for Lord Wilmington. Finding no relevant monument or portrait bust, she thought that Stanley was responsible for the elaborate plaster ceilings, which indeed in terms of relief are almost 'sculptured'. I think, however, that the evidence now available warrants more caution in attributing the work to Stanley alone.

Stanley was born in Copenhagen on 12th December, 1703, and in 1718 was apprenticed to the Danish stuccoist Sturmberg, assisting him on ceilings (1721–22) at Fredensborg Castle. After further study in Amsterdam under Jan Van Luchtern, he left in 1727 for England and was soon working with the sculptors Peter Scheemakers and Laurent Delveaux.[1] Instead of leaving for Italy with his two friends and the painter Pieter Angellis, he stayed to work at Eastbourne and it is here that the story becomes a little more involved.

The main ceiling at Compton Place (Fig. 44) depicts in bold relief the *amours* of Venus and Adonis, and two small reliefs show Paris, and Helen and Diana with Endymion. In the border, with its sphinx-like figures, modelled *putti* and elaborate shells and foliage, richness abounds, but the dominant impression is the centre panel. Venus has alighted from a shell-like coach drawn by fluttering birds. All around are the swirling modelled clouds, which Mrs Esdaile suggested were Stanley's most recognisable characteristic, but which appear in work by most of the Italians.[2]

Both Mr Tipping and Mrs Esdaile were only able to examine Lord Compton's account-book, which mentions the 'plasterers' collectively. My examination of this account-book, together with an extensive series of correspondence and vouchers, proves certainly that Stanley was not solely responsible for the plasterwork. On four occasions the letters to Lord Wilmington from his gardener William Stuart are helpful and show that 'German plasterers' working under a London plasterer were used.

> April 8, 1728 . . . Mr Hewes ye Plaster'r was here Satterday last & thinks of sending some of his men shortly to worke.

This refers to John Hughes of London who did the plasterwork at Burlington House and, as Stuart makes clear, employed, in addition to English workers, three German plasterers.

> July 14 . . . The German plasterers are gon from Bourn (Eastbourne) today, to Coll fains[3] . . .

[1] Stanley did two monuments in Denmark *c.* 1749–50 based on designs of Delveaux and Scheemakers. The best recent accounts of Stanley are those by Ogveke Helsted in *Weilbachs Kunstler lexikon*, III, 1952, pp. 262–4, and R. Gunnis, *Dictionary of British Sculptors*, 1954. For the work of Italian stuccoists in Denmark see Bibliography (p. 200) under *Grandjean, B. L.*

[2] Bagutti and Artari's ceiling at St Martin-in-the-Fields, London, 1725, for example.

[3] Presumably Mereworth, Kent, built by Colin Campbell for Colonel John Fane, later seventh Earl of Westmorland. The main plasterwork here is by Giovanni Bagutti. The 'Germans' probably provided enrichments to Francesco Sleter's decorative paintings (Fig. 49).

The Italian Plasterers

August 11 . . . Mr Hughes's men & ye Plasterers are all gon . . .

Mr Tipping noted the text of a letter of 3rd June, 1728, from Thomas Willard, the steward, which he had sent to Lord Wilmington. ' . . . the Plasterers have bin at work sometime last weeke they had a flight to London on p'tence they wanted to gett some tooles. They Return'd last night. I have paid them subsistence money . . . '

I have traced the statements of this subsistence money and an account of the materials used among the accounts and vouchers which the steward preserved. They show that from October, 1728, to October, 1729, John Hughes was paid £211 16s. Five guineas of this was paid to Hughes's 'servant', Richard Taylor, 'for three Germans p. order Mr Hewes'. The materials included five bags of hair and sixty bundles of laths brought from Hastings and more hair and laths came from London.

The following conclusions may be drawn from the Eastbourne documents and the Danish biography by Busching: (*a*) no payment occurs to Stanley throughout Lord Wilmington's personal account-book in which payments to the woodcarver (James Richards) and other craftsmen appear: (*b*) if Stanley did work there he would have to be one of the 'three German' plasterers working under Hughes, and in consequence cannot be given sole credit for the plasterwork: (*c*) some connection, as yet untraced, existed between Lord Wilmington and Stanley (as the Danish biography records) because the marriage of Charles Stanley and Anne Allen is recorded on 21st May, 1730, in the Parish Registers of Old St Mary's Church, Eastbourne. Busching recorded that Lord Wilmington paid Stanley so well for his work that he could afford to marry his Eastbourne landlady's daughter.

The other letters from Stuart enable a chronology to be fixed when certain parts of the house were plastered. Plain plasterwork was started in November, 1728. By 19th May of the following year the decorative plasterers were working on the Gallery ceiling and in early June on the Great Staircase. At the end of July the 'German workers' left and by the middle of August, 1729, most of the plastering was complete.

On the strength of a statement in volume 3 of Neale's *Seats* . . . (1823) – 'Saloon, Alto Relievo in Stucco, Stanley' – the plasterwork in the saloon at Langley Park, Norfolk, is regarded as Stanley's work. He is said to have worked at Barnsley Park, Gloucestershire, Hall Place, Maidenhead, Honington Hall, Warwickshire, Easton Neston, Northamptonshire, and at Stratton Park, Hampshire, which was destroyed in 1790. It should be said that all these are merely attributions. Mrs Esdaile thought he was responsible for the plasterwork at Kirtlington Park, Oxfordshire, and this seems possible. He certainly worked at Okeover, Staffordshire, and with Thomas Roberts at the Radcliffe Camera, Oxford, and it is fair to assume, bearing in mind his residence of twenty years in England and the fact that only two monuments are known from his hand, that stucco work, possibly at many of the houses noted above, formed a chief occupation with him. (Figs 46–48).

Barnsley Park lies near to Cirencester on the road to Bibury. It was built in 1720–1 for Henry Perrot, a Member of Parliament for Oxford, and a frequenter of the circle of friends surrounding James Brydges, 1st Duke of Chandos. The house seems to have been complete by 1731 and was possibly designed by John Price (?–1736), although the evidence, or lack of it, allows many other alternatives.

Price was architect-builder to the Duke of Chandos in 1720–1 and these dates appear on rain-water heads at Barnsley Park. There is also a resemblance between the house and Price's elevation for Canons. At Canons the Duke employed many stuccoists including Bagutti, Artari and Serena. The general design and decoration of the hall (Figs 43, 47) at Barnsley portends the work of Gibbs in such a house as Ragley twenty years later.

There were few stuccoists in England at this period, other than the Italians and the mysterious 'Germans' we have noted at Compton Place, skilled enough to produce such convincing results, and Rudder's *Gloucestershire* (1779) says that the ceilings are 'by the best Italian Masters'. Need we therefore regard Stanley as the plasterer at Barnsley as Mrs Esdaile suggested? It is true that the treatment of clouds in the ceilings at Compton Place, Hall Place, Maidenhead, and Barnsley Park is similar and almost identical chimney-pieces (Figs 46–47) are in the last two houses, and this fact has led some writers to assume that Stanley worked at both houses. Mrs Esdaile, however, pointed out[1] in reviewing a book which illustrated the Barnsley chimney-piece as Stanley's work that it was certainly 'by a sculptor-plasterer trained in the London tradition of canopy work and curtain, laureate medallion and volute, such as one finds on a hundred monuments from London masons between 1690 and 1730. The Hall Place chimney-piece is by the same hand, and the design rendered more effective by the dark background of some of the principal features; from neither of his masters, Sturmberg or Scheemakers, did Stanley derive details such as these.' I feel the Italians rather than Stanley must be credited with the work.

In 1742 Charles Stanley was working with the Oxford plasterer Thomas Roberts at the Radcliffe Camera, Oxford, under the supervision of William Smith. It is this fact and a connection here suggested which may allow that together they were responsible for the stucco decoration of nearby Kirtlington Park, built by William Smith to the designs of John Sanderson.

The building of Kirtlington was begun in April, 1742. Sir James Dashwood succeeded his grandfather in 1734 at the age of nineteen. Indeed he heard of his succession on the Grand Tour. In 1738 he married Elizabeth Spencer, but it was not until August, 1746, that his house was sufficiently well advanced for Sir James and his family to move in. The architecture and decoration of Kirtlington have occupied several writers[2] and I need only add fragments from Sir James's unpublished eighteenth-century bank account (p. 192). This acts as an analysis of the building accounts; neither source, however, mentions the plasterers and they presumably worked to a sub-contract. Seventeen payments were made of 'William Smith's accot' between 23rd October, 1742, and 24th December, 1746, totalling £5,370. A payment of £186 was made to Henry Cheere on 1st July, 1745, presumably for chimney-pieces.

[1] *Country Life*, 28th September, 1940, p. 283.
[2] *Country Life*, 13th April, 1912; James Townsend, *The Oxfordshire Dashwoods*, 1922; Christopher Hussey, *English Country Houses, Early Georgian*, 1955.

In the Kirtlington accounts payments are made to the architect John Sanderson and together with 'Smith' he is credited with the design in Woolfe and Gandon's *Vitruvius Britannicus* (1767). Some letters from a Joseph Sanderson, probably a relative, which mention Stanley were written to Leak Okeover of Okeover Hall, Staffordshire, and are preserved at the house.

2nd June, 1745. 'Mr Stanley . . . the week after next is to meet Ld. Maynard to conclude a design of a marble monument to his late brother.'

16th October, 1746. 'I was informed that our friend Stanley had gone off . . . However I got scent of him, but could not see him till this evening when he made over a large sum due to him for Mr Barrington.'

25th October, 1746. 'Stanley went last Saturday on shipboard without any formal leave of his friends . . . he was never so civil to let me see either the busts or chimneypiece.'

9th December, 1746. 'One thing we must allow of him [Stanley] is your ceiling is well done and cheap.'

These valuable references show that Joseph Sanderson and Stanley were well acquainted, that the plasterer worked at Okeover, and that the Kirtlington plasterwork and that at Stratton Place, Hampshire (a house which John Sanderson remodelled) may be attributed to him.

The Dining Room from Kirtlington was acquired by the Metropolitan Museum of Art, New York, in 1931 and installed there as a period room in 1955. 'It was removed from the house in nearly two hundred and fifty sections with the old laths and timber attached. For the better part of a year a team of ornamental plasterers were employed in preparing these sections for installation. This involved the removal of the ornament, section by section, from the laths and timbers, from which in the course of the years it had often become detached to a hazardous degree. It was then reapplied to a new background of wire lath and steel armatures. The restoration of such breakage as had inevitably occurred in transportation was next undertaken, after which the sections were hoisted into place and firmly fastened to the ceiling and walls. The narrow cracks between the different sections were then filled in. Since the woodwork had been previously installed, the flat plastering of the walls was next in order and finally the laying of the original floor of wide parallel oak boards.'[1]

The plaster medallions in the Library at Kirtlington, as at Nuthall Temple, Nottinghamshire (demolished in 1929), and at Heythrop are subjects from *Aesop's Fables*. Those at Kirtlington are based on engravings by Francis Barlow. In 1778 Mrs Lybbe Powys said the work at Heythrop was by 'the famous Roberts of Oxford' and it seems therefore possible that Thomas Roberts worked at all these three houses using his Aesop medallions, and that he probably learned his craft (bearing in mind his collaboration with Stanley at the Radcliffe Camera) from the enigmatic Dane.

The architect of the Radcliffe Camera, James Gibbs, tells of different ways to adorn ceilings in plaster, and gives three examples in his *A Book of Architecture* published in 1728. 'One with large square panels, another with large octagon panels, a third with large octagons and rhombs,

---

[1] Metropolitan Museum, *Bulletin*, March, 1956.

all with roses in the middle of their panels and bordered with fret and guilochis.' The classical theme and mythological representation were of course the main features of plasterwork by the Italian *stuccatori* and their English counterparts. At Holkham in Norfolk the London plasterer Thomas Clark 'with great accuracy followed the antique manner'. The entablature in the Drawing Room is modelled after the frieze of the portico of the Temple of Antoninus and Faustina at Rome. Preoccupation with Roman pattern was to become as important, if not more so, a few years later when Robert Adam came on the scene.

III

Iron and Paint

IRON

WHILE the decorative workers in iron contributed less to a house than the plasterers, their activities enhanced staircases, balconies, and gave fitting and dignified approaches through huge gates with coats of arms in the overthrow. The principal worker in the first few years of the century was Jean Tijou. His first recorded appearance in England was in 1689 when he was working at Hampton Court, the great house he was to work at, on and off, until 1700. He alternated work here with commissions under Wren at St Paul's, and went out to Chatsworth, Burghley, Stoneyhurst, Ampthill and Kiveton. He published his *A new Booke of Drawings* . . . in 1693[1] and, as was the case with other publications in the latter part of the century, it had a considerable improving effect. Tijou left England in about 1712; in November, 1712, Mrs Tijou was paid £109 'in full of my Lord's note for the Iron Balusters and Railes for the staire case made by her Husband'. This was probably payment for the work carried out at Ampthill for Lord Ashburnham in 1706–7.[2]

Tijou stated on the title-page of his book that he hoped it would be used by 'them that will worke Iron in Perfection and with Art' and his influence can be traced in many workers, such as Robert Davies, Robert Bakewell, John Gardom and Thomas Robinson. In a casual footnote to an 'Estimate of Works to bee done att Kiveton, Aug. 3rd, 1699[3], we read 'ther is a man yt will make very good Ironworke, lives near Chirk, nr Rth [Ruthin] yt wrought with Tishan, ye French Smith, a Longe time'. Tijou had worked at Kiveton and this note refers to Robert Davies whose use of eagle heads and masks particularly in the Chirk Castle gates (dated 1719) is similar to Tijou's work at Hampton Court. Recent research[4] into Davies's career shows that he worked gates of an elaborate kind for 5d. a lb. Perhaps the finest works by Robert Davies are the White Gates and Screen at Leeswold, Mold (Fig. 24). 'Its hundred foot length consists of a series of broken pediments, with solid cornices.' Each section has the

---

[1] The title page was designed by the decorative painter Louis Laguerre, who married Tijou's daughter Eleanor (Edward Croft-Murray, *Decorative Painting in England, 1530–1837*, 1962, Vol. 1, p. 250).

[2] *Survey of London*, Vol. XXIX, 1960, p. 85, citing Ashburnham MS, 3000, 4190, East Sussex Record Office. The architect William Winde advised the owner and Laguerre (paintings), Tijou (ironwork) and Symms (joinery) were some of the craftsmen used.

[3] Yorkshire Arch. Soc. Library, Duke of Leeds MSS, Box 35.

[4] Ifor Edwards, 'Robert Davies of Croes Foel', *Denbighs Hist. Soc. Trans.* VI, 1957; 'Art in Iron', *ibid.*, XII, 1963; *Country Life*, 27th September, 1962.

Wynne dolphin in the centre, with the cupolas of the piers bearing vases of flowers. They take their place among the finest pieces of ironwork in Europe and were probably erected in 1726–7 for Sir George Wynne, who is notable more for his patronage of Richard Wilson and of leading the sort of life Hogarth was to satirise in *The Rake's Progress.*

It is not known whether Davies worked with the Derby smith Robert Bakewell (1685–1752), or whether Bakewell himself had any connection with Tijou. The earliest recorded mentions of him seem to be in the Castle Donington registers and rent rolls of the Melbourne estate in Derbyshire. The Coke property extended into Leicestershire and the rolls for 'Donington' – presumably Castle Donington – contain the names of Robert, Thomas and John Bakewell from 1707 onwards.[1] This town is only a few miles from Melbourne and Staunton Harold where there is work (Figs 21–22) by this talented Midland smith. Indeed the Iron Arbour (Fig. 21) at Melbourne is his best-known work. In my search of the archives for information it is clear that it was finished by late 1707–8. There is a note in the Coke correspondence[2] of 29th February, 1707–8, saying the 'Ironwork is done'. Henry Green was to pave it with 'ye Park Stone at 3d p. foot' and John Thorp of Bakewell (principally a marble-worker, p. 181) was asked 'to line Inside of ye Brickwork of ye Iron Arbour with flatt pilasters and slabs of ye Grey marble'. This is no longer to be seen.

It is difficult to trace how much Bakewell was paid for the arbour: £130 has been suggested.[3] Documents I have seen – particularly Elizabeth Coke's account book – show that Bakewell was working there for many years, although, when Elizabeth wrote to her brother Thomas on 3rd March, 1710–11,[4] she said, 'I hasten Mr Bakewell with the finishing your work for his behaviour is not to be born with in respect to this place which is bad enough of itself but I will not be tedious in perticulars . . .'. A few years previously, in an undated letter[5] – probably of 1708 – to her brother she says:

> Mr Bakewell has finisht your work of the arbor and has not brought in any account of this last but sais when you have seen it he will referr himself to you, so if you would have him make an Estimate please to lett me know, he has had twelve pound odd money in Iron of Mr fossbrook, which must be stop't I believe in your payment, as also five pound due from Bakewell to Mr hardinge upon the parish acount, he has gott a shop fitting up at derby but is so miserable poor that I believe he cannt remove till he has some money so as farr as five pound I have promised to lett him have till I hear from you to leave him without excuse in goeing, he has just sent home a very noble piece of work for my lord Gore, and is further ingaged in work for my lord Chesterfield, & my lord ferrers has lately sent to him also, so I have been unwilling to press him goeing to expose him so much, since his lively hood depends on it. . . .

[1] For biographical details of Bakewell see p. 173. [2] Melbourne, Coke Correspondence, Parcel 96.
[3] *Country Life*, 12th April, 1913, p. 580. [4] *Ibid.*, Parcel 97.
[5] M. Ayrton and A. Silcock, *Wrought Iron and its Decorative Use*, 1929, p. 130, reproduced in facsimile.

There has been little reason over the years to quarrel with the generally accepted lists[1] of Bakewell's work, but a few additions can be made. The smith had early worked under James Gibbs in providing the Chancel Screen and Gates (*c.* 1724) at All Saints Church, Derby, and twenty years later (1744–6) he worked for the architect again in doing seven ornamental gates to fill the outer arcades at the Radcliffe Camera, Oxford. At Okeover, Staffordshire, Bakewell, assisted by his pupil Benjamin Yates, did the Entrance Gates and other work (some now destroyed), receiving £451. The Okeover gates are partly based on plates in Gibbs's *A Book of Architecture*, and the house archives[2] record payments over many years.

Bakewell died in 1752. Three years previously, the Reverend Rowland Cotton, writing on 6th December, 1749, to his friend Charles Lyttelton, then Dean of Exeter, said that he had been trying, such was the antiquarian enthusiasm of the day, to get a drawing of the Norman west door of Tutbury Church, Staffordshire. He tells Lyttelton, 'I apply'd first to Bakewell famous all over England for Ironwork & who drawes to perfection, but he declined it, I believe upon account of his Eyes which begin to fail him . . .'.[3]

While work in North Wales was dominated by the Davies brothers and that in the Midlands by Robert Bakewell, there were many other workers. Francis Foljamb provided the gates at Arbury Hall, Warwickshire. His contract[4] of 3rd August, 1719, reads: 'It is agreed between Sʳ Richard Newdigate and Francis Foljamb of Nottingham that the said Francis Foljamb is to make two pair of Iron Gates the height ten foot to open and twelve foot wide, the Main barrs inch and half: the Small barrs 3 qrs of an inch with Sir R.N's Coat of Armes and Crest, with Locks and Bolts with a proper Scroll at each side the gates for fifty-five pounds. He the sd. Mr Foljamb to allow the said Sʳ. Richard Newdigate after the rate of Sixteen Shillings a hundred for all his old Iron and the sd. Foljamb to bring and Set the sd. Gates up at Arbury at his own proper cost to be according to the Draft with Sʳ R. Newdigates name over it . . .

'It is further agreed between the partys within named that the sd Mr Foljamb shall make the Iron work about the Altar in the Chapel at Arbury two foot four inches high from the Wainscott to the return to be three foot Eight inches the front Six foot 5 inches for five guineas and half ½ guiney for Carriage and leave All Iron.'

It is interesting how a precise contract of this kind can wreak havoc with previous attributions. Starkie Gardner writing in 1911 in his book on Wrought Ironwork says (p. 230) that the Arbury Gates 'may be Robinson's work . . . although they correspond in some details with Edney's work'. These are the London smith Thomas Robinson and the Bristol smith William Edney. Ayrton and Silcock in their book (1929) say that probably one of Wren's 'London smiths made the gates'.

---

[1] *Ibid.*, p. 129; K. Mantell, *Derbyshire Countryside*, July–September, 1951; *Country Life*, 27th September, 1962; M. Whiffen, *Stuart and Georgian Churches outside London*, 1947, pp. 33, 95.

[2] Okeover Archives, Bills, Vol. I, ff. 3–5; *Country Life*, 23rd and 30th January, 12th and 19th March, 1964; 21st January, 1965.

[3] G. W. Beard, *Country Life*, 2nd May, 1952, p. 1338.

[4] Warwickshire County Record Office, Newdigate MSS B2418.

The fact that there was more than one member of a family at work in the same trade also leads to confusion. The fine gates at St Mary Redcliffe, Bristol, dated about 1710, are by William Edney. I assume that this Edney, who was made a free burgess of Bristol on 18th December, 1706,[1] was the son or brother of the Simon Edney who was working in 1694 to provide the 'iron rails before the hous' at Dyrham, a few miles from Bristol. William's gates at St Mary Redcliffe were originally made in 1710 to separate the nave and chancel. He received £110 for the work. William Edney, who may have been responsible for gates at St Nicholas and the Temple Church in Bristol (the churches, but not the ironwork, were destroyed in the Second World War), has been credited with the gates at Tewkesbury Abbey. We have seen, however, by the Arbury example that attributions, while necessary, are often easily upset.

A worker in the Tijou style in the north Midlands was John Gardom of Baslow in Derbyshire. He worked with Tijou at Chatsworth and at Kiveton and was also employed at Castle Howard. Other workers included the Paris family of Warwick which worked under Sir William Wilson in providing ironwork at St Mary's Church, Warwick, which was being restored after the fire of 1694. The original plan had been to employ Birmingham smiths, but the Paris family claimed that as natives of the town they were entitled to do the work. They were to receive '£1.12.6d for every hundred weight . . . for all the Ironwork of ye Church and Tower'. It may well be that gates at Ragley Hall, and St John's House, Warwick, are by them. They did work for the Leigh family at Stoneleigh and turned their hand to making and mending clocks, pistols and fire-engines.[2]

Research on the makers of ironwork has yet told us little of their lives. We know nothing of Joshua Lord who provided the entrance gates and side wickets to Burley-on-the-Hill, Rutland; or of Bell of Sheffield who did the staircase balustrades (Fig. 20) at Vanbrugh's Grimsthorpe Castle, Lincolnshire. John and Thomas Warren are recorded or suggested for a few commissions;[3] but iron gates and staircase balusters as a form of decoration were to die away for a time. In interior decoration the joiner and the carver now held the day until Robert Adam gave employment to such metal-workers as Thomas Tilston, Robert Blockley and William Kinman.

DECORATIVE PAINTING

The fashions which had been set by Charles II at Windsor attracted many artists, by impulse or invitation, to England.[4] One such was the Italian painter Antonio Verrio (1634?–1707).

---

[1] W. Ison, *Georgian Buildings of Bristol*, 1952, p. 33.

[2] *Transactions* Birmingham Archaeol. Soc., Vol LXV, 1949, pp. 22–6; Vol. LIX, pp. 72–3, records work at the Court House, Warwick, by Thomas Paris and Benjamin Taylor.

[3] Warren: Denham Place, Bucks, 1692; possibly at Belton, Lincs; gates at Trinity and Clare Colleges, Cambridge (1713–14). J. Harris, *Records of Bucks.*, XVI (1957–8), p. 196. Robinson did the gates at New College, Oxford (1711). He worked for Tijou at St Paul's and had a yard at Hyde Park Corner (Ayrton and Silcock, *op. cit.*, p. 90). He is noted as 'that ingenious Artist' by John Ayliffe in *The Antient . . . State of the University of Oxford*, 1714.

[4] Fully examined by Edward Croft-Murray, *Decorative Painting in England, 1537–1837*, Vol. I, 1962.

His work at Windsor, Hampton Court and Burghley House shows him as a leading exponent in forms of baroque painted decoration. He worked with a large party of craftsmen including a colour-grinder, gilder, flower-painter, and architectural painter. While Burghley House contains all that is the best and most spectacular in Verrio's work, he was by then beginning to feel his age. He worked intermittently at Windsor until 1702, but as a force in the eighteenth century he is hardly to be reckoned. His eyesight began to fail and he retired shortly after 1704 on a royal pension and died at his house at Hampton Court on 15th June, 1707.

Apart from Verrio the other notable foreign painter of this period at work in England was the Frenchman Louis Laguerre (1663–1721), one of Verrio's early assistants. He worked on many royal commissions, at Chatsworth and at Burghley in 1698. Captain Winde, writing to Lady Mary Bridgeman on 2nd July, 1698, says: 'Mr Lager is gon in to ye Northe, withe ye Earl of Exeter'. He was explaining the delays which prevented Laguerre from painting the overmantels and staircase ceiling at Castle Bromwich Hall, Warwickshire. At Verrio's death Laguerre became the foremost historical and decorative painter and his talents were early used by the Duke of Chandos at Canons – said to be the original of Alexander Pope's Timon's villa 'where sprawl the saints of Verrio and Laguerre' – for the Duke of Marlborough at Blenheim, and at Petworth for the sixth Duke of Somerset. At Blenheim Laguerre succeeded Sir James Thornhill (p. 142), who had been dismissed by the Duchess for, in her view, excessive charges. The lofty colonnades are crowded with painted figures, Laguerre among them, but it was his last important commission. He died on 20th April, 1721, and at his death the leadership of the decorative painters which had come to him from Verrio – and against which Thornhill was partly protected by influential patronage – passed to lesser hands.

Gerard Lanscroon (*fl.* 1677–1737) probably came to England with his father, a wood-carver, who worked at Chatsworth. He worked under Verrio, but is best known for his staircases at Burley-on-the-Hill, Rutland (*c.* 1700), Powis Castle, Montgomeryshire (1705), and Drayton House, Northamptonshire (1712). The French decorative artists who worked at Montagu House in the late seventeenth century included James Parmentier, a high-spirited mediocre worker. Vertue says he was encouraged to come to London from Yorkshire at Laguerre's death. He notes that the staircase at Worksop Manor (1709) was his best work. A modern critic has indicated that his altar piece at Hull representing the 'Lord's Supper, which he made a present of in gratification and acknowledgment to that town . . .', is deplorable. He died in London in 1730.

Decorative painting was conceived usually in mythological terms. Its techniques were not very complex, being usually confined to distemper or oil on plaster, panels or canvas, and fresco. This is a method of painting with water-colours on freshly laid plaster while it remains wet. The colours mingle and on drying the whole presents a durable surface. Archaeological excavation has revealed good examples and Michelangelo and Raphael worked in the medium.

Care in preparation characterised good work and care in giving exact instruction was usually evident. In October, 1698, Captain Winde asked Lady Bridgeman to indicate 'what sune does comm in to lighten ye window, weather North, South, West, etc, that so I may inform him [Laguerre] to give the proper shadow to his picture to make it looke the moore butifull when it is seen in its proper lighte . . . '.

This same care was observed by the most celebrated of the native painters, Sir James Thornhill (1676–1734). After assiduous study, travels on the Continent, and the acquisition of a collection he turned to painting. According to Vertue his techniques owed much to Laguerre, but he was in sympathy with baroque trends. He soon had reason to be satisfied with his practice and his success at wresting two important commissions from the Venetian Sebastiano Ricci. These were the painting of certain rooms at Hampton Court (before 1715) and the Dome of St Paul's Cathedral (1715–17).

The best known of Thornhill's important works, however, is undoubtedly the Painted Hall at Greenwich, where he worked on and off from 1708 to 1726. During this time he did at least half of his other known paintings. Mr Croft-Murray has listed forty-seven separate schemes of decorative painting on which he worked; some twenty are now destroyed in whole or part. In its length the Greenwich ceiling presented a difficult problem and there were few English examples of a similar nature which could be studied. Here were some five thousand square feet of flat ceiling with no divisions or compartments to divide the subject matter. The Glorification of William and Mary occupies the large feigned oval in the centre and at each end is an elliptical arch held up by Atlantes. Some twenty figures sprawl in frozen muscular poses before the sterns of baroque-like English and Spanish ships. All the work was finally complete by 1726 and Thornhill received £6,685 in all for this, the finest example of baroque decorative painting by an English artist.

In the intervals of this major task Thornhill, as noted, was very busy with other work, particularly the painting of the Dome of St Paul's. The prospect of this important commission attracted many Venetian artists[1] to England, the most notable being Antonio Pellegrini and Marco Ricci in 1708–9, Sebastiano Ricci in 1710–11, and Cassana, Damini, Grisoni and the two Belluccis in the few years following to 1716. After many set-backs, which included Laguerre's nomination as the Commissioners' first choice, staid English Protestantism triumphed and Thornhill was asked in June, 1715, 'to paint the great Dome of St Paul'. Regrettably it was to be in monochrome. One might contrast this against the rich colours Pellegrini had used in painting the High Saloon and Dome at Castle Howard five or six years earlier. Had he been given the commission – his oil sketch of 1710 is in the Victoria and Albert Museum – we should have had a swirling colourful display to brighten Wren's classical interior. Appropriately Thornhill painted eight scenes from the life of St Paul, and by the time the commission, including the continuation of the theme into the Whispering Gallery was complete in 1721 he had received £6,575.

In the next three years he worked principally at Wimpole and Moor Park. At Moor Park after a law suit, which cost the owner, Benjamin Styles, the full amount of the bill at the end of long negotiation and an out-of-court settlement, Venetian paintings were put with the rich

[1] Fully treated in Croft-Murray, *op. cit.*, Vol. 2 (forthcoming), and by Francis Watson, *Arte Veneta*, 1954, pp. 295–302; *Journal Royal Inst. of Brit. Architects*, March, 1954, p. 174.

plasterwork by Bagutti and Artari (Figs 36–38). But after this, like the work of the plasterer Edward Goudge twenty years earlier, commissions dwindled away and at his death in 1734 the style of decoration involving immense portrayals of scenes and allegories on vast areas of wall was at an end.

Throughout the last twenty years of his life Thornhill had needed to be ever wary of the inclination of patrons to give work to the Venetians. Lord Carlisle had used Pellegrini and Marco Ricci at Castle Howard. The Duke of Manchester employed Pellegrini to decorate Kimbolton. Lord Chandos gave the important commission of painting twenty-three canvases for the private chapel at his princely palace of Canons at Edgware on the outskirts of London to Antonio Bellucci. When Canons was demolished in 1747 the second Lord Foley purchased these paintings and the painted glass by Joshua Price[1] of York and inserted them as the glory of Great Witley Church, Worcestershire. Price's windows were designed by Francesco Sleter who worked at Canons, Mereworth and Moor Park (Figs 38, 49). He worked in the style of Ricci, but in weaker vein, and his name is often anglicised to Slater.

The last Venetian painter we need to mention is Giacomo Amiconi (1675–1752), who came to England about 1729 and established himself as a successful portrait painter. In 1731 he was asked to decorate the Temple of the Four Winds at Castle Howard – Mrs Hawksmoor listed her late husband's charges in coach and chair hire 'about making the bargain with Snr. Amiconi to paint the Temple' – and there are four letters from the painter about this commission at Castle Howard. In one of these, dated 6th October, 1736, he writes to Lord Carlisle: '. . . it is true Milord that so far as I can remember that at my first coming in this country, after I had painted Milord Tankerville's stairs, that Mr Hawksmoore acquainted me with yr Lordship's desires, but after five or six years time past, i cannot well recollect the prices I ask for, because in that time i mind nothing else but for been known by my own works, and accordingly since that time, by the kindness of the English lords and others i had always something to do and found great encouragement . . .'

He worked at Wentworth Castle (p. 51) and with Sleter at Moor Park, but left England before the full onrush of the rococo style made itself felt.

The only English painter to work to any great effect during the Thornhill years, apart from some commissions executed by William Hogarth, was William Kent. His decorations at the Cupola Room, Kensington Palace, in 1722 are the earliest we know by him. At Ditchley, working alongside the Italian *stuccatori*, he painted the centre of the ceiling of the Hall in 1726 with an Assembly of the Gods, for which he was paid £50. His painted imitations of techniques and styles that he had noted on his Italian tour were, however, not too good and he was much more successful as an architect and landscape gardener. At Rousham he painted a version of the grotesque ornament in an antique Roman manner, but could not compete in this style with Giuseppe Borgnis who worked at West Wycombe, Buckinghamshire, and at the Ionic Temple in Duncombe Park, Yorkshire (Figs 93–94). Another Venetian, Antonio Jolli, came to

[1] John A. Knowles, 'The Price Family of Glass-Painters', *The Antiquaries' Journal*, July–October, 1953, pp. 184–92.

England in the early seventeen-forties and decorated a house for the impresario John James Heidegger (Fig. 81). The seventh Viscount Irwin also inserted canvases by Jolli in the Long Gallery chimney-pieces (Fig. 67) at Temple Newsam House, Leeds.

This brief note on painters must end with one of the most famous. In 1746 Antonio Canaletto came to England. He had already established good connections with many Englishmen travelling or resident abroad, of whom the most important were Owen MacSwinny and the British Consul at Venice, Joseph Smith. Through the latter's intercessions the Royal Collections at Windsor contain fifty paintings and more than one hundred and forty drawings by Canaletto. In wall decoration he worked principally at Farnborough Hall, Warwickshire.[1] His paintings were mounted in frames of rococo plasterwork, but in 1929 were removed and sold; skilful copies take their place. Canaletto left England for the last time in 1756 and died in his native city of Venice in 1768. The sun was already rising on new strange styles: everything was to be Chinese, Gothick or rococo.

[1] *Country Life*, 11th and 18th February, 1954.

IV

Great Fine Houses

' . . . the expense of living in this Great fine house, do's not amount to above a hundred pounds a year, more than what was spent in the Old one.'

Sir John Vanbrugh, writing of Castle Howard, to James Craggs, October, 1713.

IN the late seventeenth century society suddenly found itself preoccupied with the work of a young dramatist-soldier, John Vanbrugh. Talk of his plays *The Relapse* and *The Provok'd Wife* echoed through the drawing rooms and introduced to the civilised Whig nobles a dramatic author worthy of joining in the activities of their elegant Kit Cat Club. Among its titled members were the Earls of Carlisle and Manchester who, besides a love of music and drama, were attracted to anyone possessing originality and invention in architecture. In John Vanbrugh they found such a person. The third Earl of Carlisle was thirty years old when in 1699 he engaged Vanbrugh (five years older than himself) to design Castle Howard. Earlier plans for the house had been submitted by William Talman, but he demanded a high price for them and Lord Carlisle refused to pay. The rivalry existing between Talman and Vanbrugh was to be given sharper emphasis at the death of William III when Vanbrugh succeeded Talman as Comptroller of the King's Works.

The architectural history of Castle Howard has been given considerable attention[1] over the years. A study of the building books yields valuable information about the interior decoration. A group of talented workers was assembled, including 'Mr Nadauld' and Samuel Carpenter, carvers in wood and stone, with Nadauld's man, Robinson, Giovanni Bagutti the *stuccatore* with a partner, Plura, the London and York plasterer Isaac Mansfield, John Hervé (Harvey) the painter, his relative Daniel, a sculptor, and Gian Antonio Pellegrini and Marco Ricci the decorative painters.

Nadauld, often called 'Mr Nedos' and 'Needo' in the accounts, was also employed at Chatsworth. He worked in wood in many of the rooms at Castle Howard and did stone carving on the south front. Perhaps the most important item to emerge from a study of the

---

[1] The complicated story of the building of Castle Howard is found in *English Homes* IV, Vol. 2, 1928, *The Work of Vanbrugh and his School* (ed. H. Avray Tipping and Christopher Hussey); Laurence Whistler, *The Imagination of Vanbrugh and his Fellow Artists*, 1954; and Kerry Downes, *Hawksmoor*, 1961. I have used the original 'Building Books' at the house to give the details recorded here.

accounts is the employment, 1710–12, of the *stuccatori*, Giovanni Bagutti ('Mr Bargotee') and 'Mr Plura'. It seems reasonable to assume they provided the stucco fireplace and the scagliola[1] niche in the Great Hall (Figs 1, 3), which takes a foremost place among the finest achievements of this period. John Storey and 'Sellar' acted as their labourers, and the plasterer Isaac Mansfield, who had settled at York in 1704 and moved about the country to Blenheim and London, assisted and worked in five other rooms. In all Mansfield received £105 2s. 6d. in contrast to the £321 17s. paid to Bagutti and Plura.

York was, as we have noted, the important centre for carpentry and joinery and 'deales and wainscot' were provided by 'Mr Stephenson', presumably William Stephenson. The joiner Sabyn was paid for '2 days at Yorke choosing out deals for floores'. There is also a memorandum for 3rd January, 1700–1, concerning 'deals fetched from Norway and delivered at Scarborow'. Sabyn worked on the cornices, friezes and bolection mouldings in 1706, and among the building bills is a measurement of his work by Nicholas Hawksmoor and William Etty. The York joiner William Thornton was also there and in 1708 agreed 'to wainscott the Rooms called Saloon [Fig. 2], Dining Room and Anty roome. The Saloon with a good Cornich & Collours according to ye draft at the Price of 2s 6d p. Superficiall Yarde'. The Dining room was to be 'thoroughly wainscoted with Good Cornich, Base, surbase and bolection after the best and usual way at the price of 2s. 2d per yard'. Thornton's detailed knowledge of window sizes at Castle Howard appear in his correspondence (p. 48) with Lord Strafford and indicates that he was probably responsible, with carpenter John Milburn's help, for (among much else) the window frames and sash bars.

Apart from Nadauld's carved work in wood 'Mr Tushaine' did 'beding mold' and Daniel Harvey carved door, picture and chimney frames. Samuel Carpenter's bill[2] for woodcarving is an extensive one. It ranges from '11 Cartozzas' to 'roses, moulding Corinthian Capitals, door scrowles and wooden scrowles in the Belconey of the Hall'.

It seems likely that John Harvey (1681–1735) and Daniel Harvey (1683–1733) were at least relatives (if not brothers), and were probably French Protestants who escaped persecution after the revocation of the Edict of Nantes. John not only worked in the house but was consulted by Hawksmoor about work in the Castle Howard park at the Temple of the Four Winds. One of Daniel's accounts for woodcarving survives, written in French, and signed 'Daniel Hervé'. He worked also for Etty, and in south Yorkshire at Wentworth Castle. He is buried, like Thornton, at St Olave's, York.

On 4th July, 1708, John Gardom of Baslow, Derbyshire, was paid for 'Iron Gates for ye Garding' and we may assume he was responsible for the wrought-iron staircase rail in the Hall.

---

[1] A coloured plaster which imitates marble. Used in ancient times in Egypt and Greece, its acceptance in England was cautious and late. The Alcove closet at Ham House has a chimney-piece and wide hearth slab of the material, *c.* 1674. It was also used at Castle Howard in 1710 and in the Temple of the Four Winds there in 1736. See entry under R. B. Wragg, p. 201.

[2] He charged 4s. each for his 'cartozzas', 2s. 6d. for his roses, 3s. a foot for his enriched friezes (6d. a foot without enrichment), £2 each for his 'scrowles' in the balcony, and 3s. each for his 'door scrowles'.

Little is known of Gardom, but as a pupil of Tijou he worked at Chatsworth and Kiveton. Keys and hinges came in 1709–10 from Josiah Kay and all the marble work was provided from Derbyshire by John Thorp of Bakewell. He worked also for the Hotham family at Beverley and at the Mansion House, York. At Castle Howard he erected five marble chimney-pieces, door casings to several rooms, and worked in the corridors leading from the Hall as well as the Hall 'margents'. The Hall floor was made up of two hundred and sixteen marble squares, sixty half squares and four quarter squares and stands to this day precise in the mathematical disciplines of its design.

In 1709 it was agreed with Antonio Pellegrini to paint the Dome. The surviving bills show various payments to him in the next three years and on 25th September, 1712, he signed a document to the effect that he had received 'Eight Hundred fifty two pounds five Shills in full of all Demands to this day by me'.

When Dr Waagen visited Castle Howard in 1835 to describe its picture collections for his *Art Treasures in Great Britain* he was not pleased with Pellegrini's decoration. 'According to the tasteless fashion of that age', he says, 'the cupola is painted with the fall of Phaeton . . . so that a person standing beneath it feels as if the four horses of the sun were going to fall upon his head'. On 9th November, 1940, fire broke out at Castle Howard, destroying the state rooms of the eastern range, including the fine decorations in the High Saloon (Fig. 2), and eventually the entire dome fell in. The long work of restoration, carefully supervised by Mr George Howard, still goes on. The Dome and Cupola were replaced in 1962 and the subject of Pellegrini's painting was re-created in tempera by a Canadian artist, Scott Medd. As soon as this was done it was possible for a younger generation to feel again the full effect of Vanbrugh's intentions and to appreciate the conception of Pellegrini's fiery steeds in their swirling clouds far overhead.

Further south in Yorkshire, at Wentworth Castle (or Stainborough as it was called until 1731) and nearby Wentworth Woodhouse, an old but petty rivalry existed between the families. At the death of William, second Earl of Strafford, in 1695 many things happened besides the erection of a grand monument, probably by John van Nost, in York Minster. He had no children and left Wentworth Woodhouse to his nephew, Thomas Watson, a cadet of the Rockingham Castle family. His honours became extinct except for the Barony of Raby, which went through special remainder to his younger brother's grandson, Thomas Wentworth.

The rival family, Lord Raby, his mother and brother Peter, were at an immediate disadvantage in not owning a great house such as the Jacobean Wentworth Woodhouse. In 1703, however, the wind of fortune veered slightly with the appointment of Lord Raby as Ambassador at Berlin. He accumulated capital and bought Stainborough when it came on the market in 1708; it had a most remunerative rent roll. Money was necessary to Lord Raby in more than ordinary quantity for he was seeking the restoration to him of the Strafford earldom. It was at length Lord Harley who gave him the coveted title in 1711, and every attention was given to building and altering at Stainborough. There is extensive documentation.[1]

[1] British Museum, Strafford papers, especially Add. MSS 22221–2; 22238–9; 22257–62.

In 1709 Peter Wentworth wrote to his brother, then still in Berlin, mentioning that he had showed the plans to their mother and Lady Bathurst. They 'stood amased at it and said the least such a building would cost inside and out wou'd be ten thousand pounds . . .'. The rest of the letter establishes that it is the plan of the north-east front of Wentworth Castle which Peter is writing about; and Horace Walpole in a letter to Richard Bentley recorded that the architect, under Raby's direction in Berlin, was Johann von Bodt (1670–1745). It has been noted that Bodt's plans[1] for the house survive, with elevations which 'conform to the stylistic trend of early eighteenth-century Franco-Prussian architecture and of his own work'. Directing affairs from Berlin cannot have been easy for Raby, and his brother Peter Wentworth writes on 22nd May, 1711: 'when I was at the Duke of Shrewsbury's my Lord Scarborough was there and he was talking of his building, and they did agree there was no Building without a Surveyor, even when they agreed by the great; wch agrees with the advise Mr Benson is always desiring to send you word, you must be at the expence and lost in time and labour'. This mention of Robert Benson, first Lord Bingley, is interesting in that as a knowledgeable man he was supervising the building of his own house at Bramham, Yorkshire, with advice from Thomas Archer. Payments to 'Mr Archer' appear in Benson's bank account[2] as early as 1699 and Archer was also consulted by Raby,[3] perhaps at Benson's suggestion.

Building a house on this scale and attending to much of the detail from great distance caused some trouble and delay. Strafford went on from Berlin to the Hague embassy, where he negotiated the Treaty of Utrecht. He was allowed to continue there until 1714, but, as a pillar of strength to the Tories, he was not welcome to the active Whigs who assumed control at the accession of George I. While in foreign parts he seized the opportunity of buying Brussels tapestries, and of sending Dutch elms and other trees and plants to his gardener, John Arnold. His stewards wrote frequently in answer to his many questions – 'you have not sent me word what the masons Bullock & Thackerly are now doing' is an example of the repeated enquiries about the activities of a varied range of craftsmen.

The most interesting facts to emerge (and before Strafford retired from the Hague and came home to Yorkshire) are in the letters[4] written to him by the York joiner William Thornton. That of 22nd March, 1713–14, is filled with details about the thickness of glazing bars and dimensions of sash windows. He says 'the largest of my Ld Carliles glass is 18½ p 11½ Inches. My Lord Bingleys is not so large'. We know he worked at Castle Howard and the mentions of Lord Bingley lead us to assume he was at Bramham also. He continues: 'I Recd yor Lordships Contract for yr windows, but since yor Lordsp is pleased to write that yor prices & paymts

---

[1] Victoria and Albert Museum, 1890, 212, and Album 92.0.46. John Harris, 'Bodt and Stainborough', *Architectural Review*, July, 1961.

[2] Hoare's Bank: '1699, April 8. To Mr Archer £28.10.0; 1700, May 7. To Mr Archer £845.17.6.'

[3] J. J. Cartwright, *The Wentworth Papers*, 1705–39, 1883, pp. 15, 84, 133; Marcus Whiffen, *Thomas Archer*, 1950, pp. 15–16.

[4] British Museum Add. MSS 22, 238, ff. 145, 146, 150, 165, 169. Also references in Add. MSS 22, 239, ff. 88, 90.

shall be as good as My Lord Bingleys & others I shall go on with the rest of yor work without troubling yor Honr with any more Contracts till you have seen som of my work at Stainbrough.'

Thornton suggested the staircase steps leading to the Long Gallery should be of stone – 'I think Stepps for yr Great Stairs will be better of Stone than wood – as to ye fashon of ye Banester . . . the woodwork and setting up such a banester to be made of oak will cost 14 pence & to be of deal ten pence'. The thickness of the sashes and glazing bars was finally decided, '& that it is ye same thickness I have done for Mr Bourchier and others wch hath proved to turn well better than those of thinner stuff'. This is valuable confirmation in an otherwise humdrum note that Thornton did the joinery work at least for John Bourchier at Beningbrough (p. 51) in north Yorkshire.

In September, 1714, Thornton writes again – stone steps had now been decided on – and says: 'I am going to Hull next Monday so if I find anything in Mr Perritt's[1] hand, they shall be sent up to Doncaster'. Goods were frequently sent by Strafford from the Hague to Hull, and then along the rivers Humber and Ouse towards Doncaster. The agent also noted in January, 1719–20, that 'I writ to Mr Thornton concerning ye Marble pedestals' (his opinion was to be asked about false corners in wood to cut down the expense on marble) '& have heard since that he went to London with my Lady Betty Hastings so I suppose he never got my letter'. Thornton had perhaps gone to help Lady Betty in the choice of something he was dealing with for her Yorkshire home at Ledston.

Work however was to go slowly. Despite his remunerative ambassadorial posts Strafford brought work to a halt from time to time. He used his position, however, to arrange for ships – 'the men of war' – to call in 'either at Genoa or Lighorne to take in any marble or Statues' and he wrote to the British Consul at Leghorn, Christopher Crowe, on 10th August, 1714, asking him to gather up the bronze statues which were being done for him by the great sculptor Massimiliano Soldani.[2] He goes on: 'but there is a second favour I would beg of you . . . I have built a pritty large house in which I have a large gallery'. He asks Crowe to get four marble columns, and enough marble for pedestals and capitals of pilasters. Crowe replies to say he has ordered all this 'of a fine white marble with a blue vein which is the best & prettyest this Country affords'.

Strafford, like most of his contemporaries, seems to have held considerable stock in the South Sea Company and frequently consulted his banker, Francis Child, about purchase and disposal. In 1718–19 he had some £14,000 in his account, but many letters to him show that on occasion trades-people and craftsmen waited up to five years for their money. The delays and avoidance of payment meant that eventually other hands were engaged to do work. Thornton died in 1721 and his assistant, John Goodyear,[3] agreed in November 'to lay ye Gallery floor for

---

[1] A timber merchant who was probably connected with the mason-builder family of York of that name (p. 169).

[2] Hugh Honour, *Connoisseur*, May, 1958, pp. 222–3.

[3] In *Country Life*, 25th October, 1924, a quotation from a MS diary, 1726–35, calls him Jonathan

sixpence p. yard. Mr Thornton he says had twelve pence p. yard for laying yr Lordships other Floors'.

The family had owned a house at Twickenham since 1701 and would know the Octagon House which James Gibbs was building for James Johnston, joint Secretary for Scotland under William III. What more natural than to seek help from the same architect, joiner, and Italian plasterers? The document which indicates this may have been done is the agreement[1] of 28th July, 1724, with Charles Griffiths, a London joiner – '. . . to wainscoat ye Gallery att Staineborough as Desined by Mr Gibbs in manner following for £225 inc. Carriage'. On 3rd September Griffiths writes that he is 'now very forward with ye Gallery . . . ye pitture of ye 3 Kings is ye same size as ye Chimney piece att Secretrey Johnsons att Twickenham. I wish your Lordship would let me know whether ye other can't be made ye same bigness . . .'. He also asks whether he has to flute the pilasters and notes that his 870 yards of deal work at 6s. a yard would include this, 'compass worke and mouldings at ye same price'. The 'right wainscoat in Shutters, Suffeets & window boards, compass worke included' was at 7s. 6d. a yard and 'all ye Pannels to be yellow Deale & one Inch in thickness'. Richard Huss, a plasterer used by Thomas Archer at St Philip's Church, Birmingham, did plain work in the Gallery. It is a little difficult to date the Italian plasterwork on the stairs (Fig. 7), but the likeliest theory is that Bagutti and Artari, having been used by Gibbs in London, and at the Octagon House[2] at Twickenham, came up to Yorkshire in 1724 to the house where the architect was bringing a Palladian correctness to Bodt's earlier Long Gallery treatment.

It had been agreed in August, 1720, that Daniel Harvey should carve capitals in wood and stone, but delay seems to have attended parts of his work also. Griffiths tried to secure the work for a London man, and the steward writing on 20th November, 1724, says he 'finds there is a mistake between Mr Harvey and him for Mr Harvey at his price proposes finding stuff for them as well as working them and by Mr Griffiths contract he is to find ye Stuff for them, and his Man tells me they are accordingly come down putt together for Carving'. The quality of stone carving on the East front, however, with the '4 Capitals after ye Corinthian order' of Harvey's 1720 agreement, is such as to suggest he carried this out. Strafford's friend, Lord Bathurst, called there in the autumn of 1725 and thought that 'the Gallery is a very magnificent room now that the pillars are up'.

The great doorway in the centre of the East front opens into a Great Hall, a square of some forty feet into which Strafford was to introduce the last grand touch – decorative ceiling paintings. Lord Strafford and his friends approached the East front (one hundred and eighty feet in length) through fine wrought iron gates which were probably the work of Richard Booth. Seven grand windows were passed, divided into twenty-four panes each and six broad stone steps ascended to the great door, surmounted by the Strafford arms and rich stone carving.

Godier and states that he died at Doncaster in June, 1732: 'he did most of the joyner's work at Stainborough Hall being then servant to Mr Thornton.'

[1] British Museum Add. MSS, 22239, f. 128.

[2] James Gibbs, *A Book of Architecture*, 1728, p. xix; G. W. Beard, *Apollo*, July, 1964, p. 52.

Within, the span demanded pillars supporting entablatures to divide the ceiling into one central and eight side panels. It was painted for Strafford in 1735 by Giacomo Amiconi. The general house painting was done by William Addinall of Wakefield (he seemed to count gilding, picture-framing and funeral arrangements among his accomplishments). In June, 1729, he writes to Strafford about a ceiling which will 'not be drie enough to gild this 3 months. I will say nothing to ye Italions about it'. It does not appear, however, whether this related to ceiling painting or indeed plasterwork. The work of decoration by Amiconi was in Strafford's last years. He died in 1739, having spent most of his lifetime planning one of the greatest houses in the north.

The employment of William Thornton at Wentworth Castle is useful to us in that his work can be compared to that he did at Beningbrough, seventy miles away to the north. Certain parts of the panelling[1] have similarities to that at Wentworth Castle, and a cryptic note in a *Builder's Dictionary* of 1730[2] says that Beningbrough was designed by Thornton. I have given the brief line of confirmation which appears in the Strafford papers as to Thornton's woodwork there. While it is a little startling to think that a house as competent as Beningbrough was designed by a York joiner, groping in this direction has been going on for many years. In 1928 the editors of *The Work of Sir John Vanbrugh and his School* wondered if the Etty family could be connected 'with both the designing and decorating of the house, thus accounting for some percolation of the Vanbrughian *ichor* into the flesh and bone' of Beningbrough. Vanbrugh would know Thornton's work at Castle Howard, but here at Beningbrough it is the faint echoes only of that almost indefinable style, as practised by the Vanbrugh followers, which is at work.

Within the house the wood-carving (Figs 12–14) is of a very high order, but a little out of the contemporary mood. It has been pointed out to me (by Dr Eric Gee) that the unusual square knop (Fig. 12) on the staircase balusters also appears on the staircase of the Treasurer's House, York. The imposing staircase at Beningbrough has for its 'documentation' a parquetry insert on a quarter-landing, of the Bourchier cross impaling the Bellwood caltraps – John Bourchier married Mary Bellwood – while an encircling border has the Stafford knot on each side, the initials 'J.B.M' at the top and the date '1716' at the bottom. The same initials are carved in stone over the front door on the north front and freely introduced in the wood carving in the cornice of the west drawing room. The house was presumably finished in time for the festivities attending John Bourchier becoming Sheriff of York in 1719–20.

Before turning to the work of Vanbrugh's follower in the north, William Wakefield, and his connections with the Etty family in building matters, another architect of greater importance merits our attention again. In 1716 Colin Campbell designed a house at Beverley for Sir Charles Hotham.[3] He used William Thornton as joiner and carver and John Bagnall, the

---

[1] In particular the use of capitals with in-turned volutes, a feature used by Borromini, and in England by Thomas Archer and Francis Smith in particular. Whiffen, *Archer, op. cit.*, p. 45; H. M. Colvin, *Archaeological Journal*, CIV (1948), pp. 193–5.

[2] This information is to be published by Dr Eileen Harris and Mr Howard Colvin.

[3] See K. A. Macmahon, *Trans. East Riding Georgian Society*, 1956–8, based on the Hotham MSS, Beverley Record Office. William Thornton received £1,116 for work done by May, 1720.

York plasterer, who had been employed on plain work at Castle Howard, did similar decoration. A year or so later, in 1718, Campbell was designing Ebberston Hall on the slopes of the Yorkshire moors for Hotham's relative, William Thompson. Campbell says in *Vitruvius Britannicus* that 'this small rustick Edifice stands in a fine park well planted, with a River, which forms a Cascade and Canal 1200 feet long, and runs under the Loggio in the back Front'. Campbell in these years was not able to use the Italian plasterers.[1]

Campbell's authorship of Baldersby (formerly Newby Park) near Ripon for Sir William Robinson (1655–1736) was already known from its appearance in *Vitruvius Britannicus*, but documents[2] at Studley Royal and Leeds fill in some of the detail. Sir William writes on 3rd May, 1720–1, to his son Metcalfe, on whom he is settling the estate, 'I shall goe to Newby for this summer, shall have enough trouble in pulling down an old house and Building a Wing of a new one'. On 26th May he hopes that when Metcalfe has 'settled all yr matters & discours'd Mr Campbell about yr Library & Gallery you will come down & see it finished to yr mind'. His letter of 2nd June makes it clear that the 'main house' was by Campbell, and to be left in detail to his son's fancy, and that the wings which 'wee are busy building' were by William Etty who 'assures me that it will not cost above £200'. Three days later he writes again to his son 'yr house at Newby begins to appear above ground. I am very intent on that design, having near fifty workmen. Etty has been here all this work, is gone to Admirall De Lavalls [Seaton Delaval] to lay ye foundation of his house and will return next week. . . .'

The documents at Leeds provide the names of the craftsmen used. Campbell is not mentioned. Etty is in complete charge, allows the bills and settles all disputes.

Lime	Christopher Pinckney of Sutton Grange.
Stone	Francis Gill (Rainton Quarry).
Mason	John Simpson.
Carpenters	William Etty and William Mudd.
Plasterwork	Jonathan Perritt.
Carvers	Henry and Edward Raper, John Carpenter and Daniel Harvey
Glaziers and Plumbers	Robert Barugh, Thomas Allanson[3] and Charles Chawnor.

The documents (which at times have been confused with those in the collection relating to the nearby Blackett-Weddell house, Newby Hall) show that Etty and Mudd worked in partnership, and that John Carpenter (presumably a relative of Samuel, p. 46) and Daniel

[1] The note in the Burlington account book at Chatsworth (22nd January, 1719) about 'lodging the Italians at Chiswick' relates to Italian singers, not plasterers, as the entry for 16th April, 1720, makes clear. He was to use the *stuccatori* at Houghton, Mereworth and Compton Place, after their active introduction to England in about 1720 (p. 27).

[2] Studley Royal, Ripon, Estate Office MSS, especially Parcel 286; G. W. Beard, *Country Life*, 10th August, 1961; Leeds Reference Library, Newby Hall MSS 2277/6/17–21.

[3] Allanson worked at the York Mansion House in November, 1731: York Reference Library, Mansion House, Chamberlain's Accounts.

Harvey were also together. It may be assumed that these men were those used by Etty and William Wakefield in creating the houses of this period around York. When the house was complete Sir William subscribed to the third volume of Campbell's book in which it was described, and the architect acknowledged, by receipt, 'two pounds seventeen shilling in full for ye 3d. vol of my *Vitruvius Britannicus*, Whitehall, 10 February 1725'.

Robinson's relative, John Aislabie, Chancellor of the Exchequer in 1721 at the time of the South Sea Bubble, also employed York and London craftsmen. He was building at Studley Royal and also sought Campbell's advice at a late stage – just before the architect's death in 1729. In 1716 the Tudor house of the Mallory family at Studley Royal was destroyed by fire – probably the mischievous work of a servant, Ann Gill. After the initial inconvenience, however, Aislabie saw that here was the opportunity to rebuild and to surround the house with an impressive garden setting. A mile away lay the ruins of Fountains Abbey, and while Aislabie was destined to disappointment in trying to add them to his possessions they acted as a constant reminder that his schemes must match them in grandeur.

We know nothing of the work of 1717 and almost nothing of Aislabie's architect and garden designer, if indeed he used one. There is evidence in the archives of his own abilities and considerable interest in the running of his estate and he was friendly with the knowledgeable Lord Bingley. Sir John Vanbrugh had often stayed in the same house when visiting the Robinson family. John Aislabie's sister Mary had married Sir William Robinson, and she writes to her son, Metcalfe: ' . . . we have had dined here Mr Vanbrook and all ye broaken officers in town', and again, 'yesterday at Lady Vanbrugh's, I had nothing to do but criticise in my own mind Sr John's wonderfull taste in Architecture felicitating myself upon yr having none of his thick walls to pull down . . . '.

All that is now certain is that Aislabie entrusted the early work at Studley itself to the care of his agent, John Storaker, his two masons, John Simpson and at Simpson's death on 7th December, 1728, the experienced Westminster man Robert Doe, and to his gardener, William Fisher. Doe had worked at Castle Howard and pronounces himself in a bond among the Studley manuscripts to be 'of the Parish of St Ann's in the liberty of Westminster, mason' and to be 'held and firmly bound unto Rt Hon John Aislabie for £130'. He emerges as a competent mason, working also at Temple Newsam House, Leeds, where he may have erected the fine Long Gallery chimney-pieces (Fig. 67). Unfortunately Aislabie's troubles with the South Sea Company led him to prolong for some years completion of the house and park. The stables were not built until 1728-9, and the main construction of the garden features took place from 1727 to 1732. Effective cascades and canals were mainly created by using the little River Skell flowing swiftly past the Abbey ruins. By 1730 Doe had twenty-one men working under him on various garden temples and the stables.

It is here that belatedly Colin Campbell again comes on the scene. One letter of his about his connection with the project, dated 26th August, 1729, survives. He tells Aislabie that he is glad the stables are in active construction and continues: 'when R. Morris returned from the north he told me he had called at Studley and brought me three different designs for the Arcade of which two were very ugley . . . '. A further letter from Morris is relevant, and indicates a closer connection with Campbell than has perhaps hitherto been suspected.[1] Writing from London on 11th August, 1729, he says: 'Mr Campbell have examined the Arcade and thinks this Desine will be the best, he would have wright to you on this Afaire but was Taken Ill in Norfolke and with grate Dificulty Gott to London and Contineus very bad. The Grove must be Equlatral Triangles and 1 Forth of the High of the Rusticks.'[2]

In these years, when Campbell was introducing the Palladian villa to Yorkshire, William Wakefield was still parading the grand masses of the Vanbrugh style and working at Gilling Castle and Duncombe Park. The Fairfax front at Gilling resembles the stables by James Gibbs at Compton Verney, Warwickshire, while Duncombe Park shows strong Vanbrugh influence. He may well have been working to the design or advice of others or using craftsmen like Etty who were steeped in the patterns required. Whatever the truth no mention of him appears in the documentation[3] for either house. Campbell's *Vitruvius Britannicus* records that Wakefield made a design for Sir Thomas Robinson's house in north Yorkshire at Rokeby, but the house was not built to it. Sir Thomas must have enjoyed long friendship with Wakefield for, writing to his father-in-law, the third Earl of Carlisle, in 1730, he says that he had thought it, 'but doing a justice to my late dear friend Mr Wakefield, to believe that had he lived he would have made plans for the York Assembly Rooms full as convenient as Lord Burlington's and certainly cheaper, tho' perhaps [with] not so many Palladian strokes in 'em.'

Wakefield did however collaborate with William Etty in 1720 in work at a house in Yorkshire at Holme-on-Spalding Moor. The documents[4] show that Mr Wakefield instructed the steward, William Martin, 'what quantities of materials of all sorts to provide'. He had 'been here att Holme setting out the Foundation for the new Building and giveing his Directions to the Bricklayers and Carpandars'. Etty was to give a 'draught' for a bow window, 'but being for London in Easter Weeke (1725) where he was in Hopes to see something that might be newer fashoned & better, desired me to defarr writeing . . . '. It would be useful to know why Wakefield (as the correspondence shows) went into Lincolnshire in July, 1720, but such riddles seem to shadow his career as completely as he shadowed the style of others. At Duncombe Park Wakefield was at work by 1713, if the inscription on Campbell's plans and elevations in *Vitruvius Britannicus* is to be believed; and as they appear in the first volume, published in 1715, the statement would seem reliable enough. There is no evidence, however, for such an

---

[1] Roger Morris (1695–1749) was born at Netherby in Yorkshire and may have come to Campbell's attention when the architect was working in Yorkshire. Campbell may also have introduced Morris to the Duke of Argyll, his own patron and head of his Clan, and to the 'architect Earl of Pembroke', with whose work Morris was closely associated. See H. M. Colvin, *Biographical Dictionary of English Architects* (1954), p. 395; James Lees-Milne, *Earls of Creation*, 1962, Chapter 2.

[2] This refers to the rustication of the Stable arcade.

[3] North Riding, Yorks., Record Office, Northallerton (Duncombe); Mrs V. M. Wombwell (Coxwold), and Newburgh MSS, Yorks. Arch. Soc. Library, Leeds (Gilling). I am indebted to Father Hugh Aveling, O.S.B., for communicating his findings on the architectural history of Gilling.

[4] East Riding, Yorks., Record Office, Harford (Holme) MSS DDHA 14/25–26. I am indebted to Mr Derek Sherborn for this reference.

early start at Gilling, and indeed the stucco decorations by Giuseppe Cortese belong to the 1740s.

Wakefield's other main essay in building that we know a little of was for Richard Atherton at Atherton Hall, Lancashire. The foundation stone bore the inscription 'Marcij 28, 1723, Rics. Atherton Ar. W.W.Ar.Archs:'. The house was demolished in 1825, but fortunately a surviving account book[1] gives some details, and the house itself appears in the background of a painting (Fig. 11) by Arthur Devis of 'Richard Vernon Atherton of Atherton Hall with his family in the grounds of his house'. The account book commences in 1724, but makes no mention of Wakefield. We may assume that he took little interest after providing the plan, and practical matters seem to have been the concern again, as at Holme, of Samuel Sidall or Sidell. On 16th February, 1727, he was paid £564 6s. 2¼d. 'by sundry sorts of work and stuff measured and valued, together with Mr Siddell's allowance of 10s. 6d p. week for Inspecting ye workmen p. Bill'. He was given ten guineas 'by allowance att ye Differance of Mr Etty and Mr Blomley's valuations'. Most of the other craftsmen used at this Lancashire house probably came from that county except the York carvers Henry Raper, John Carpenter and Daniel Harvey.[2]

By the time of Campbell's death in 1729 and that of Wakefield a year later the Palladian style was well established. In York a Building Committee, having failed to get possession of Sir William Robinson's house, determined on a new building and the 1730 (and 1732) General List of the Subscribers shows most of the county gentry, including (posthumously) Wakefield, subscribing sums of £25 and £50. Lord and Lady Burlington and the Dowager Lady Burlington, Sir Thomas Robinson, the Earl of Carlisle, James Moyser and John Wood (perhaps the Bath architect, who early in his career, worked in Yorkshire) are among the hundred and ninety or so names which between them raised the required £5,500.

Burlington of course had been asked by the Directors in May, 1730, to provide a design for the new building 'which we entirely leave to your Lordship to do in what manner you shall think proper'. The Chatsworth book records Lord Burlington receiving £52 10s. when 'going to Yorkshire in April, 1732'. The Assembly Rooms opened in August during race week and Sir Thomas Robinson presented the 'compliments of Thanks for his Lordships great Goodness and favour in designing and so generously contributing towards ye Carrying on of this Building'. This 'Carrying on' was a direct adaptation of the Egyptian Hall from Palladio's *Quattro Libri*, 1570, and while criticized at the time – the old Duchess of Marlborough and later Dr Johnson were scathing enough – survives as probably the 'most severely classical building of the early eighteenth century in Europe'. Into its interior went plainer decorations than those being practised by Burlington's friend William Kent, or by the Italian plasterers working under Francis Smith of Warwick.

[1] Lancs Co. Record Office, Lilford MSS Account Book, 1724–37. When the collection is fully available 'Estate Correspondence, 1718–?' may give more details.

[2] They worked with William Bibby (brickwork); George Crawford (lead-work); William Dandy (flooring, windows etc); Joshua Longfield (mason); Adam Stirrup (plain plastering) and John Runigar (painter).

Lying some four miles north-east of Bridgnorth in Shropshire is Davenport House which was built for Henry Davenport by Francis Smith in 1726. Here the interest is not in Italianate plasterwork but in the convenient plan, the oak staircase with its mahogany veneered hand-rail inlaid with bone and ebony, and the Inlaid room, which has parallels with that at nearby Mawley Hall. In this room the doors and panels are inlaid in a variety of mahogany, and the heraldic marquetry over the doors is particularly successful. Mr Christopher Hussey has suggested 'that when the elaborate marquetried furniture of Queen Anne's reign went out of fashion many of the skilled craftsmen responsible for it found themselves faced with unemployment'. It is possible that these two inlaid rooms at Davenport and Mawley were the work of a firm of cabinet-makers which had been responsible for some of the finest marquetried furniture a few years before. 'In the pilasters which flank the chimneypiece no fewer than eleven vertical strips of contrasting veneers occur.'

In panelling Smith did not always break away from the Wren tradition. Until the discovery of the bills dating between 1723 and 1730, it was thought that the main block of Ombersley Hall, Worcestershire, was decorated in the 1690s. The Saloon has handsome oak panelling and the arms of Sandys impaling Tipping appear on a carved shield above the door (Fig. 32), dating it to after 1725. As a room it is similar in treatment to the Velvet Drawing Room at Stoneleigh and the Oak Drawing Room at Wingerworth Hall, Derbyshire, a house attributed to Smith but now demolished. The Corinthian columns and carved door-case show that the Warwick architect again employed a talented carver. Perhaps the carver, joiner and carpenter he used at Sutton Scarsdale came to Ombersley. Worcester at this period had few talented craftsmen and they were mainly working on Thomas White's Guildhall. White himself, a Worcester mason-sculptor, confined his attention in the main to mason's work, carving (Fig. 15) and monuments.

Opening out from the Saloon at Ombersley are two rooms similarly wainscoted in oak – the Red Drawing Room and the Rose Boudoir (Fig. 31). In the boudoir the capitals of the pilasters flanking the chimney-piece have the inward turning volutes which appear also at Davenport House and Mawley Hall. Apart from its use in Thornton's 'houses' it was a trick extensively used by Thomas Archer, and Smith would have come into contact with him when working for Andrew Archer at Umberslade Hall, Warwickshire. His elder brother, William Smith (1661–1724), is also mentioned as having supervised the delivery of two hundred loads of stone for St Philip's Church, Birmingham, which was designed by Archer.

In a memoir of Francis Smith we read of 'the far famed architect of his day from whose plans the great mansions of Ombersley Court, Kinlet, Patshull, Davenport House, etc., arose . . .'. Kinlet is in Shropshire and was built for William Lacon Childe in 1727–29. Patshull, Staffordshire, and its little church, dominated by the towering Astley monument, were designed by Gibbs but presumably built by Smith. It is difficult to decide if Smith designed Mawley Hall, Shropshire, built for Sir Edward Blount about 1730.[1] Most of the family docu-

---

[1] Mr Arthur Oswald has suggested Thomas White of Worcester (*c.* 1674–1748), but this would be for the exterior only, *Country Life*, 11th July, 1948, p. 115.

ments, including even title-deeds, were destroyed by fire in 1808 and I have not traced any account Sir Edward may have had with a London bank.

The close parallel between the inlaid rooms at Davenport and Mawley suggests the same group of craftsmen. The trophy of arms above the mantelpiece in the entrance hall is similar to that at The Drum, Edinburgh, and to White's carving (Fig. 15) at Worcester Guildhall. The naturalistic carvings on the staircase and the undulating handrail which is fashioned as a serpent with a twisted tail are interesting features.

It seems to have been Smith's method to get his patrons to supply timber for his buildings from their estates. In 1720 Smith estimated for the 'workmanship of ye Carcis of a Hous for Martin Baldwin Esqr at Meriden [near Coventry] according to a draught given in by ffran Smith, Master finding all materialls that may be wanting for the said building . . . '. Smith was responsible for the 'Stone, Brick & Carpenters worke and alsoe for the Lead worke'. Planks and stair risers came from John Adcock of Coventry who also did the flooring and wainscoting. The accounts, which indicate only a modest outlay, have been preserved.[1]

At Lamport, Northamptonshire, Smith was perhaps recommended by the Leighs of Stone-leigh who were cousins of the Ishams. In 1732 the third Sir Justinian Isham employed Smith to add a library wing on the north side of the John Webb block. There exists at Lamport[2] a pen and wash drawing, almost certainly by Francis Smith, of the new elevation of the south-west front. Neither Smith nor his employer, the fifth baronet, lived long enough to see this front completed. Sir Justinian died in 1737 and on 19th April, 1738, Sir Edmund Isham writes to his wife that 'our honest Builder, Mr Smith of Warwick, I have just now heard that he dyd of a Fever about ten days ago. I really think it a great loss to all that were concern'd with him'.[3]

Again Sir Justinian was to find 'all manner of materials for ye aforesaid building'. Oak and larch for the floors were brought from the Isham estate at Shangton in Leicestershire. A fine chimney-piece of dove-grey marble was put up in the Library and a simple plaster ceiling inserted. This was the work of John Woolston of Northampton, who provided the more elaborate Music Room ceiling at a cost of £200 2s. 2d. His detailed bill survives and includes such items as: '7 Heads as big as the life with a moulding round each of them and Ornaments of leather work with shells over and under them in ye height of ye Attick at £10. 10.'

A similar but less elaborate ceiling was provided for the staircase. Sir Justinian left five hundred pounds in his will towards 're-edifying and beautifying' the nearby church. William Smith was employed and again Woolston provided flat ceilings and heraldic embellishments in chancel and nave, and over the chancel-arch the arms of George II were set up.

Woolston may have been responsible for the plaster decoration of the dining room at Easton Neston.[4] This suggestion by Dr Margaret Whinney accords a little more to form than

[1] Birmingham Reference Library, Digby MSS.

[2] I am indebted to Sir Gyles Isham, Bt, for loaning me notes based on his family papers now at the Northants. Co. Record Office.

[3] He was buried in St Mary's Church, Warwick, on 9th April, 1738.

[4] It would seem possible on stylistic grounds that the early eighteenth-century plasterwork on the

Mrs Esdaile's suggestion that the room was by Charles Stanley. The 'design is ill adjusted to the room and might be the work of a local craftsman'. One wonders if Woolston also worked at Althrop, where the third Earl Spencer decorated the two-storeyed hall in 1733, and filled it with nine large sporting canvases by John Wootton. The plasterwork, however, has a beauty which I think transcends any creation of a Northamptonshire plasterer.

The Age of Orders was almost at an end and the patrons of the mercurial indefinable rococo, Gothick and Chinese styles were soon to erect new shrines at which to worship the creators of such intriguing confusion.

---

staircase is by Edward Goudge who was working at the Northampton Sessions House, 1684–88, *Archaeological Journal*, CX, 1953, p. 181.

V

Visions and Revivals

As the great exponents of the Palladian style went their way a new feeling was coming to interior decoration and the rococo style was making itself very evident in the 1740s. It had been introduced from France and the swirling asymmetry which is its main characteristic found ready acceptance, not only with the Italian *stuccatori* but with their English counterparts working in plaster and wood.

In 1740 the seventh Viscount Irwin commissioned Thomas Perritt of York to provide the plaster ceilings at Temple Newsam House, Leeds. Perritt had been apprenticed to his father Jonathan, a York bricklayer. By 1737–8 he had been made a freeman of the City, and with his father was employed at the York Assembly Rooms in 1741 (and for several years after) cleaning various rooms and colouring the stucco work. At Temple Newsam, Perritt with the apprentice he had taken in 1738, Joseph Rose senior (*c*. 1723–80), provided the plasterwork and received in all £419 16s. 1d. of which sum £190 10s. 9d. was for the execution of the Long Gallery ceiling. This fine piece of work presents an iconographical problem in that its design incorporates what the accounts[1] call '13 Medals at 10s. 6d each. £6. 16s. 6d' (Figs 69–70) These plasterers were to use similar 'medals' at other houses.[2]

Perritt's principal commissions, however, were given to him by the architect James Paine. These were at Cusworth Hall, Nostell Priory and the Doncaster Mansion House. Like Colin Campbell twenty years before, James Paine found ready encouragement for his talents from Yorkshire gentlemen. He put it neatly in the Preface to his book of 1751, *Plans, Elevations, Sections and other ornaments of the Mansion House Belonging to the Corporation of Doncaster*: 'Having at that Time the Honour to be engaged in several Gentlemen's Buildings in that County, I was made Choice of for their Architect. . . .' He notes that the foundation stone of this splendid town house was laid in the spring of 1745, but the Jacobite rebellion stopped the work for a time. It was finished by 1748 'with the Approbation of the Gentlemen who engaged to inspect into it, on behalf of the Corporation . . .'.

The manuscript *Courtiers Book* and other documents[3] give evidence for some theories about

[1] Leeds Reference Library, Temple Newsam MSS E.A.12/10.

[2] N. and S. Staircase, Nostell Priory; Whistle-jacket room, Wentworth Woodhouse. They are also shown on Plate XXI of Paine's book on the Doncaster Mansion House, 1751, but were not executed. Medallions are also depicted in *The Gentleman's or Builder's Companion* . . . 1739, by William Jones, Plate 57.

[3] Doncaster Corporation MSS, *Courtiers Book*, Vol. III, and Parcel 26. The mason was George Gibson; interior mason's work by John Beal, *ibid.*, 14th December, 1744. The carpenter was William Rickard who married in 1727 Elizabeth Platt, daughter of the Rotherham architect George Platt (1700–43) who, with Rickard, was employed at Cusworth Hall (p. 61).

the decoration. But firstly the entry for 8th December, 1744, shows that the committee appointed to 'get plans . . . drawn by such persons as they think fit' accepted 'Dr Stead's plan for a Mansion House' and that 'such variations in ye sd. Plan as shall be advised and thought necessary' were to be by 'Mr Pain of Wragby'. Then, as Paine noted, came the Jacobite troubles, the first Committee's powers were revoked and a new one appointed. 'Deals and Polls bought by the former Comēe at Hull at ye same prices they gave for them there & Charges of bringing ye same from thence' were allowed. Paine inspected the accounts in November, 1745, and on 26th February, 1745–6, it was agreed 'that Mr James Paine of Pontefract is to finish the Mansion House according to the Designs he has this day given in the Estimate of the whole amounting to four thousand five Hundred, twenty three pounds four shillings and sixpence'. He was to receive £700 before Ladyday, a second payment of £500 in twelve months, and a third payment 'when the House is finished which shall be against Michaelmas 1747'. This remaining sum was to be paid at £500 a year with interest added at four per cent. John Stead was appointed one of the 'Inspectors' and is presumably the 'Dr Stead' who provided a first plan. Paine notes him as 'John Stead. M.D' in the dedicatory epistle of the 1751 volume.

While the house was finished in 1748 – there is a note in the 'Money disbursed for the Corporation, 15th April, 1749',[1] 'Paid ye Musick at opening the Mansion House, 5s. 0d.' – it was not exactly as he had planned it. In the note to Plate XXI of the descriptive volume of 1751 he first observes that 'the ornaments in it [the Banqueting Room], and on the Sides of the Room, are of stucco (executed by Mr Rose, and Mr Thomas Perritt), inferior to none of the Performances of the best *Italians* that ever work'd in this Kingdom'. These various designs and sections show elaborate ceiling paintings within the stucco framework, and in the Dedication Paine says that 'stucco work forming Compartments for Painting' is 'much more elegant than Cieling and Sides finish'd entirely with either painting, or stucco. I have therefore design'd, and with my own Hands drawn, suitable compartments of Ornament, and that nothing should be wanting to render the Work compleat, have been at the Expence to have them filled with proper Subjects for Paintings'.

The surviving documents do not mention any paintings and I am sure they were not executed.[2] Paine had left a generous cove to the ceiling for them and three years after completion was still trying to indicate to the City fathers in the book devoted to their Mansion House that paintings would 'render the Work compleat'.

A few clues are available to suggest the painter Paine had in mind. The title-page of the book shows a portrait of the architect drawn by Francis Hayman and engraved by Grignion. Hayman also did decorative paintings and it is significant that Paine employed him at Cusworth Hall, some two miles north-west of Doncaster. The spaces in Paine's book filled 'with proper subjects for Paintings' are an indication of what Hayman intended and were presumably

---

[1] *Ibid.*, Parcel 26.

[2] The entry in *Courtiers Book*, III, of 26th September, 1747–8, about 'Mr Paine giving security to ye Corporacon to finish ye painting yet to be done in the sd. house at such times as the Corporacon shall direct' relates, it seems, to ordinary painting and not decorative treatments.

drawn by him. But apart from considering a chandelier from Ranelagh, which eventually Paine could not obtain 'at the price proposed', no 'outside' touches were allowed. Perritt and Rose's swirling rococo plasterwork alone captivated the dour Yorkshire committee as they danced in their assemblies to the 'town musick' and sipped the wines provided by Mr Jaques.

The many gentlemen who visited Paine's work here – he was also using Perritt and Rose at nearby Nostell about this time – may have included William Wrightson of Cusworth Hall, Doncaster. He had started to build his house[1] in 1740 to his own design with the help of the Rotherham architect George Platt. The central hall was completed by 1745, but, his second wife having died, building was temporarily abandoned. The work went on in due course, but Wrightson's son-in-law complained that he considered the south front 'too tall for its length' and Paine was asked to design two wings which would help to correct this impression. The west wing was to contain a chapel and that on the east and south side a Library. Eleven letters from Paine, and estimates and bills for materials document the work in considerable detail. Wrightson tried to arrange for economies in the original estimate of £894 8s. 11½d. and Paine suggested that he could lessen it 'by finishing plainer' and that the owner might find his 'own timber, Bricks, Lime, Sand & Common Wall Stones, and as the Laths and Nails will be but a trifle I would Advise you Also to Provide them . . .'. Paine's attention to detail is indicated in his statement of 18th January, 1749–50: 'I made three different Designs for y[r] intended Additions 'ere I cou'd Please my Self.' His busy life within these years is hinted at when he tells Wrightson in a letter of 3rd July, 1750: 'I have got the Drawing of the Front very Forward (Altho I never was so hurried in Business in me life).'

The work at Cusworth was in the hands of a team of Yorkshire workers,[2] with the addition of two accomplished craftsmen, Joseph Rose senior for plasterwork and Francis Hayman for the paintings in the Chapel (Fig. 76). Rose's detailed bill shows his rates for work, per foot.

| Running of enrichment | 2d. | Laurel leaf | 1/0d. |
| Enriched Astragal, | 4d. | Festoon of Leaves | 1/6d. |

Hayman provided a fresco, *The Ascension*, for the Chapel ceiling, and a painting, *The Good Samaritan*, for the altar piece. He was paid £26 5s. 'in full' on 19th March, 1752. Rose then surrounded it with four 'flowers' at 23s. each, and added cherubims, festoons and carved trusses elsewhere. He framed Hayman's altar painting with a stucco border for £4, and received £226 8s. 2d. for all his work. His man Luke Green assisted.

Paine meanwhile was still busy. He sent instructions through his clerk, Joseph Rumball, to

---

[1] Leeds Reference Library, Battie-Wrightson MSS A22–32.

[2] The workers under George Platt, *c.* 1740, included, as carpenters, his son-in-law, William Rickard, John Morton and John Bower; plasterer Richard Wilkinson of Wakefield; bricks (163,000 at 6s. 6d. a thousand), Samuel Brookesbank; slater, Thomas Aldom; lead, William Harwood. Paine used John Mosley as mason (stone from nearby Brodsworth); carver in wood and stone, Christopher Richardson; painter, William Cave; decorative painting, Francis Hayman; plasterer, Joseph Rose; carpenters, James Norris, Lionel Garlick and John Wilson. Doors and windows were by Richard Middlebrook.

the carpenter, John Wilson, who was working at Cowick some twenty miles from Doncaster. Paine was reconstructing the house for Viscount Downe and needed to know 'whether Ld. Downe gave Orders for a New Chimney Piece for his Bed Chamber or not' and 'how forward all the works are at Cowick'. As well as being busy with buildings, a letter to Wrightson of 8th February, 1749, indicates that Paine had married again (his first wife was Sarah Jennings of Wragby, near to Nostell Priory, in March, 1740–1) to a Charlotte Beaumont.[1]

Cusworth Hall was, however, a much less significant commission for Paine than Serlby Hall,[2] near Bawtry, for Viscount Galway, or Felbrigg,[3] Norfolk, for William Windham. For Felbrigg Paine again used Joseph Rose as plasterer, assisted by George Green, who may have been a relative of Luke Green, Rose's man at Cusworth. In February, 1752, an incompetent plasterer (unnamed) had been sent down, and Hull (Paine's foreman at Felbrigg) 'must write to Mr Rose for another'. In April Rose was there himself working on the staircase and again in June, executing to Paine's designs the reliefs of the four Seasons on the dining room ceiling. Green did the Library ceiling, that of the Cabinet and further work on the staircase. There is a letter to Green from Joseph Rumball, writing from Paine's office in Holles Street enclosing a drawing of this ceiling. By 1753 the work was complete, but even with the money paid to him Paine was writing from London to Wrightson, on 19th March, 1754 ' . . . I need not tell you that Building is expensive As you have been so large a Benefactor but permitt me to Acquaint you its more so here than in the Country which ocasions a Scarcity of Money with me . . . '. It was April, 1761, before he opened his bank account at Coutts, preparatory to work at Sandbeck, Alnwick, Gopsal, Thorndon and a variety of the kind of commissions which in exterior style remained Palladian. The interior work was composed of an individual variation of Adamesque which showed, as Hardwicke said, 'the superiority of his taste in the nicer and more delicate parts of decoration'.

While Paine designed good rococo ceilings for Perritt and Rose to execute – those at Nostell are superb – they did not quite match in skill of execution the unknown stuccoist working at Norfolk House, London,[4] in about 1750, a house designed for the ninth Duke of Norfolk by Matthew Brettingham. The collections at the house were dispersed in 1938, but fortunately the Music Room was saved and re-erected at the Victoria and Albert Museum. Musical instruments and the flowing lines of decoration, some rich with gilding and worked with rare skill, must have required considerable care from craftsmen and architect. An account book[5] notes that Brettingham was paid £800 'for my trouble, Jorneys, Drawings and expences and atten-

---

[1] Charlotte Beaumont (1722–66) of Whitley Beaumont, Yorks. Joseph Foster, *Pedigrees of the County Families of Yorkshire*, 1874.

[2] Nottingham University Library, Galway MSS 12415 is headed 'Prices of different kinds of work allow'd at Serlby p. Jnº. Carr & Jas Paine, Esqrs.'. As the book is dated 1774 it does not seem that Paine and Carr were working together at Serlby.

[3] R. W. Ketton-Cremer, *Felbrigg*, 1962, pp. 131–43.

[4] Described and illustrated in detail, *Survey of London*, Vols XXIX–XXX, 1960.

[5] P.R.O., C108/362. This lists the craftsmen but apparently not the skilled stuccoist. Clark, a plasterer, is mentioned. This is probably Thomas Clark, who worked for Brettingham at Holkham.

dance'. This contrasts sharply with the £60 Paine received for his attendance at Cusworth. Wrightson had been always struggling for economy and one suspects Paine of a *double entendre* when he wrote to his patron 'I need not tell you that Building is expensive . . .'.

One of the stucco decorations at the Doncaster Mansion House is of music and instruments and this accorded well with a statement of the architect, Isaac Ware. Writing in his *A Complete Body of Architecture*, 1756, he was concerned to naturalise the French style and introduce 'the flowers of our country . . . wind instruments . . . and the representation of books of music'. He deprecated ceilings 'straggled over with unmeaning C's and O's and tangled semi-circles', but at Chesterfield House, the building he designed for the fourth Earl of Chesterfield, 1747–9, he was forced to bow to his patron's demands in these directions. The representation of music and wind instruments certainly came. Apart from the examples at Norfolk House, at Doncaster and Fairfax House, York, the Italian plasterer Francesco Vassalli put them in his stucco decoration of the saloon at Hagley about 1759. Whoever did the plasterwork at Nuthall Temple, Nottinghamshire (about 1756, now destroyed), also favoured the motif. The work is attributed to Thomas Roberts of Oxford.

Within four years of Ware's book decoration was to be as naturalistic as the trailing vines which cover the staircase walls of the Royal Fort, Bristol. At Kirtlington, Oxfordshire, the cove of the Library ceiling, decorated about 1745, is rococo in feeling and is one of the few English ceilings which bears comparison with the rococo plasterwork, *c.* 1754, which was being produced for the young Adam brothers at Hopetoun, near Edinburgh. The author of this Scottish plasterwork was probably Thomas Clayton who had a yard at Leith and worked at various Scottish houses.[1] One of his bills for work at Blair Castle in 1747 is quoted elsewhere (p. 188). In his second bill, dated 20th June, 1753 (but including work to July, 1756), he charges for 'Palmyra ceiling' and 'Palmyra Cornice' and, it seems, he based these on Robert Wood's book, *The Ruins of Palmyra*, of 1753. This splendid folio of measured drawings was produced under the patronage of the Dilettanti Society following an expedition to Syria Wood made in 1750 in the company of James Dawkins and John Bouverie. These were archaeological exercises which Paine, the ardent Palladian, thought little of – he said that 'although Palmyra and Baalbec are curious (and in some respects useful) works, they furnish no new light in the great parts of architecture, and are only valuable for the ornaments . . .'.

It was, however, preoccupation with ornament of this nature which caused the 'milords' returning from the Grand Tour to concern themselves not only with the rococo style but with the Gothick and Chinese rages. In Worcestershire George Lyttelton and his architect Sanderson Miller were busy erecting at Hagley a ruined castle and bringing Gothick into the church. The Bateman family were doing the same at Shobdon in Herefordshire, and Horace Walpole and his 'Committee of Taste' were working hard to remain the leaders of the strange style of the moment which owed so much to medieval precedent. At Strawberry Hill Walpole used William Robinson, the Clerk of Works at Greenwich Hospital, to supervise his workmen.

[1] John Fleming, *Robert Adam and his Circle*, 1962, p. 333; *Country Life*, 17th December, 1964, 11th February, 1965, p. 301.

There was a need to create atmosphere – it was left to Robinson to see that the effect was structurally sound, for as 'Gilly' Williams[1] said, 'Mr Walpole had already outlived three sets of his battlements', and noted on another occasion that 'Horry is now as much a curiosity to all foreigners as the tombs and lions'. Bewildered Frenchmen, accustomed to the niceties of rococo, struggled to understand the Gothick of Strawberry Hill, to which they were welcomed with music playing in the cloister and complimentary verses for the ladies set up in type at the printing house. It was built, as Walpole said,[2] ' . . . to please my own taste, and in some degree to realise my own visions'.

The Gothick style, the origins and details of which have often been discussed,[3] had strongly entrenched itself by the late 1750s. In 1757 James Adam was writing to the portrait painter Allan Ramsay 'with respect to the treatise on Gothic architecture', and in the Soane Museum and elsewhere are a number of sketches which show the study the Adam brothers gave to this vogue.[4] Gradually all obstacles were being cleared by Robert Adam for his début in London. He returned from his Italian tour in the winter of 1758. Within a year or two a new young monarch who was a patron of the arts was to come to the throne. By 1762, when Walpole wrote 'if there are any talents among us, this seems the crisis for their appearance', the 'Adam style' had taken hold. The long years of apprenticeship in Scotland and study in Italy had brought success within grasp.

The sixty years of an age which had involved itself so fully with the architectural orders and had bred patrons, architects and craftsmen dedicated to following them strictly, although there had been divergences and frivolities, was over. It was to be no longer easy to choose rococo, Gothick or Chinese. True to the pattern of his muddled life Sir George Lyttelton was one of the last to decorate his house at Hagley in 1759 with rococo plasterwork by the Italians.[5] By 1761 they had gone abroad and everyone was ready to turn to Adam's 'regiment of artificers'. The visions of what might be and the revivals of ancient style were now in one hand and directed by one mind.

[1] George James Williams – 'Gilly' – was a friend and correspondent of Walpole and his circle.
[2] Horace Walpole, Preface to 'A Description of the Villa . . . at Strawberry Hill', *Works*, 1798, II, p. 398.
[3] R. W. Ketton-Cremer, *Horace Walpole*, 1940, p. 226. For Walpole and the Gothick Revival see Sir Kenneth Clark, *The Gothic Revival*, 1950, and W. S. Lewis, *Horace Walpole*, 1961.
[4] Fleming, *op. cit.*, p. 85.
[5] Late commissions were Hagley (Vassalli, 1759), Ragley (Artari, 1759), and Croome Court (Vassalli, 1758–9).

PART TWO

A Regiment of Artificers

1760—1800

'*He came at the head of a regiment of artificers, an hour after the time he had promised: the bricklayer talked about the alterations to be made in a wall; the stonemason was as eloquent about the coping of the said wall; the carpenter thought the internal fitting up of the house not less important; then came the painter, who is painting my ceilings in various colours, according to the fashion.*'

Mrs Montagu to the Duchess of Portland, 20th July, 1779 (referring to Robert Adam).

' . . . *we have introduced a great variety of ceilings, freezes, and decorated pilasters and have added grace and beauty to the whole* . . . '

The Works in Architecture of Robert and James Adam, 1778.

I

Launching a Style

THE achievements of Robert Adam at some forty-five country houses are comparatively well known. They have given rise to his reputation for elegance, good workmanship and the employing of skilled craftsmen. Students of his work are fortunate in being able to turn to the nine thousand Adam drawings acquired by Sir John Soane in 1833, and housed in the museum which bears his name. They show, however, that the career of the brothers cannot be assessed solely in terms of interior decoration and that their minds constantly conceived on a much grander scale than the minutiae of designing door-knobs and window catches.

Their name is casually connected with any mid or late Georgian building in the generic way in which every piece of wood-carving is 'Grinling Gibbons', and every item of furniture 'Chippendale'. The term 'Adam style' has become more or less a household word even if it often denotes the strugglings of a rich world to imitate it. The activities which led to this flowering and the career of the most talented of the four brothers, Robert, lasted a little over thirty years.

Robert Adam was the second of four distinguished brothers and was born at Kirkcaldy, Fifeshire, on 3rd July, 1728. His father, William, was the first strictly classical architect that Scotland produced, and those who only know the late Adam interiors would do well to look at a house like Mellerstain, near Kelso, where the centre block is by Robert and James, put up in the 1770s, and the wings, previously unconnected, by their father in 1725. Here is a castellated style, severe, battlemented and a stern foil to the delicate ceilings and paintings within.

When William Adam died in 1748 the practice was continued by his sons. The second Earl of Hopetoun suggested that Robert should go on the Grand Tour with him. He and his younger brother, Charles, intended to spend the winter of 1754 in Italy and the Earl asked Robert to accompany them and share the expense of the journey. They would travel as social equals, an advantage Adam eagerly seized. He wanted to qualify as an architect and prepare himself to be the supplier of 'some new and undiscovered resources for the internal decoration of private apartments by introducing elegance, gaiety and variety instead of that dull and elaborate floridity', and secondly to issue a large imposing folio on architecture which would in the engraved splendours of its title page, dedication and context herald his return to England and introduce him with, he hoped, 'a great puff conducive to raising all at once one's name & Character'.[1] Both these aims he realised in spectacular fashion even though his folio *The Ruins of the Palace of the Emperor Diocletian at Spalatro in Dalmatia* was not published until 1764.

[1] For the years in Scotland and Italy see Fleming, *op. cit.*

The years in Italy, with the many contacts made and lessons learned, were full and fruitful, but in 1756 his family began to press him to return home. His elder brother John was apprehensive of the mounting cost if the architect lingered much longer abroad. He had been spending some eight or nine hundred pounds a year, apart from his purchases of works of art. While he hoped to recover some of the outlay by selling pictures and engravings in London, he too became increasingly concerned about money and with reluctance started his leisurely return to England.

On the way back he visited Florence, where he went to the opera with Walpole's friend Sir Horace Mann. A couple of months were spent inspecting Venice and the nearby towns, but even here creditors were pressing. Finally he landed at Harwich, was lucky through the Customs in that the official was a virtuoso and a lover of drawings, and was set fair, he hoped, for a good future. A year or so was spent in consolidating his position and making new contacts by meeting such people as the Earls of Bute and Mansfield. At the accession of King George III in 1760 his career was fairly launched. He was appointed with his rival Sir William Chambers 'Joint Architect of His Majesty's Works' and a year or two later his book on Diocletian's Palace was issued with its dedication to the King.

Such patronage as was now to be Adam's demanded a talented team of craftsmen to put his ideas into effect. He early made use of the family firm of Rose (p. 70) for the execution of his plasterwork and used them almost without exception. While documentation is not complete, they must have worked at almost every commission he undertook. At one of the first decorative tasks at Croome Court, Worcestershire, Adam used as his carver John Gilbert who had worked at the Mansion House twenty years earlier, and such work was also done by John Linnell and Sefferin Alken. His mason was usually John Devall, and Matthew Boulton at his Soho, Birmingham, works produced ormolu, steel, and silver work. Thomas Blockley, 'the foremost locksmith in the Kingdom', supplied door furniture. In addition a skilled team of decorative painters (p. 84), all foreign except for William Hamilton, were used. Cipriani, Zucchi, Angelica Kauffmann, Biagio Rebecca and Michele Angelo Pergolesi are the names most frequently encountered. John Voyez, who modelled for the potter Josiah Wedgwood, was a carver who 'had been two or three years carving in wood and marble for Mr Adam'.

Chimney-pieces were provided by Thomas Carter, John Hinchcliff, Joseph Wilton, and other stone and marble carving by John Baptist Locatelli and Michael Henry Spang. Some of the iron and copper-work such as skylights, lining domes, and staircase balustrades was entrusted to Thomas Tilston and William Kinman. Carpets to Adam's design in such houses as Syon and 20, St James's Square were woven by Thomas Moore, who in 1756 was given a grant by the Royal Society of Arts for excellence in carpet-making; but on one occasion at least, for Mersham-le-Hatch, Adam provided an Axminster carpet. Furniture[1] was made by Ince and Mayhew, Cobb and Vile, Thomas Chippendale, and many other skilled cabinet-makers, including, as at Croome, the Frenchman Peter Langlois. The mode was the antique and Adam

[1] Eileen Harris, *The Furniture of Robert Adam*, 1963; Clifford Musgrave, *Adam, Hepplewhite and other Neo-classical Furniture*, 1966.

was praised a generation later by Sir John Soane for his 'light and elegant ornaments . . . imitated from the Ancient works in the Baths and Villas of the Romans'.

All this activity provided and demanded a secure financial standing. Adam's bank account at Drummonds commences in 1764 and shows that while he had a balance of £6,620 in that year the amount had increased to £12,359 5s. 11d. by 1768 and to £40,123 11s. 11d. by 1771. For the painters out-payments are made only to Antonio Zucchi and William Hamilton and there is no mention of Rebecca or Angelica Kauffmann. Joseph Rose and George Richardson, John Gilbert, William Kinman, Oliver Alkin (probably a relative of Sefferin Alken the carver) are all there and are names we shall often meet in connection with the Adam style in terms of plaster, wood and metal-work. The retaining fee[1] to Adam's tutor and friend Charles-Louis Clérisseau was still being paid in 1766, but there is no later payment than this. The imparted knowledge was now used in hard work. The style was launched drawing freely on youthful memories of Scottish architecture and the advantages of knowledge garnered in Italy. There was no turning back for 'my dearest Mother's British boy'.

[1] Fleming, *op. cit.*, pp. 242, 365. Drummonds Bank, Adam account, 5th June, 1765, £300; 1st August, £300; 19th December, 1766, £163 10s.

II

'The Ingenious Mr Rose'

Joseph Rose – 'his father before him and his grandfather before him were plaisterers: and we almost all know the great name of the family'.

Mr Wallace in the law-suit Liardet *v* Johnson, 1778.

THE name of Joseph Rose, junior, has long been associated with the plasterwork he produced to the designs of Robert Adam and, to a lesser degree, James Wyatt and Sir William Chambers. He is mentioned in *The Works in Architecture of Robert and James Adam* as having worked at Syon and elsewhere, but otherwise very little is to be found about him in any of the existing books on architecture and plasterwork. His work is also frequently confused with that of his uncle Joseph, whom we have noted (p. 59) working for James Paine. After a long period of research with many baffling features some account of his life is now possible.

Joseph junior was baptised on 7th April, 1745, at Norton, Derbyshire. He was presumably apprenticed to his father Jonathan or his uncle Joseph, but the fact is not recorded. His grandfather Jacob had been a plasterer, his father and uncle were, and his brother Jonathan was. The use of the same christian name in two generations has frequently led to confusion. In 1768, three years after he was made free of the Worshipful Company of Plaisterers, he visited Rome, where, like the Adam brothers, he presumably laid the foundations of his knowledge of classical design. In 1769 he went on an eighteen-day excursion into other parts of Italy with a distinguished party[1] which included the landscape painters James Forrester and George Robertson, Mr and Mrs Richard Dalton, a Miss Robinson, Gavin Hamilton, Peter de Angelis, and Joseph Nollekens, the sculptor. (Dalton had been sent to Italy by King George III to collect pictures and James Wyatt met him there and formed a life-long friendship). Maps of Rome and Venice, together with French architectural books, were included in the sale after Rose's death in 1799.

Returning to England, he married in 1774, became Master of the Plaisterers' Company in the same year, and from then onwards was one of the best known and busiest craftsmen in

---

[1] *Walpole Society*, Vol. XXXVI, p. 58, note 16, confirming Richard Hayward's statement in his MS List of English visitors to Italy (British Museum, Dept. of Prints and Drawings) that Rose was in Rome in 1768. I am indebted to Mr Brinsley Ford for his help in this matter.

England. His uncle Joseph died in 1780 and left him the very successful business they had built up together.

The confusion in Christian names has meant that Joseph junior has been credited, for example, with the Wentworth Woodhouse work (1751–63) carried out by his father and uncle. Joseph junior can actively be reckoned into the picture from about 1765, when he was almost twenty, but he was probably present at most of the family commissions from his early teens. He was a formative influence in turning the firm's attention to the Adam style which first appears in their work at Croome Court, Worcestershire, in the early 1760s. Almost all work prior to Joseph senior's death in 1780 was on behalf of the family firm. At Harewood House, Yorkshire, for example, when Rose junior received payment he states that it is for the use of his uncle Joseph. For Alnwick it is by 'Joseph Rose & Co.'.

Turning from the forms of rococo decoration practised by Rose senior in the 1740s, they built up an unrivalled set of moulds in the 'new' antique taste. A book of friezes by them (now in the Library of the Royal Institute of British Architects) shows no other style being followed. Only once in later years to my knowledge did Rose senior revert to a version of his earlier style in the work he did (significantly while the nephew was in Italy) at Claydon under its architect, Sir Thomas Robinson, where, accompanied by Luke Lightfoot's amazing carving, the medallions reappear in the Saloon ceiling and cornice, with draped swags of flowers, in a technique whose freedom belongs to the 1740s rather than to 1768. The firm monopolised English plasterwork for nearly fifty years, throughout the second half of the eighteenth century. As Rose senior was only fifty-seven when he died he was presumably active after the change of style but may well, after about 1770, have confined himself more to organising and administration. Their annual income, as implied in the wills of both uncle and nephew and in the many commissions I have noted,[1] must have been measured in thousands of pounds.

When Joseph Rose junior died in February, 1799, it was stipulated in his will[2] that his equipment and collections should be sold. The sale took place at Christie's on 10th and 12th April, 1799, and a study of the priced catalogue is useful in that it reveals not only something of the organisation of Rose's business, but also indicates the books he possessed. These give some idea of the sources of his work. The first day's sale of the 'late ingenious Mr Joseph Rose' was of equipment and architectural models. His premises in Queen Anne Street East comprised: '*Casting Rooms* containing vases, crests, Arms, medallions and various ornaments, a *Loft* and the *Wax Room* which contained vases and candelabras, sculls, masks, boys, figures, tripods, vases, griffins, pateras, flowers, medallions and birds.'

Friezes, lions and sphinxes were also in the *Hay Loft*, while Lot 38 in the *Gallery* was 'a marble floor from Rome'. The *Mill Room*, Stables, Counting House, Cellars, Room under Gallery and the Cart House, all contained similar items including thirteen casks of composition. At the Riding House Lane premises Rose had an *Exhibition Room* in which bas-reliefs, a model for which a premium was granted, medallions and other models were shown alongside busts of Homer, Sir Isaac Newton and '14 other heads'. Lot 122 was 'A Capital and model of the

---

[1] *Apollo*, November, 1966.   [2] P.C.C., 138 Howe.

Cornice of the Temple of Jupiter Stator at Rome'. In the *Mould Room* were, of course, wax moulds and a quantity of plaster casts and basso relievos, while the *Coach House* contained the boards and poles, ladders and trestles for scaffolding erection. On the last page of this first day's catalogue 'Clement Cryer, Plasterer' announces that he intends to continue Rose's business, having been his assistant for 'near Thirty Years'. The first day's sale raised £157 14s. and Rose's assistants Richard Mott and Rothwell bought several lots.

The second day's sale, on 12th April, realised £246 11s. 6d. and was mainly given over to books. In view of Rose's importance as a plasterer I have listed the relevant items as they are written with their lot numbers. Sometimes two or three titles are grouped together as one lot.

122	Inconologia di Ripa, Forestiere Instrutto – Brook Taylor's Perspective.
123	Richardson's Iconology. 2 vols., with plates.
133	Montfaucon's Antiquities & Supplement. 7 vols.
134	2nd vol. of Piranesi & 1st Part Rossi's Civil Architecture.
135	Vitruvius Britannicus, 5 vols.
136	Sketches of Friezes by Mr Joseph Rose.
137	Ruins of Palmyra.
138	Ruins of Balbec.
139	Major's Ruins of Paestum.
140	Stuart's Athens, 3 vols.
141	Ionian Antiquities.
142	Bartoli's Admiranda Romanorum.
143	Logge del Vaticano.
144	Chambers Civil Architecture, Elevations and Plans of Houghton.
145	Leoni's Palladio.
146	Adam's Architecture.
147	Richardson's Five Orders of Architecture.
148	Parallele d'Architecture, 2 vols. and Desgodet's Antiquities de Rome.
149	Swan's British Architect.
153	Richardson's Architectural Designs. 10 nos.
154	Richardson's Ceilings. 8 nos.
155	Fourteen Views in Rome engraved from Clérisseau.
156	Piranesi's Vases.
157	Six Maps of Rome, Venice, etc.

Decoration in stucco of the Adam period must be considered in relation to the law action in 1778, 'Liardet *v.* Johnson'. The facts are set out in two rare pamphlets, *Observations on Two Trials at Law respecting Messieurs Adams's new-invented Patent Stucco* and a *Reply* thereto, with 'the summary of the evidence and charge to the Jury'. They were published in 1778. The stucco was mainly used for exterior plastering, but Adam found it easy to use it for panels, picture-frames and swags. The 1778 pamphlet asserted: 'that the antients possessed the art of making such a composition . . . and in the year 1726 Leoni Baptista Alberti, an ingenious Italian architect published receipts for the composition of a stucco or cement of this kind. In the year 1732 Governor Pyke communicated to Dr Halley the receipt for compounding such stucco as used in the East Indies . . . Notwithstanding this, one Dr David Wark of Haddington in Scotland obtained a patent in the year 1765 for such a compost, as a new invention of his own, and in the year 1773, one Liardet, a Swiss clergyman, obtained another for a similar invention; both which patents, it seems, were purchased of the respective patentees by Messrs Adams, the celebrated builders of the Adelphi; whose name the stucco in question now goes by, under the appellation of ADAMS'S new invented patent Stucco . . .'

The Adam brothers obtained an Act of Parliament in 1776 (Robert Adam was still a Member of Parliament) which vested them with the exclusive right to make and sell the composition. In this Act the specification was much amended, though still left rather vague and indefinite. Thus the brothers were now in a position to prosecute anyone selling a composition resembling Liardet's. In a short time they were forced to proceed against the architect John Johnson, who claimed to have improved on a composition previous to that of Wark, Liardet or Adam and had proceeded by patent to manufacture it. The case was heard in the King's Bench before the Lord Chief Justice, Lord Mansfield, a fellow Scot and friend of the Adam brothers, who had worked at Kenwood for him.

In the *Reply to Observations* . . . , the summing up by counsel, Mr Wallace, briefly notes the evidence of many architects and plasterers, including Rose, who spoke for the Adam brothers. 'Mr Dance, a man of experience, observation and character in this way . . . never used it (the stucco) himself', but thought it 'a most excellent composition indeed'. The opposition were scathing enough about this! They called Robert Mylne and James Wyatt and Wyatt is noted as having employed 'Mr Milner, a witness, to do a house for Lord Thanet'.[1] They were followed by the further opposition support of Sir Robert Taylor, James Paine, Paul Sandby and James Stuart. The last said that 'he has no experience in stuccos; but he speaks to its being the desideratum; for Mr Anson, he says, whom everybody knows is a great encourager of all arts and sciences, had his house in Staffordshire [Shugborough], in a bad situation, covered with stucco, which failed'.

The pamphlet continues: 'then they called several witnesses, who had had it used . . . and there is a great list of plaisterers, who join with the architects. The first of whom is Mr Rose, whose father before him, and his grandfather before him, were plaisterers; and we almost all know the great name of the family, and he himself for thirty-four years; and, he says, this is quite new to him – "he never knew of any thing like it". That it is much superior to any thing he did know; and where his would not last a year and an half, this has lasted four years; and, he says, where he has seen it, succeeded; and in all his experience, he was never taught to do

[1] Assigned by Colvin to Chambers, but Antony Dale (*James Wyatt*, 1956, p. 43) notes a design by Wyatt for the ceiling in Lord Thanet's dressing room at the Victoria and Albert Museum and support is given to his authorship by the 1778 pamphlet.

such a thing before . . .' Dobbins, a plaisterer, said 'he had tried it – it would not do; he tried festoons for Lord Coventry, they would not do; he never knew any that promised to do like this'. John Davies, a plasterer, said more or less the same. Support, however, for the superiority of the Adam stucco continued. The mason John Devall the younger, who had worked at Adam houses, spoke in favour of it: 'and he thinks this is the best he ever heard of'.

After a long hearing Lord Mansfield, having confessed to the jury that he 'was too much fatigued' to sum up the evidence, said: 'this cause hath taken up a *monstrous* deal of time – I should not wonder if you are spent – for I am.' The unknown observer of the 'attack' noted in a footnote: 'no fewer than six (of the witnesses) having their eyes closed, at one time, during Mr Wallace's reply . . . but whether they slept in earnest, or only dozed a dog's sleep, it cannot positively be affirmed.'

The various patents and the *Philosophical Transactions of the Royal Society*[1] enable us to check the 1778 facts. Isaac Pyke, who was Governor of St Helena in 1717, spent much time in building a tomb ten feet in height by seven feet broad in memory of his wife. He presumably gained the experience which enabled him to report to Edmund Halley, Vice-President of the Royal Society, of 'a method of making the best mortar'. From such developments, David Wark, a Doctor of Divinity, claimed in his specification (1765, No 834) 'a composition of stone paste made with oils and various other things'. This could be used to cover walls, roofs, domes and to line water cisterns, and was somewhat different from the stucco used later inside houses.

In 1773 'John Liardet of Great Suffolk Street in the Parish of St Martin's-in-the-Fields in the City of Westminster, Clerk' claimed in his specification of Patent (1773, No 1040) to have invented 'A Composition or Cement for all the Branches concerning Buildings to which the same is applicable . . . ' The cement was composed of 'drying oil, any kind of absorbent matters, white or any coloured lead, solid whatsoever (gravel, sand, &c), as circumstances will require it'. George Jackson (1756–1840) carved reverse moulds in boxwood to press out the Liardet composition. His enterprise laid the foundation in 1780 of the present firm of G. Jackson and Sons whose collection of moulds now numbers many thousands.

The Adam brothers, by Lord Mansfield's verdict in their favour, obtained control of this composition. 'John Johnson of Berners Street in the Parish of St Mary le Bone in the County of Middlesex, Architect' had dared by his specification of Patent (1777, No 1150) to claim that he had 'a cheap and Durable Composition for the Covering the Fronts and Tops and ornamenting of Houses and buildings . . . which will adhere to surfaces that are wet as well as those that are dry at any season of the year'. He reckoned however without Scottish tenacity, and the tremendous influence the Adam name exerted. Surely Joseph Rose would say the Adam variety was good. He had earned £2,829 17s. in the years 1761 to 1770 at Harewood, £2,684 in two years, 1766–7, at 20, St James's Square, and £1,822 3s. at Nostell.

It is now time, however, to follow the Adam brothers, secure in their book knowledge and the esteem of many patrons. They had assembled a talented team of craftsmen, ready to add 'grace and beauty to the whole'.

[1] Vol. 37, 1731–2, p. 231.

III

Something Like Truth

'But their substitution of the Greek fret, the honey-suckle, the husk, and other ornaments of graceful contour, instead of the nondescript angular flourishes, was an approach to something like truth.'

Mary Berry to Horace Walpole (*referring to the Adam brothers*).

CROOME COURT, WORCESTERSHIRE

ONE of the patrons most ready to recognise the skill and talent of Robert Adam was the sixth Earl of Coventry who was building at Croome Court in Worcestershire. He used 'Capability' Brown as his architect and landscape gardener and probably accepted much advice – some unlooked for – from his friend, the gentleman architect, Sanderson Miller. In December, 1752, Lord Deerhurst (as he then was) wrote to Miller and said: 'what ever merits it (Croome) may in future time boast it will be ungrateful not to acknowledge you the Primary Author . . . .' This was interpreted many years ago as conclusive support to the theory that, because Croome resembled Hagley (which in turn, according to Horace Walpole, resembled, and was 'stolen' from, Holkham), Miller must have designed both houses. In 1951 the family papers indicated Brown's share in the design of the house and the nearby church; and the close resemblance to Claremont and Redgrave (houses indisputably by Brown) was pointed out.[1] The Sanderson Miller letters (at the Warwickshire County Record Office) show that as the busy squire of Radway he took only a spasmodic interest in an advisory capacity. Lord Guernsey writes to Miller: ' . . . I am glad of your surprise at what Deerhurst has done at Cromb, as I wish him success in his undertakings.'

The Croome Estate Trustees have kindly made available to me an account book, a series of accounts and furniture bills (and one letter), sent to the sixth Earl of Coventry (1721–1809) by Robert Adam and others for work at Croome Court and the family's London house, 106, Piccadilly (now St James' Club). They cover in great detail the years 1760–81 and represent a large proportion of Adam's working career. The accounts add interest to the Adam drawings for Croome preserved at Sir John Soane's Museum and the few drawings in the possession of the Estate Trustees.

The Adam accounts, neatly tabulated on folio sheets, begin in August, 1760, with an

[1] Dorothy Stroud, *Capability Brown*, 1st edn., 1951, pp. 47–9.

elevation and plan of the Greenhouse or Orangery (£15 15s.), and the first 'Design of a Ceiling for the Gallery' was submitted in September at £12 12s. This was speedily rejected and in March, 1761, 'A new design (as executed) for the Ceiling of the Gallery' finds its place at £9 9s. It was intended to fit the Gallery up as a Library and the ceiling design of the early Syon type depicted elongated octagons and lozenges which harmonised well with the rest of the lavish decoration. In May, 1761, an 'Elevation and Plan of a Bridge' (£15 15s.) – possibly the bridge in Richard Wilson's painting of the house – preceded the 'Sections of the Inside Finishings of the Gothic Church'. The 'new' church at Croome, in which material from the old church appears to have been incorporated, was designed, as Repton has said, by Brown, but we know that his work was 'confined to the carcase while the internal treatment, as in the case of the principal rooms of the house, was handed over to Adam'.

As in most architectural accounts a certain number of items listed were never executed or failed to satisfy Lord Coventry. Some were repeated at full size for the craftsmen and others slightly adapted. The design in the Soane Museum for the Library ceiling of January, 1763, was used for the Tapestry Room ceiling. This is now in the Metropolitan Museum of Art, New York.[1] In June, 1763, Adam sent a section of the Gallery 'finished in the Antique Taste with Statues, Bas Reliefes etc' and all the 'mouldings at large for Messrs Cobb and Vyle', the cabinet-makers, and 'the ornaments for Mr Alken for the Bookcases of the Library'. This is Sefferin Alken (p. 172) who worked at Shardeloes for Adam and was at Croome, 1763–5. He carved friezes, architraves to doors, windows and probably the fine guilloche moulding around the windows, the dentils of the chair rail and the fascia and leaf moulding around the base-board of the Tapestry Room.

Adam visited the site in October, 1763, and a month later sections of the 'Tapestry Room, Staircase and Dairy Offices' were sent for Lord Coventry's approval. His Lordship had visited the Gobelins tapestry manufactory in August, 1763, and had ordered a set of Boucher Neilson tapestries; these were finally ready by 1771. The Tapestry Room ceiling on fir laths was by now painted bluish white, and the chimney-piece was given a red Veronese marble background and trims in white and lapis lazuli. Joseph Wilton, the State coach carver and sculptor to his Majesty, possibly carved this and certainly did the caryatid chimney-piece for the Gallery.

The master carpenter was John Hobcraft who worked in the house carrying out Adam's Gothic designs. The family firm of Joseph Rose and Co. were the plasterers, and John Gilbert provided the brass furniture such as doorknobs and lock plates.

It was at this stage of submitting the accounts that a note of discord crept into the relationship of architect and client, Lord Coventry having rendered but £250 in settlement. Adam retaliates in a long letter of 3rd April, 1764, which is worth quoting in full as an indication of the more material attentions an architect needed to give his livelihood.

---

[1] The history of the room and its tapestries is given by James Parker and Elizabeth Standen, Metropolitan Museum, *Bulletin*, November, 1959; and in *Decorative Art from the S. H. Kress Collection at the Metropolitan Museum of Art*, 1965. Dr Eileen Harris dealt with Lord Coventry's visit to the Gobelins factory, *Apollo*, April, 1962, and in her book *The Furniture of Robert Adam*, 1963, pp. 10–12.

'I received the Honor of your Lordship's Letter with the draught for £250 and have returned the Bill discharged to your Lordship. I am extrimely sorry your Lordship should have thought of deducting any part of the Money, as almost every person I have done designs for, upon considering that it is my only Branch of business, and that I have never stated a sixpence for Surveying (which every Carpentar [sic] & Bricklayer who call themselves Architects, claim with not half the justice I might) have generally sent me a present over and above the Bill itself, and not long since upon delivering one of seventy five pounds, I received a Hundred, with this Compliment That he knew how many thousands I had spent in acquiring knowledge, and if he was to offer seventimes that sum he did not know where he could have got Designs that would have pleased him so well.

'I am very far from either asking or expecting anything of that kind from your Lod'p But cannot help wishing from the Respect & E'teem I have for your Lod'p that you had considered me as incapable of stating more than I thought was just, when I compute the Time employed by my clerks, the high wages I pay them, and the particular attention I have always given & will continue to bestow on everything that is your Lordships.

'Your Lod'p will at once be convinced that it consumes the same Time & requires the Same Money from me for Drawings, Executed or not Executed, as your Lo'p knows I have charged nothing for the Execution though I have done everything that gives a title to that Claim. If I was paid 5 p.c. (for surveying I could then afford with Justice any Drawings for less money, or even made a present of them altogether).

'I must beg that your Lod'p will be so obliging not to mention any taking less than the Total of my Bill, I will with the greatest pleasure join the other things your Lod'p desires for the same money as I do assure you that it is not the difference of the payment that is capable of giving me the smallest concern. And will exert myself in the other buildings for Croome and always endeavour to show with how much esteem & Respect I have the honor to be

> My Lord,
>   Your Lordship's
> Most obedient and
>   Very Humble Servant
> [Signed] Robert Adam.'

London. 3rd April, 1764.

Lord Coventry paid the full amount the same day! He fully patronised the furniture and cabinet-makers and one hundred and twenty-eight bills survive for the period 1757 to 1800. All the main names are there – Cobb, Vile, Ince and Mayhew, statues and tables from the Carters and John Cheere, furniture from France provided by Poirier and in England by Peter Langlois. Chippendale and Rannie provided boxes, fire-screens and a shaving table. Ince and Mayhew put up Lord Coventry's Gobelins tapestries when they reached Croome in 1772. All were kept busy – all were paid.

In February, 1765, Adam sends 'Another Design of a Chair for Gallery at Croome £2.2.0.' or 'another Design of a Sopha or Scrol Chair'. We are informed that the 'parts at Large of a Sedan Chair' will cost £3 3s. od. Not only furniture and a 'richly ornamented cloaths press' did Adam design, but a 'Grate & Fender for the Gallery at Croome' and such varied work as 'Drawing at large of the Dial plate of the clock at Croome for Mr Mudge' (Thomas Mudge).

Adam visited Croome again in November, 1765, for six days and charged £20 to the account. Work continued on the Dairy and outbuildings and even the lamp-standard in the Stable yard was designed, for £3 3s. od., in January, 1766. The largest item during 1766 was £21 for the 'Plan and elevation of a Design for a Menagerie at Croome', closely approached by £20 for 'Two Ornamentall paintings in chiaroscuro for two large panels in the gallery at Croome at £10 ea'. Smaller 'pannels' were supplied at £4 each. The Gallery at Croome 'has full-size sketches in grisaille showing arabesques of the Shardeloes type' (only on the fireplace side have they been executed in stucco), in addition to the splendid fireplace with its life-sized figures and swags of flowers draped between delicately moulded fingers.

In October, 1766, Adam was busy in assisting Lord Coventry in the embellishment of 'Capability' Brown's landscaped park, with his new design of 'a Building between the woods' known now as the Panorama Tower, and possibly modified at a later date by James Wyatt. His Alcove Seat followed in the same month adding £10 10s. to the accounts. In 1760 Adam had designed the 'greenhouse' or the Doric Orangery with its delightful carved basket of flowers nestling in the pediment. Unfortunately the accounts do not reveal any description of the classical circular Garden Temple, c. 1766 (unless it be the 'Menagerie' mentioned in 1766), despite its betrayal of typical Adam decoration masking early Georgian treatment.

After attending for a number of years to the many alterations and decorations Adam turned his attention in 1767 to 'curtain cornices' and 'rings for window shutters' and other minor ornamentations. He also sent Lord Coventry a considerable number of elevations of the house 'done on stampt parchm'[ent].

The interest in France at this time and the extensive transfer of Adam's influence in design to that country is reciprocated when we note in May, 1767, that Adam designed a Tripod 'altered from a French Design for a water stand'.[1] Later, in 1767, with the majority of the main work of internal decoration at Croome completed, Adam was busy for the next few years at the London house, designing furniture, mirrors, carpets, picture-frames and 'rich mouldings'. From July, 1770, until June, 1779, we have no accounts and it is possible that very little work was executed over this period. In March, 1781, Adam submitted a 'New Design for a Bridge' and many details of the Menagerie as well as Designs of an Iron Gate (in May, 1781) 'in two different ways'.

[1] Harris, *op. cit.*, p. 11.

The accounts conclude in June, 1781, with 'A Section of the Upper part of the Staircase with the addition of a "Cove"' and, while there are drawings dated as late as 1791 for gateways, it does not seem that much more documentary evidence will come to light to reveal Adam's activities at Croome during these last years of his life. When Adam died on 3rd March, 1792, the Earl was one of the pall bearers at his funeral.

The complete Adam accounts as available total £733 12s. Today Croome Court is a school. The Tapestry Room as we have noted is a main feature at the Metropolitan Museum, New York, and some of the furniture is at both the Metropolitan and the Philadelphia Museums.

KEDLESTON, DERBYSHIRE

In 1768 Horace Walpole paid a visit to Kedleston in Derbyshire. 'The front is heavy,' he said, 'there being no windows, but niches behind the columns.' This north front (1761) was the work of James Paine who had taken over from Matthew Brettingham[1] and is illustrated in his *Plans and Elevations of Noblemen's Houses* (1783). For the interior Adam was soon designing for Lord Scarsdale. An examination of the Kedleston archives reveals the interesting fact that for this interior work Samuel Wyatt, a competent architect in his own right, was working under the supervision of Robert Adam. Wyatt had organised taking down the old Kedleston – a house probably designed by Francis Smith (p. 28) – when Sir Nathaniel Curzon (as he then was), fresh from the Grand Tour, decided on a new house. Before this work was finished he was to spend some £22,508 9s. 4¼d.[2] on carpenters, joiners, masons, plasterers, all at work under the careful guidance of the Adam brothers.

In an account book at Kedleston (1760–65) the 'state of Samuel Wyatt's Account with Rt Hon the Lord Scarsdale ending 1st December, 1764', is entered – £4701 16s. Robert Adam signed it after examination. The Roses were again busily providing the plasterwork. Their bill[3] of £1,107 16s. 8¾d. was made up as follows:

[1] Harris, *op. cit.*, p. 62, discusses an early drawing of the Great Hall at Kedleston, *c.* 1757, which may relate to Brettingham's work and to a suggested scheme of decoration, attributed to James Stuart.

[2] Masons, Joseph Hall, John Chambers, James Denston (new Bridge, 1770), £6596 1s.; bricklayers £2,685 12s.; carpenters/joiners, William Johnson, assisted by Richard Clark, Charles Sowter, Thomas Bedson, £5,104 8s.; glaziers, Joseph Taylor, William Cobbett, £477 10s.; slaters, Pratt and Co., £344 18s.; plumber, Joseph Taylor £27 15s. 6d.; leadwork, William Chapman, £1,079 9s.; painter, Thomas Smith, £113 17s.; ironmonger and smiths £478 12s.; coppersmith, William Kinman, £307; carvers, George Moneypenny and Joshua Hall, £2,501 3s.; plasterers (plain), Abraham Denston £412 15s. 9d; (decorative) Joseph Rose £1,107 16s. 8d.; Chimney-pieces to four rooms, J. M. Spang, £990. Some stone came from the Horsley Castle Quarry (John Whilton), five miles away.

[3] Kedleston Account Book, 3R, fol. 64.

	£	s.	d.
Music Room	192	19	8
Drawing Room	345	6	5¼
Library	212	7	1¼
Portico	22	12	5½
Hall	29	0	6
Saloon	35	7	3¼
Dining Room	270	3	3½

It is possible to work out the price of the component parts of each ceiling. The Drawing Room (Fig. 101) has a rose in the centre (£6 5s.), lion's masks at £1 10s. and two 'Bass Relievos & 4 Boys, 4 Terms & 4 Figures' cost £41 6s. In the Marble Hall Rose merely added touches to the earlier work (1759) of George Richardson (?1736–1817) who, when he issued his *Book of Ceilings* . . . , in 1776 (to which Joseph Rose junior, his uncle and father all subscribed), illustrated this Kedleston ceiling.

It was inevitable that the heavy, indefatigable Dr Johnson and James Boswell should find their way to Kedleston. The Doctor was a little worried by the 'massy' alabaster pillars in the Marble Hall. These splendid columns carved by Joseph Hall for £993 12s. 5d. were polished and fluted by workmen of 'Francis Battersby, mason' for £180. The contract, dated 25th September, 1775, was between Battersby and (on behalf of Lord Scarsdale) Joseph Pickford, the Derby architect who supervised the work.

To satisfy the musical tastes of his patrons Adam had provided organs at Newby in Yorkshire and at 20, St James's Square; the one for Kedleston cost £32 15s. 5d. exclusive of the £3 13s. paid to 'Mr Gravenor for carving the ornament in the freeze and festoon of Laurel leaves for the Pipes to stand upon'. A Mr Brown and the joiner William Johnson assisted and Mr Gamble was paid £6 16s. 6d. for 'Guilding the organ case'. Chimney-pieces came from John Michael Spang (£990), and in the Salon William Hamilton, a pupil of Zucchi, did ruin paintings. As at St James's Square, the coppersmith William Kinman was employed and he sent two men down from London to fix copper skylights at a cost of £268 19s.

In the Dining Room with its attractive ceiling paintings Rose's charges for the plasterwork included the gilded surrounds to the pictures by Zucarelli, Snyders, Claude and Romanelli. To the left and right of the apse William Collins moulded plaster panels. Collins (p. 164), who also provided the figures in the Marble Hall, was the usual supplier of such classical casts.

At Kedleston the work done by and for Robert Adam can claim to be among the most interesting of his career. The materials are good and solid – his favourite external stucco was as yet unexploited. Stone was used extensively and it is significant that the masons' bill is the highest individual amount. Fifty-five tons of lead was used by the plumber to cover the Dome. In the Park James Denston supervised the erection of a bridge to Adam's design. The building of Kedleston summarises perhaps as completely as any country house can do the expensive tastes of an owner – the pulling down of a splendid William and Mary house, a new house in the classical style and the use of three architects, or indeed four as we now know it to be, Matthew Brettingham, James Paine, Robert Adam and Samuel Wyatt.

SYON HOUSE, MIDDLESEX

It has been said[1] that 'the gallery at Syon may, I think, possibly be the place where the Adam style was actually initiated. This room presented to its designer a rather special challenge and elicited a correspondingly original response.' King James I had granted the old nunnery at Syon to the ninth Earl of Northumberland and round the quadrangle a Jacobean mansion was erected. The whole length of the east front was devoted to a corridor-like Long Gallery and it is this room – the glory of Syon – which provided a special challenge in bringing it to a classical pattern. In ceiling and carpet a certain amount was done to give breadth, but it is in the treatment of the walls that the architect's ingenuity held full sway. A series of thin pilasters of the Corinthian order divided the walls into bays. The whole was finished as Adam said 'in a style to afford great variety and amusement' with plenty of delicate arabesque ornamentation.

At Alnwick Castle among a rich collection of documents are a few[2] which enable us to learn a little more of the decoration of Syon at this time. Mr Butler's two volumes of 'Receipts and Disbursements' for 1760–77 together with the Duke of Northumberland's bank account, 1757–67, at Hoare's show that Michele Angelo Pergolesi (p. 86) was paid in all £160 14s. between 1765 and 1768 for ornamenting the sixty-two pilasters in the Long Gallery, of which £20 was 'a present from His Grace'.[3] Pergolesi was also paid £24 5s. for 'his Designs for the Carpet & Tapestry at Syon House'. This was presumably the design sent to Thomas Moore for the Long Gallery carpet. Zucchi did a similar drawing to send to Moore for the carpet for 20, St James's Square. The agent, Mr Butler, visited 'Mr Moors to see his Tapestry' on 13th September, 1765, two months before the payment to Pergolesi. The carpet is signed 'by · thomas · moore · 1769' and measures 34 ft. 9 in. by 14 ft. 2 in. The Drawing Room doors (Figs 104-105) at Syon have always excited admiration for their metal ornamentation. The following payments indicate the authors, one of whom, Anderson, was a bronze-founder also employed by Sir William Chambers.

> 1766. Jan. 7. Paid Mr Brimingham on
> Acc[ot] of the Gilt ornaments
> for the Drawing Room Doors
> at Syon.   £2. 2. –.

---

[1] Sir John Summerson, *The Listener*, 27th August, 1953.
[2] Alnwick Castle MSS, Library, Vol. 94; Muniment Room UI. 41/44/46.
[3] This is at variance with the first Duchess's Syon House Book '62 Pilasters by Pergolesi at 3. 3s. od. each'.

1767. Jan. 7. Paid Mr Bermingham on
              Account for the Gilt Metal
              Ornaments for the Drawing
              Room Window Shutters at
              Syon House.   £30. 0. 0.

1767. Jan. 24. Paid Mr Anderson on Accot
               of his Bill for Brass
               Edgings gilt to the Mosaic
               Tables & Medals for the
               Drawing Room Doors at Syon.   £10. 0. 0.

There is a draft of a letter dated 4th November [1764] from the Duke to Robert Adam. He wanted the Gallery to be proceeded with and for Joseph Rose to do the plastering before the frosts so that it would be dry: 'fit to be gilt early in the Spring by which Time I hope the Paintings will be ready to be fixed up. I must desire you will order those Carved Mouldings which have been so ill executed by Mr Adair[1] to be returned him & amended in such a manner as you shall approve of for I would not, upon any account, suffer any work to be fixed up at Sion that is not compleatly finished to your satisfaction.'

One of the most notable features in the Adam decoration of Syon was the use of twelve disengaged columns in verde antique said to have come from the bed of the River Tiber. James Adam in a letter to the Duke dated 22nd April, 1765, 'has the pleasure to inform his Lod[s] that by last Mail he receiv'd from Rome the Bills of Lading for the Columns & Pilasters &c. The ship sail'd from Civita Vecchia the 27th of last month with a fair wind & in a few hours was out of sight. Mr Adam has insur'd his own things & those of Lord Shelburne, but has not insur'd My Lord Northumberland's as his Lop[s] seemed rather against it.'

His Lordship's agent, Mr Butler, on 3rd July, 1765, paid £56 8s. in 'fees & dutys at Custom House on Landing the Colums & Pilasters for Syon House', and on 9th September Mr Hillier was paid £12 6s. 6d. for 'Lighterage & carrying columns &c to Syon & 2 Statues from Milbank'. We do not know the cost of the columns, but in 1762 on 2nd August Mr Butler on behalf of his master 'Paid Mr Adams for a Bill of Exchange drawn on My Lord by his brother at Rome which he had paid £125.0.0.'. This may have no connection at all with these famous columns. Adam added gilt Ionic capitals and bases in white and gold, and on 15th November, 1763, a porter was paid 1s. for 'carrying the capital of a column sent from Syon to Mr Adam's'.[2] On 30th December, 1766, John Dayon was paid £20 for 'Locks, Latches & Bolts for the Doors at Syon House', and a 'Mr Jenkins' also provided 'Locks &c.' at £30.

---

[1] For John and William Adair see Ralph Edwards and Margaret Jourdain, *Georgian Cabinet-Makers*, 3rd edn., 1955, p. 108. John Adair worked for Stuart at Shugborough.

[2] It is, however, known that some of the columns are made of scagliola so that a Tiber origin for them all must be discounted.

Something Like Truth

LONDON, 20, ST JAMES'S SQUARE

At 20, St James's Square,[1] Rose, whose bill amounted to £2,684, collaborated with the mural painter Antonio Zucchi (p. 00). The Great Drawing Room, the Music Room, Sir Watkin Wynne's Dressing Room, the Drawing Room – all were decorated by Zucchi. He also provided the drawings of a 'Bas relief representing Aurora going before the Sun and the different Hours to be executed in marble in first drawing room', as well as the 'two figures for the jambs of the said chimney', £8 in all. Zucchi's complete bill amounted to £614 14s., but he promised to 'retouch the 2 bookcases & finish them to the satisfaction of Mr Adam'. Eight chimney-pieces were provided by John Hinchcliff for £360 10s., and Thomas Moore (who provided the carpets at Syon and Osterley) charged £232 10s. 6d. for a 'Persia carpet' to match the ceiling. Zucchi provided a small pattern of the ceiling for Moore to work from. 'For Two Bookcases Extraordinary to a design of Messrs Robt. and James Adam' Richard Collins charged £15 18s. 7¼d. — there are many payments to Collins in Adam's bank account. They were of 'rich mahogany' with '12 Ovall Patterae let into the Legs' and '130 Small [Patterae] let into the Pannels of the Doors'. Hopkins and Co. provided the steel fenders, grates and various items in copper (£70 19s. 6d.) and Robert Jones, the 'Hinges Tacks & Pins and various fittings for Lady Williams Wynn's Bird Cage' (13s.). Thomas Tilston, Richard Blockley of Birmingham and Mr Gascoigne supplied the intricate locks and door furniture (£500), and Tilston did all the 'smith's work'. His complete bill was for £1,261.

The grand staircase at the St James's house was Tilston's work again in company with William Kinman. They provided the '3 Balconies, the Copper Railing of the Best Stair Case & sundry other work in the brass & cast iron way'. 'Sir William's New House' as it is frequently called in the accounts was erected by the mason and sculptor John Devall, the younger (1728–94). His bill amounted to £4,064 14s. 10d. and he was paid in instalments over six years, 1771–77. And so one could go on but accounts are not the easiest of reading. The payments to Robert and James Adam bring us to a conclusion. They charged £1,388 15s. for 'Surveying, Plans, Measuring &c' and, as late as 25th July, 1783, Robert Adam was writing to advise certain repairs in the laundry and kitchen areas. Here if anywhere 'something like truth' of the quality of his work was bound to be spoken.

[1] National Library of Wales, Williams-Wynne MSS; *Survey of London*, Vols. XXIX–XXX, 1960.

IV

In the Best Manner

'... he [Cipriani] then offered to paint for the whole room at Two Guineas each picture & to finish them in the best manner ...'

The Duke of Northumberland to Robert Adam, 4th November, 1764.

No Adam interior after the early years was complete without painted decoration and it is convenient to discuss here the more important artists.[1] They did on occasion work for architects such as Chambers and Wyatt, but to the casual mind their achievements are solely related to those of Robert Adam, and the development of his neo-classical style. In addition to the foreigners there were many native decorators; for instance the architect James 'Athenian' Stuart (1713–88), who had a vast knowledge of ancient art and antiquities, and decorated some of the interiors he designed, such as the Painted Room at Spencer House, St James's.

It is, however, with such painters as Angelica Kauffmann, her third husband Antonio Zucchi, Giovanni Battista Cipriani, Michele Angelo Pergolesi and Biagio Rebecca that we must briefly concern ourselves. Many decorations have been carelessly attributed to Angelica Kauffmann, probably because documented ceiling paintings by her are very rare.[2] Born in Switzerland, she trained in Italy and came to England in the early years of Adam's important building activities. As a foundation member of the Royal Academy – there are authenticated ceiling paintings by her at Burlington House for which she received £100 – Angelica showed regularly at the annual exhibitions. Her engravings were also used as the basis of decorative work on furniture, and for Matthew Boulton's decorative paintings 'process' (p. 87). She finally left England for Italy in 1781, the year in which she married.

Antonio Zucchi (1726-95), Angelica's husband, was probably employed by Robert Adam in 1757 to engrave plates for the *Spalatro* book[3] and at the architect's invitation he later came to England. He appears many times as a payee in Robert Adam's bank account, on one occasion in 1770 for £1,000.

[1] Full biographical details and a catalogue of their works will be given in Vol. II of Edward Croft-Murray's *Decorative Painting in England, 1537–1837*.

[2] *Angelica Kauffmann*, Exhibition of Paintings at The Iveagh Bequest, Kenwood, 1955. The catalogue cites the relevant literature about her life and work.

[3] John Fleming, *Robert Adam and his Circle*, 1962, pp. 270, 370.

In England Zucchi centred himself in London and was much visited by prospective patrons. Therese Parker, *née* Robinson, writing[1] to her brother Frederick in London on 17th September, 1769, asks that he call about the pictures ordered from Zucchi by her husband, John Parker, for the Library of their Devon house at Saltram. They are still to be seen there and form one of the chief attractions of this interesting house. Occasionally Zucchi's detailed bills survive, as for 20, St James's Square, or the one in broken French headed '*Mémoire de Mr Zucchi pour des Tableaux peints pour Son Excellence My Lord Mansfield*' at Kenwood. They show that, as with most artisans, he was subject to supervision by Robert Adam and is perhaps the painter most closely identified with the architect's work.

Giovanni Battista Cipriani came to England with the architect Sir William Chambers and within a year or two had the honour to decorate King George III's State Coach[2] designed by his new-found architect friend. Adam gave him the important commission of decorating in the Drawing Room at Syon. In the draft of the letter (partly quoted at the head of this section) of 4th November, 1764, from the Duke of Northumberland to Robert Adam the Duke mentions a price disagreement: '. . . I am sorry there appeared any mistake between us about the price fixed for the Paintings which I am persuaded will be very easy set right but it proceeded in a great degree from what Cipriani himself told me when I showed him the two Paintings, one with a Single, the other with Double Figures which were done as Specimens and which I am certain he then offered to paint for the whole room at Two Guineas each picture & to finish them in the best manner . . .'

The roundels in the Drawing Room have been repeatedly ascribed to Kauffmann rather than Cipriani yet further support of the latter's authorship is again provided by Mr Butler's Receipt and Disbursement Books (at Alnwick).

1765. July 5. Paid for Post Chaises for Mr Cipriani & myself going to Eaton to examine the Antique Paintings there.	58s.
1766. Feb. 24. Coach hire to Syon with Mr Cipriani, whole day.	16s. 10d.
Feb. 27. Paid for a Post Chaise to Syon with Mr Cipriani when he went to alter the Ground of his picture.	18s. 6d.

For many years Cipriani has been credited with the centre of the Tapestry Room ceiling at Hagley Hall, Worcestershire, although the late Margaret Jourdain doubted this in view of

[1] Edward Croft-Murray, *Country Life*, Coronation number, 1953, pp. 80–7.
[2] Studley Royal MSS, Ripon, Robinson letters, 14476.

George Lyttelton's letter[1] to Mrs Montagu in which he says that Stuart[2] is engaged to paint him 'a Flora and four pretty zephyrs'. The zephyrs, oil on tempera, are still there, but the centre painting, oil on canvas, was badly damaged in the Hagley fire on Christmas Eve, 1925, and the present painting is a copy by an Italian named Nerini employed at the time of restoration. In Sir William Chambers's letter book[3] there are letters of 1773 to Lord Melbourne telling him that 'Cipriani has finished all the paintings for the Great Room' at Melbourne House. The letter book gives an interesting idea of the care needed to prepare a room for the reception of such paintings. In 1770 Chambers was retained by the Duke of Bedford to fit up the Library and Dining Room at Woburn. Cipriani with Biagio Rebecca provided the paintings, and three extracts from Chambers's letters speak for themselves of the progress made:

19 May, 1770. . . . I believe one of the painters that is about the Library Ceiling will go downe next week to make his remarks upon the light & to verify some measures & as he cannot speak a word of English I should be obliged to you if you would desire anyone in the family that understands Italian to ask for any thing he may want of the work-men . . .

I June, 1770. . . . as I shal want to fix up some paper Patterns in the Library Ceiling at Wooburn Abbey be pleased to have 2 or 3 Plaisterers trusses in the room to form a Moving Scaffold high enough to reach to the top of the Cove.

22 November, 1770. . . . the painters have nearly finished the Ceiling for the Library at Wooburn Abbey & will be down soon to put it up. I hope therefore that all your things in the room are nearly done, as when they come the room must be cleared for them & they must have moving Trussels to stand upon . . .

By 1771 Cipriani had finished his part of the Library ceiling and Chambers writes to ask for the remainder of the money due to the artist 'which is £217.10 his Agreement being 350 Guineas or £367. 10 Mr Biagios part not being yet finished he is not entitled to the Remainder of his Mony'. Biagio Rebecca was to be paid £220 1s. 'for Painting the Ornaments' and £10 travelling expenses. Rebecca's chief skill lay in the imitation of antique bas-reliefs and his monochrome *trompe l'oeil* style was much in evidence in late Georgian interiors. He worked for Adam, Sir William Chambers and James Wyatt in particular, and his best known work is for the latter at Heveningham. At Audley End Rebecca, using Vertue engravings, created an interesting series of portraits after the sixteenth-century picture *The Visit of Queen Elizabeth to Blackfriars* attributed to Marcus Gheeraerts the younger and now at Sherborne Castle.[4]

Michele Angelo Pergolesi is only known for his work at Syon (p. 81). It is probable that he

[1] Emily J. Climenson, *Elizabeth Montagu*, 1906, Vol. 2, p. 150.
[2] Stuart had designed the Temple of Theseus at Hagley for Lyttelton in 1758 and there is a payment of £20 to him in Lyttelton's bank account for that year (Hoare's Bank).
[3] British Museum Add. MS 41133.
[4] *The Connoisseur*, April, 1957, p. 164.

was sent to London by James Adam, when on his Italian tour. Between 1777 and 1785 he issued several books of ornament and design.

Theodore de Bruyn, a Swiss artist, had a good practice. The Duchess of Queensberry, writing[1] to Sir William Chambers on 23rd November, 1772, advises him: 'that she can now acquaint him of the name and abode of that Artice sent from abroad by the Dutchesse of Norfolke, his name is de Bruyn, his dwelling place little Castle street, Cavendish Square, being near Sʳ William he will easily & soon judge by what he will shew and explain having done for Lord Radnor from designs of Montfaucon . . .', and she wonders 'whether or not such will answer well for the Chinese house . . .'; this was a temple which Chambers designed for her at Amesbury, Wiltshire, in that year. His principal work in this country was in the Dining Room at Farnley Hall, Yorkshire.[2] He painted some eighteen pictures, charging in all £59 9s. 8d. The medallions in the Dining Room, painted in sepia on canvas, are sculptural in effect and, surrounded by Joseph Rose junior's plasterwork, stand out boldly from the background. One of the overdoor panels is signed and dated 1789.

It was inevitable that this demand for ceiling paintings should make Matthew Boulton of Birmingham turn his attention to cheaper but good quality versions. Although his part in eighteenth-century industrial development is well known, less attention has been paid to his many artistic achievements. Something is known about the manufacture of silver and of Sheffield plate which went on at Boulton's factory at Soho near Birmingham, and a little has been written about his ormolu work, buttons, cut-steel trinkets, and watch-chains, but there is no really satisfactory account of these activities; and his work on coinage, for example, is an important field for research which still remains largely unexplored. Nevertheless, some valuable work has been published, especially where the significance of one group of surviving manuscripts[3] has been recognised. These record in considerable detail Boulton's work on 'mechanical paintings'.

The method used was a form of aquatint in which the engraver employed a brush and a mixture of resin and nitric acid upon a copper plate. The colour was applied in the inking-in stage and frequently only one plate seems to have been used to receive all the colours. The canvas which took the impression was covered with gum to receive the print more easily. Finally the impression, now transferred to the canvas, was touched up by hand and varnished to give the appearance of an oil painting. The touching-up process was highly skilled, and the painter most frequently employed by Boulton was Joseph Barney of Wolverhampton, who had connections with Angelica Kauffmann. He is described by Boulton and Fothergill as 'superior to any of his brother Artists in or about Birmingham'. He worked on the mechanical paintings for the ceilings of Montagu House. Other painters were Richard Wilson of Birming-

---

[1] British Museum Add. MS 41133.

[2] Illustrated in *Country Life*, 3rd June, 1954, p. 1809.

[3] Birmingham Assay Office MSS. See *Apollo*, January, March, 1950, September, 1951; *Country Life Annual*, 1950; *Annals of Science*, IX, December, 1953; *Econ. Hist. Rev.*, XVI, No. 1, 1963. Mr. Robert Rowe's *Adam Silver*, 1965, includes a careful study of the Assay Office MSS.

ham and a Mr Simmons, also of Birmingham. On some occasions the impression was taken up to London so that it could be corrected from the original; on others, the picture was brought up to the Midlands; and Boulton wrote to many owners of important paintings for permission to copy them. A very high standard of craftsmanship was demanded throughout all stages.

In 1774 Amos Green wrote from Bath to Jonathan Scale, one of Boulton's departmental superintendents at Soho, to tell him that he had seen Thomas Gainsborough, 'who has promised me a drawing. I am to see him within three days, the moment I have Mr Edgerton shall hear from me.' By 1776 Boulton and his partner John Fothergill were ready to enter into a partnership with Edward Jee (or Gee) and John Eginton to produce mechanical paintings. The partnership was intended to last fourteen years. Jee and Eginton were already in partnership in a firm which manufactured gilt frames. From Boulton's point of view, however, the key figure in the enterprise was Francis Eginton (1736–1805), who was in charge of the japanned ware department at Soho. He was also a designer and manufacturer of stained glass,[1] providing, for example, panels to the design of William Hamilton for Beckford's Fonthill Abbey, the Gothic extravaganza designed by James Wyatt.

Why was there a sale for Boulton's mechanical paintings? Some of his patrons wished to adorn their walls, doors and ceilings with such paintings. Often the repetition of a certain figure or landscape could be used to build up a large design. Where several copies of a picture were required the Soho method was much cheaper than hand-copies, and if a customer was content to choose from the Soho catalogue instead of ordering originals, another great saving could be made. Presumably all these copies were on canvas, so that the walls, doors and ceilings ornamented with them must have had mounted canvas panels. They were also used to adorn coaches and furniture.

Elizabeth Montagu, a distant cousin by marriage to Matthew Boulton, was the first to use mechanical paintings on a large scale. John Wyatt is asked to call upon Mrs Montagu in 1776. From 10th June in that year to the 5th November several letters between Soho and John Wyatt in London concern themselves with the pictures for Mrs Montagu's dressing room. These were to be inserted at Montagu (afterwards Portman) House in Portman Square, designed by James Stuart, and erecting from 1775 to 1782. It was regrettably destroyed by bombing in 1940. The paintings were designed by Biagio Rebecca and Cipriani.

In the engaging way artists occasionally have, Rebecca and Cipriani were not to be hurried, and Boulton and Fothergill became a little alarmed at the delay. The paintings were to have gilt frames from Jee, Eginton and Co., so that one part of the business dovetailed with the other. Then the services of Angelica Kauffmann were enlisted. At the end of 1776, she was commissioned to paint *Penelope with the bow of Ulysses*, and this proved to be one of the more popular subjects among the mechanical paintings. Her next picture for Boulton was not until 1778, when she painted a companion piece to the *Penelope* entitled *Calypso, mournful after the departure of Ulysses*. Eventually she painted in the region of thirty pictures for the mechanical project. On 25th July, 1778, Mrs Montagu wrote to Boulton that she had 'no opinion of any

[1] *Journal, British Society, Master Glass Painters*, Vol. 2, 1927–8.

room of beauty or state without embellishments from Mr Boulton', and he replied, in August, 1778, in similar terms, that: 'Mr Egginton and I shall attend to the ornaments for your house in Town. If our success should be equal to my wishes, I shall impute it to the earnest desire we feel that our Execution should not be unworthy of your patronage. . .'

By October, 1778, Mrs Montagu was enlisting Boulton's help with the decoration of her Great Room, and in January, 1779, Boulton and Fothergill were awaiting designs from her architect, James Stuart, for that purpose.

It was in November, 1778, that Boulton made a real effort to enlist the architect James Wyatt's attentions in the promotion of mechanical paintings. It was obvious that architects would be the best persons to introduce commissions of this kind to Soho. Boulton therefore wrote to John Wyatt on 23rd November asking him to make the following enquiries from his cousin, James: '1st. Would Mr James Wyatt like to introduce Soho paintings supposing it to be done well and upon such terms as he would be satisfyd with if so – 2nd will Mr Jam^s Wyatt favour Soho with two or three of the figures he was so kind to offer Eginton when hear [sic]. 3rd – Can he oblige Soho with the sight of any other specimens of such kind of Painting which he thinks most likely to be useful. 4th Can he send a Design either in Painting, Drawing or writing for either Compartments in Cielings, Pannels or Ornaments for Soho to execute and thereby give an Idea of their work and price. 5th He should be inform'd that although such subjects that will bear repetition are the most proper for our purpose yet if he wants any Single subject Painted it can be done at Soho as cheap or cheaper than he can have it done in London of the same Quality . . .'

It may have been the mechanical painting which led Mrs Montagu to renew her acquaintance with James Wyatt, whose genius, she wrote, 'is so universal that he cd. design the most beautiful temple or Superb palace or prettiest cottage'. She had long been tiring of James Stuart's delays, and she considered him 'idle and inattentive'. As for Stuart's assistant, Gandon, she declared, 'I believe Mr Stuart made choice of him as men do of their Wives for their passive qualities rather than Serviceable talents'. Gradually she turned more and more to Wyatt for the completion of her great designs, though, in view of Wyatt's later characteristics, the change is perhaps ironic.

James Stuart and James Wyatt were not the only architects to be approached by Boulton on the subject of mechanical paintings. In 1777 Boulton and Fothergill sent samples to Robert Mylne, who was then architect for Lord Arundell.

Despite the display at Montagu House of ceiling paintings, door panels, etc., and the attention which they undoubtedly attracted, the mechanical painting business was not a financial success. Boulton, busy with steam-engine business, was ready by 1781 to try to bring the trade to an end. Some paintings were commissioned for export by Messrs Clark and Green in this year, but by the time Isaac Hawkins Browne, M.P., inquired about such paintings for his Shropshire house, Badger Hall,[1] which James Wyatt was building for him, it was too expensive to revive the process. Browne was referred to Joseph Barney, but for Boulton a remarkable

[1] Demolished 1952. Barney's paintings are now at Buscot Park.

enterprise was ended.[1] The historian is left wondering how many paintings 'in the best manner' of Angelica Kauffmann may yet be recognized as Boulton's mechanical paintings.

[1] A list of subjects with dimensions appears in the Boulton and Fothergill out-going Letter Book, 23rd December, 1780 (pp. 667–8), and in the 22nd June portion of the 1782 *Inventory of the Contents of Soho* (Assay Office, Birmingham). I am indebted to Mr Eric Robinson for much information on this subject.

V

Rivals and Claimants

*' . . . Melbourne House, decorated in a manner almost diametrically opposite
to theirs, and more, as I flatter myself in the true style . . . of the Ancients.'*

Sir William Chambers to Lord Grantham, 1773.

THERE were rivals and claimants to Adam's position, but, while he worked with many whom he replaced in the patrons' esteem, few spoke ill of him. John Carr and Capability Brown wrote favourably of him, Robert Mylne remained on friendly terms and also James Stuart. Sir William Chambers, James Wyatt and Horace Walpole were less tolerant of the brothers – the 'brace of self-puffing Scotch coxcombs' as the Reverend William Mason called them.

It is not difficult to establish which craftsmen Chambers[1] used to support and extend his claim (*above*). An early liaison 'William Chambers and Thomas Collins' to the extent of a joint bank account at Drummonds (continued in later years in Chambers's name only) is a useful starting-point. It explains Chambers's long association,[2] until the Somerset House days, with this plasterer; they also worked together in the 1760s at Milton House, Northamptonshire, for Lord Fitzwilliam. Chambers was an 'official' architect in the sense that he became in 1761 (as did Robert Adam) one of the two 'Architects of the Works' to King George III, to whom, when Prince of Wales, he had been architectural tutor.

Sir William's letter books give some idea of his views on interior decoration. The Duchess of Queensberry, writing to him on 23rd November, 1772, about colours, says: 'Sir William knows that the assemblage & blending of couleurs are Great Principals of his own masterfull supream taste.' Chambers was decorating Lord Melbourne's house in Piccadilly, using, as we have seen, the decorative painter, Cipriani. Thomas Chippendale was providing furniture. On 14th August, 1773, Chambers writes to Lord Melbourne: ' . . . Chippendale called upon me yesterday with some Designs for furnishing the rooms wch upon the whole seem very well but I wish to be a little consulted about these as I am really a very pretty Conoisseur in furniture . . .'

He wanted 'fewer sophas & more chairs' in the great room, thinking this better 'than as

[1] The architect's career and works are fully discussed in a forthcoming biography by Mr John Harris.
[2] The active partnership seems to have concluded in 1773. Chambers to Henry Errington (B.M. Add. MS 41133, 12th May, 1773).

Chippendale has designed'. Lord Melbourne writes on 13th October, 1774, to indicate that he 'is averse to admitt any gilding whatever in the furniture, in my opinion the Elegance of that room is from the lightness of well disposed, well executed ornaments . . . '. Chambers replies that he thinks the 'Glasses and Soffas in the Niches should be gilt for glasses without gilding are large black spots that kill the effect of everything about them, and the dead coloured silk with which the Soffas are to be covered must have gold to relieve it . . . '.

In May, 1770, he is telling Gilbert Mason, 'merchant at Leith', that 'with regard to the painting Your Parlours, if they are for Common use Stone Colour will last best & is cheapest but if you mean them to be very neat pea green and white, Buff Colour & white, or pearl or what is called Paris Gray and White is the Handsomest'. Good advice still. This period gave attention to minute detail – 'would your Lordship have brass rising hinges to the doors' – 'I think from his small Drawings that some parts may be improved a little' and so on.

During the early years of the 'seventies, Chambers reconstructed Milton Abbas, Dorset, for Joseph Damer, Lord Milton. In October, 1771, 'the painting is going on as fast as possible. Ansell has not yet been able to make out his Estimate for the Gilding . . . I find it is to be like some Gilding done by Norman at the Queens House. I hope it will not be so dear for the Cornice of one room there was charged at near £200.' Ansell also provided mirror frames and consoles at Blenheim to Chambers's design and the reference to 'Norman' is probably to the cabinet-maker Samuel Norman who worked at Woburn and supplied the Dundas family with furniture for their Adam house in Arlington Street.

Sir William of course claimed that he interpreted the classical style in more chaste form than Adam. He had referred to Adam's filigrane toy work and had presumably supported Walpole's invectives about the Scottish architect. By the time the *Works* were published the adoption of the 'ancient style' was held paramount in interior decorations by followers and opponents of the brothers or of Robert Mylne. A principal rival was the architect James Wyatt, the sixth son of a Staffordshire builder and timber merchant.

In 1762 he travelled to Italy with Lord Northampton and his secretary Richard Bagot[1] of the Staffordshire Bagots seated at Blithfield, for whom James Wyatt's family worked. He is said to have stayed in Italy for four years studying part of the time under Antonio Viscentini. Bagot's brother, Sir William Bagot, was an amateur architect and employed James 'Athenian' Stuart (who was also working for Bagot's friend Thomas Anson at nearby Shugborough) and James's brother, Samuel. They would surely encourage the young Wyatts.

Shortly after his return, London society was excited about the important building he designed – the Pantheon in Oxford Street in which the interior plasterwork was by Joseph Rose. Walpole thought it 'the most beautiful edifice in England' and recorded in the issue of *The Gentleman's Magazine*, 27th January, 1772, that 'imagination cannot well surpass the elegance and magnificence of the apartments, the boldness of the paintings, or the disposition

[1] A source for this journey, in addition to the State Papers, Foreign, Venice 1762–3 at the Public Record Office, is that at Compton Place, Eastbourne, Box Q. Wyatt is not mentioned but Northampton's activities are well detailed. He died at Venice in 1763 and Bagot's bank account as his executor is at Drummonds.

of the lights . . . Besides the splendid ornaments which decorate the rotundo, or great room, there are a number of statues, in niches, below the dome'.[1]

Wyatt's career has been tangled with the large and complex family from which he sprang. His relationship in a working capacity with his brother Samuel, for example, has been underestimated. The problems surrounding them both are complicated and we are not always ready to admit that on many occasions their work surpassed that in the 'Adam style'. In addition, as at Fonthill, James created an essentially picturesque if structurally unsound Gothic pile which William Beckford and the age clamoured for. The effects of overwhelming splendour for which he strove at Salisbury he achieved here. He was full of ideas, but in the execution of his schemes[2] he would often lose his first ardour – many of his clients grumbled at his dilatory and unbusinesslike ways – and he lacked the ability to conceive and appreciate mass as Vanbrugh did so well at Blenheim. Perhaps a capable 'Hawksmoor' to Wyatt would have enabled firm realisation as it did on the earlier occasion with Vanbrugh's restless pencillings. His character was weak, his mind untidy, and he chose according to Lord Liverpool 'to engage in a great deal more business than he was capable of'.

In his mausolea at Cobham and Brocklesby Wyatt reveals his debt to Sir William Chambers, but we need to turn to one of his late classical houses, Dodington, Gloucestershire, built for Christopher Codrington, to appreciate the expenditure and effort involved in a Wyatt house. There are detailed accounts and over seven hundred drawings and plans, but only a small number are signed or dated. Wyatt received £4,026 17s., but this amount also included reimbursement for sundry outlays. Some £3,000 a year was spent until 1817. Bartoli and Alcott were used for the scagliola work[3] and Edward Wyatt (1757–1833) did woodcarving. The arrangement of the staircase was designed to incorporate wrought ironwork from old Fonthill House which was demolished in about 1808.

In the Drawing Room there is splendid joinery and the original chimney-piece with Wedgwood medallions was supplied in 1810 by Richard Westmacott at a cost of £98 15s. James Wyatt had little chance to dine in the splendid scagliola dining room, with its black and gold marble chimney-piece, for on 14th September, 1813, travelling from Dodington to London in his patron's coach, there was an accident in which the coach overturned. Codrington escaped unhurt (and indeed lived until 1843), but Wyatt received a blow on the head which killed him instantly. Unpredictable in life, he died in the same way.

I have left to the end one of the most accomplished provincial workers in the Adam style – the northern architect John Carr (1723–1807).[4] In his early years he was following the Palla-

---

[1] See *Survey of London*, Vol. XXXI, 1964.

[2] Anthony Dale, *James Wyatt*, 2nd edn., 1956.

[3] Sir William Chambers writing to William Key, 13th October, 1773, said: 'Messrs Ritter Bartoli, Newport Street, near Newport Market London, imitate almost any sort of marble . . .' John Richter took out a patent (1770, No 978) for 'my invention of "an Art or Method of inlaying Scagliola or Plaister in and upon Marble and Metals to imitate flowers, trees, fruits, birds . . . and all sorts of ornaments"'. He was living at this time at Berwick-upon-Tweed. See p. 46 for early uses of scagliola.

[4] The researches of Mr R. B. Wragg have done much to establish this architect's activities (York

dianism of Lord Burlington – he had been clerk of works at Kirby Hall, Yorkshire, designed by Burlington and Roger Morris – but soon saw that he must adopt – and adapt – in interior decoration at least, the new ideas of Adam. He did not look back to other styles, except for the odd essay in revived Gothic, and when he added a south wing to the Elizabethan Farnley Hall for the Fawkes family it was not in imitation Elizabethan but in the best style of which he was capable. At Harewood, Carr, a distant relative of the Lascelles family, did most of the supervisory work and the State Rooms were decorated under Adam's care; it is evident that Carr did not himself use the fashionable talent of the day. No work by Zucchi or Rebecca was done under his supervision and at Cannon Hall, Barnsley, he used in 1766 the York plasterer James Henderson rather than the Rose family. It is possible that Carr as well as Henderson did use the services of the Italian stuccoist Giuseppe Cortese, for Henderson acted as executor (together with the Wakefield upholsterer Edward Elwick) at Cortese's death in 1778. The two were obviously in some form of partnership.

One of Carr's most interesting houses is Everingham Park in the East Riding of Yorkshire near to Market Weighton. The documents[1] show that work was started in 1757 and finished about 1764. The brickwork was done by Richard Swale, the carpenter's work by Richard Bainton and James Cade, and Bainton then joined William Taylor for the joinery work. The skilled carver was Daniel Shillito, who also worked at Harewood, Fairfax House in York and Tabley Hall in Cheshire. At Tabley Carr's model of the house and stables is preserved. The building accounts give Thomas Oliver as plasterer and a carver, Matthew Bertram, assisted Shillito. The timber was bought in Liverpool and, as at Cannon Hall, most of the chimney-pieces were obtained at York, probably from John Fisher, with some coming from William Atkinson at 'Hyde Park Corner', London.

Carr's early work had been improved on by his contact with Robert Adam, but he was often still hindered by the absence of good craftsmen to carry out his wishes, and by his insistence, for instance, that York men, like the gilder Blakesley, could do the gilding for the drawing room at Wentworth Woodhouse 'as well as any man in this county, and he certainly will do it as well as anybody out of London'. The supremacy of York and Bristol had declined during the years when the foreign painters were at work under Adam and in which the cabinet-makers of London were competent at doing everything from debugging the bed – as Vile did for Lord Coventry – to carving the mirror frames and hanging the tapestries.

Carr of course retained at least the sense to try to make his patrons go on London buying expeditions. Walter Spencer Stanhope recorded in his Diary[2] for 29th April, 1768: 'Mr Carr went with me to Mr Tyler the Notary and paid him his bill, from there he went with me to Cobbs, Chippendales and several other of the most eminent Cabinet makers for the order of proper furniture for my Drawing Room.' Amusingly enough some of the costs were probably

---

Georgian Society, *Report*, 1955–6, pp. 55–65). Dr Eric Gee has established a large number of York town houses by him, many having common external characteristics.

[1] East Riding, Yorks., Co. Record Office, Beverley.

[2] Sheffield Reference Library, Spencer-Stanhope MSS.

too high and on 18th May 'Mr Carr called upon me, discoursed him about furniture of my drawing room. Said he would speak to Ellick & write to me'. Elwick lived at Wakefield, nine miles away, and the provincial man won part of the day, as the diary records for 21st May. Some furniture did, however, arrive from London on 9th November and 'Ellick's man' put it up and cleaned and measured it. Stanhope must have been satisfied and Carr often dined at Cannon Hall, attending to alterations on three more occasions and as late as 1804.

By this time Adam had been dead twelve years and Chambers for eight and Dance and Soane were the successors. The latter in his Royal Academy lectures spoke kindly of 'Messrs Adam' to whom 'we are more particularly indebted for breaking the talismanic charm which the fashion of the day had imposed, and for the introduction from Ancient works of a light and fanciful style of Decoration . . .'. But within a few years Joseph Gwilt was comparing James Stuart against 'the opposite and vile taste of Robert Adam'. The new men for the moment were raised triumphant until the great nineteenth-century exhibitions of Adam style furniture and a resurgence of books again focused attention on the superb realisations of a man and a style. They gave to craftsmen the chance for their finest achievements, in striving beyond competence to virtuosity.

1. Castle Howard, Great Hall; Bagutti and Plura's stucco chimney-piece. *c.* 1710.

2. Castle Howard, the High Saloon; painted by Pellegrini *c.* 1710, destroyed by fire, 1940.

3. Castle Howard, Great Hall; detail of the stucco chimney-piece. *c.* 1710.

4. (*Below*) Blenheim Palace, Duchess's Bedroom; marble chimney-piece. 1712.

5. (*Above*) Blenheim Palace, Saloon; marble doorcase by Grinling Gibbons. 1712.

6. Blenheim Palace, Duke's Study; detail of window-sash.

7. Wentworth Castle, Yorks.; stucco-work probably by Giovanni Bagutti and Giuseppe Artari. *c.* 1724.

SIC · DEVS · DI · · · LEX · ET · MVNDVM

8. St Michael-le-Belfry, York;
reredos by John Etty. *c.* 1708.

9. St Michael-le-Belfry, York;
detail of Etty's altar rail.

10. Duncombe Park, Yorks.; west entrance front by William Wakefield. *c.* 1713.

11. Atherton Hall, Lancs., by William Wakefield. 1722. Shown in a painting by Arthur Devis of *Richard Vernon Atherton and his family in the grounds of his house* (Paul Mellon Collection).

12. Beningbrough Hall, Yorks.; staircase by William Thornton, 1716.

13. Beningbrough, staircase; parquetry inlay with initials 'J.B.M.' (John and Mary Bourchier) and date, 1716.

14. Beningbrough, West Drawing Room; Thornton's carving in the cornice. c. 1716.

15. The Guildhall, Worcester; Thomas White's carving in the pediment signed 'T. White' and dated 1722.

16. Wimpole Hall, Cambs., the Chapel; painted by Sir James Thornhill. 1724.

17. Hanbury Hall, Worcs., staircase ceiling; *An Assembly of the Gods*, painted by Sir James Thornhill. *c.* 1710.

18. All Soul's College Chapel, Oxford; a drawing by Sir James Thornhill for the decoration of the east end. Before 1719, destroyed 1871. (Drawing, formerly Collection of Sir Bruce Ingram.)

19. Wimpole Hall, the Chapel, east end; *The Adoration of the Magi*, painted by Sir James Thornhill. 1724.

20. Grimsthorpe Hall, Lincs., staircase; iron balustrade by Bell of Sheffield. *c.* 1724.

21. Melbourne, Derbys.; the Iron Arbour by Robert Bakewell. *c.* 1708.

22. Staunton Harold Church, Leics.; iron screen by Robert Bakewell. *c.* 1710.

23. Chirk Castle, Denbighs.; detail of the gates by Robert Davies. 1719.

24. Leeswood, Mold, Flints.; detail of the White Gates by Robert Davies. 1726.

25. Eaton Hall, Cheshire;
detail of the Golden Gates,
attributed to Robert Davies.
c. 1730.

26. Okeover Hall, Staffs.;
gates at the sides of the
courtyard. Piers, 1748–9;
gates, 1756 by Benjamin Yates,
a pupil of Robert Bakewell.

27. The Octagon
House, Twickenham;
plasterwork by Bagutti
and Artari. *c.* 1722.

28. The Octagon
House, Twickenham;
detail of chimney-piece
with stucco-work by
Bagutti and Artari,
joinery and wood-
carving by Charles
Griffiths. *c.* 1722.

29. Giuseppe Artari (1697–1769), Italian stuccoist.
(Portrait from Füesslin, *Die besten Kunstler der
Schweiz*, IV, 1774.)

30. Stoneleigh, Warwicks., architect, Francis Smith, the Saloon; stucco panels by the Italian *stuccatori. c.* 1730

31. Ombersley, Worcs., the Rose Boudoir; panelling by craftsmen working to the orders of the architect, Francis Smith. *c.* 1728.

32. Ombersley; a doorway in the Saloon.
33. Bramham, Yorks.; a doorway by a York carver. *c.* 1730.

34. Ditchley, Oxon., east side of the Hall; plaster panels and bustos by the Italian *stuccatori*. *c*. 1726. Chimney-piece by Edward Stanton III and Christopher Horsenaile.

35. Ditchley. The Saloon; ceiling *Flora with zephyrs* by Artari, Vassalli and Serena in partnership. *c*. 1726.

36. Moor Park, Herts., the Hall; stucco decoration probably by Giovanni Bagutti and Giuseppe Artari. *c.* 1732.

37. Moor Park, the White Drawing Room; stucco decoration reminiscent of that at Houghton (Fig. 58), Bedale (Fig. 57) and Mereworth.

38. Moor Park, the upper part of the Hall; *chiaroscuro* paintings by Francesco Sleter, signed and dated, 1732.

39. Houghton Hall, Norfolk; the Stone Hall chimney-piece, with a marble relief of a classical sacrifice, by Michael Rysbrack. *c.* 1730.

40. Mereworth, Kent, the Gallery, architect, Colin Campbell; a doorway, probably by James Richards. *c.* 1723.

41. Mawley Hall,
Salop., the head of
the staircase; stucco-
work by the
Italians, probably
Francesco Vassalli.
c. 1730.

42. Lumley Castle,
Durham, the
Banqueting Hall;
stucco-work,
probably by
Francesco Vassalli.
c. 1730.

43. Barnsley Park, Gloucs., the Inner Hall; gallery and ceiling 'by the best Italian masters'. *c.* 1730.

44. Compton Place, Eastbourne, the King's Bedroom; ceiling by Charles Stanley and others. c. 1729.

45. Compton Place; detail of stucco portrait of the architect of the house, Colin Campbell (d. 1729).

46. Hall Place, Maidenhead, Berks., the Drawing Room; stucco-work probably by Charles Stanley, and a chimney-piece similar to the one at Barnsley Park.

47. (*Left*) Barnsley Park, Gloucs., chimney-piece in the Oak Room. (Compare with Fig. 46.)

48. (*Below*) Hall Place, Drawing Room; portraits of Anne, Princess Royal, and William, Prince of Orange, married in 1734. The marbling simulates brocatello, Siena, and (in the dado) Verde Antico. The medallions after engravings by Faber.

49. Mereworth Castle, Kent, the Gallery ceiling; five compartments, *Apollo and the Muses*, painted (and signed) by Francesco Sleter. *c.* 1730.

50. Clandon Park, Surrey, the Hall; stucco-work by Bagutti and Artari, chimney-piece (one of two) by Michael Rysbrack. *c.* 1730.

51. Clandon, Hall ceiling;
detail of the centre panel.
52. Clandon, Hall ceiling;
detail of one of the stucco
figures.

53. Clandon, the Saloon.

54. Towneley Hall,
Lancs., the Hall;
stucco-work by
Francesco Vassalli
and Martino
Quadry. 1730–1.

55, 56. Towneley
Hall; details of the
stucco medallions.

57. Bedale Hall, Yorks., the
Hall; stucco-work attributed to
Giuseppe Artari. *c.* 1730.
(Compare with Fig. 58.)

58. Houghton Hall, Norfolk,
Stone Hall; detail of the stucco-
work by Giuseppe Artari. *c.* 1730.

59. Althorp, Northants., Entrance Hall; plasterwork by John Woolston, paintings by John Wootton. *c.* 1733.

60. No 12, North Audley Street, London, Lord Ligonier's Long-room; the design is attributed to Sir Edward Lovet Pearce (d. 1733), using craftsmen of the Campbell school. *c.* 1730.

61. Badminton, Gloucs., Worcester Lodge; designed by William Kent. *c.* 1740.

I

129

62. Rousham, Oxon., the
Parlour Chimney-piece;
designed by William Kent.
c. 1740.
63. Rousham, Kent's
chimney-piece in the
former Library; above
General James Dormer
painted by J. B. Van Loo.

64. Chiswick, Middx.,
Octagon Room; detail of
the chimney-piece by
William Kent. *c.* 1729.

65. The Mansion House, London, architect, George Dance, senior, Entrance Hall; plasterwork by George Fewkes. c. 1750.

66. House of St Barnabas, Soho Square, London; detail of the Council Room, east wall, showing the dragon of the City of London.

68. (*Above*) Isaac Ware, *Designs of Inigo Jones and others* (1735, Plate 36), Sir Matthew Decker's chimney-piece at Richmond. Used as pattern for Fig. 67.

67. Temple Newsam, Leeds, Long Gallery; chimney-piece (one of two) based on Isaac Ware, erected March/April, 1739–40.

69, 70, Temple Newsam, Leeds, Long Gallery; two plaster medallions by Thomas Perritt and Joseph Rose, senior. *c.* 1744. Two of thirteen charged at 10s. 6d. each.

72. Temple Newsam, Leeds, Blue
Damask Room; detail of chimney-
piece by York wood-carver. *c.* 1745.

133

73. Nostell Priory Yorks., the State Bedroom; ceiling by Thomas Perritt and Joseph Rose senior to James Paine's design. *c.* 1745. Green lacquer furniture and Chinese wallpaper supplied and hung by Thomas Chippendale, 1771.

74. Nostell Priory; detail of the State Bedroom ceiling.

75. Felbrigg Hall, Norfolk, architect, James Paine, 1752, the Cabinet; plasterwork by George Green, 'man' of Joseph Rose, senior.

76. Cusworth Hall, Yorks., architect, James Paine, Chapel ceiling; painting of *The Ascension* by Francis Hayman, plasterwork, Joseph Rose senior. 1752.

77. Powderham Castle, Devon, the staircase; plaster-work by John Jenkins. *c.* 1757.

78. (*Above left*) Powderham; detail of the decoration on the staircase wall.

79, 80. (*Above and left*) Somerset House, Halifax; details of the plaster decoration, probably by Giuseppe Cortese (d. 1778). *c.* 1760.

81. No 4, Maids of
Honour Row,
Richmond, Surrey,
Entrance Hall;
panelling painted by
Antonio Jolli, for
John James
Heidegger, *c.* 1745.

82. Fonmon Castle,
Glam.; the chimney-
piece resembles a
design (dated 1766)
in Thomas Johnson's
*One Hundred and
Fifty New Designs.*

83. Hopetoun House, West Lothian, Scotland, the Red Drawing Room; decorated by John and Robert Adam. *c.* 1752. Plasterer, probably Thomas Clayton.

84. Blair Castle, Perthshire, Scotland, the Dining Room; plastered by Thomas Clayton for £217 8s. 9½d. *c.* 1755.

85. Blair Castle, Front Staircase;
designed by Abraham Swan.
c. 1757.
86. Abraham Swan, one of the
four engravings of the staircase at
Blair Castle which appear in his
Collection of Designs in Architecture,
(1757, Vol 1. Plate 31).

87. Hopetoun House, Red
Drawing Room; marble chimney-
piece by Michael Rysbrack,
possibly based on a design sent
from Rome in 1755 by Robert
Adam. 1756.

114. Newby Hall, Yorks., the Tapestry Room; Boucher-Neilson Gobelins tapestries, *Les Amours des Dieux* (south wall set signed), *c.* 1766. Carpet to Adam design, 1775.

115. Newby Hall, Entrance Hall; plasterwork by Joseph Rose junior. The date '1771' is incorporated in the panel to the right of the *Cattle Piece* by Rosa de Tivoli.

116. Corsham
Court, Wilts., the
Picture Gallery;
designed by Capa-
bility Brown for
Paul Methuen. *c.*
1762. Plasterwork by
Thomas Stocking
senior.

117. Sledmere,
Yorks., the Library;
the house was
designed for Sir
Christopher Sykes
by Joseph Rose
junior and the
plasterwork is by
him. 1788–90.

118. Arbury Hall, Warwicks., the Saloon; Gothic-style plasterwork for Sir Roger Newdegate by W. Hanwell. 1786.

119. (*Below*) Arbury Hall; detail of Hanwell's plasterwork in the bow window of the Saloon. 1786.

120. (*Below*) Mellerstain, Berwick, the Library; stucco panel in the frieze *From the Tomb of the Emperor Severus at Monte del Grano*, stuccoist unknown. *c.* 1770.

121. Cranbury, Hants, architect, probably George Dance junior, the Ballroom; looking north beyond pairs of yellow scagliola pillars. The room, with its inlaid floor, was almost certainly designed by George Dance junior (although his pupil Soane provided chimney-pieces, 1781–4) for his brother, Sir Nathaniel Dance Holland, Bt, owner of the house. *c.* 1785.

122. Wimpole, Cambs., the Saloon; designed by Sir John Soane, 1791–3, the room has a glazed lantern, and painted tympanum.

123. Cranbury, the Ballroom Ceiling; this rises to an eight-pointed star with formal honeysuckle and vase patterns. *c.* 1785.

Selected Lists of Craftsmen of the Georgian Period

The following lists make no claim to be exhaustive, but contain those names most likely to be found in relation to eighteenth-century building and decorative activity. A number of names are also included to indicate the strength of the regional 'schools' at York and Bristol. Many of the full details of the nature and cost of the work have had to be omitted for reasons of space. Some specimen costs of work at various dates are given on pp. 184–9. I have included craftsmen whose date of death was likely to have been within the period discussed, or those of the seventeenth century who played important and formative parts in style and technique. The lists do not overlap the existing Dictionaries of Architects, Decorative Painters or Sculptors (Colvin, Croft-Murray, Gunnis), unless I have material to add. Attributions are clearly marked.

The lists are arranged alphabetically by surname, dates of activity, place of work followed by date, when known, and the evidence for the statement.

ABBREVIATIONS

Arch. Jnl.	*Archaeological Journal.*	Hussey, *E.C.H.*	Christopher Hussey, *English Country Houses: Early Georgian* (1955). *Mid-Georgian* (1956). *Late-Georgian* (1958).
Arch. Rev.	*Architectural Review.*		
Baker, *Brydges*	C. H. C. and M. I. Baker, *The Life and Circumstances of James Brydges, 1st Duke of Chandos,* 1949.		
		Jourdain, 1926	Margaret Jourdain, *English Decorative Plasterwork of the Late Renaissance,* 1926.
B.M.	British Museum.		
Burl. Mag.	*Burlington Magazine.*	Little, *Gibbs*	Bryan Little, *The Life and Work of James Gibbs,* 1955.
Colvin	H. M. Colvin, *A Biographical Dictionary of English Architects, 1660–1840* (1954).	P.R.O.	Public Record Office.
		Turner	Laurence Turner, *English Decorative Plasterwork,* 1927.
C. Life	*Country Life.*		
Croft-Murray	Edward Croft-Murray, *Decorative Painting in England, 1530–1837.* 2 vols. (Vol. 1, 1962).	Vertue	Notebooks of George Vertue, *Walpole Society,* 6 vols. and index, 1930–47.
		Willis and Clark	R. Willis and J. W. Clark, *Architectural History of The University of Cambridge.* 4 vols., 1896.
Gunnis	Rupert Gunnis, *Dictionary of British Sculptors, 1660–1851* (1954).		
Heal	Sir Ambrose Heal, *London Furniture Makers,* 1600–1840 (1953).	*Wren Soc.*	*Wren Society.* 20 volumes (Vol. 20, detailed Index).

PLASTERERS

Abbott family. Devonshire plasterers (17th and 18th cent.). Worked at Exeter Customs House, 1680, etc. *Devonshire Association Transactions*, 89, 1957, pp. 124–44.

Addinal (fl. 1772). Kilnwick Hall, Yorks. Edward Ingram, *Leaves from a Family Tree*, 1951.

Aflet, W. (fl. 1708–10). St Paul's Cathedral. *Wren Soc.*, XV, pp. 169, 196.

Alborn, Thomas (fl. 1674–8). Worked under George Danserfield and John Halbet at Holyroodhouse.

Allen, Antony (fl. 1683). St Paul's Cathedral; made model. *Wren Soc.*, XIII, p. 168.

Artari, Giovanni Battista Alberti (1660–after 1725). Worked at Fulda Cathedral (1710); Sutton Scarsdale, Derbyshire (1724); Ditchley, Oxon. (1725).

Artari, Giuseppe (1697–1769). Twickenham, Octagon House (1720); St Martin-in-the-Fields, London (1722–6); Aachen Cathedral (1720–30); Cambridge, Senate House (1722–30); St Peter, Vere Street, London (1723–4); Ditchley, Oxon., (1725); Houghton, Norfolk (1726); Moulsham, Essex (1730–1); Castle Howard, submitted drawing for Temple of Four Winds (1736); Wimpole, Cambs. (1743–5); Oxford, Radcliffe Camera (1744–5); Schloss Bruhl, near Cologne (1748); Ragley Hall, Warwicks (1759–60).

For full details of the two Artaris see G. W. Beard, *Apollo*, July, 1964.

Artima, Baltassar. Whitehall Palace, London. *Wren Soc.*, VII, p. 116.

Atherton, Charles (mid 17th cent.) Sir Robert Hooke, *Diary*, 1935 edn., p. 311.

Audsley, David (fl. 1726). Subscribed to Leoni's *Alberti*, 1726.

Bacon, George (fl. 1779–89). Osterley, Middx. Archives, Victoria and Albert Museum.

Bagnall, John (fl. 1710–35). Castle Howard, Yorks. (1712), MSS Building Books; Temple Newsam, Leeds (1726), Leeds Reference Library EA 12/10; York Assembly Rooms (1731–4), York Reference Library Minute Book, various entries 1731–4.

Bagutti, Giovanni. The important senior partner to Giuseppe Artari. In England by 1710, but it is doubtful if he came from Italy with James Gibbs. Canons,

Middx. (before 1720); Castle Howard, Yorks. (1710); Twickenham, Octagon House (1720); Mereworth, Kent (1722–5); St Martin-in-the-Fields, London (1722–6); St Peter, Vere Street, London (1723–4); Cambridge, Senate House (1725–6); Moulsham, Essex (1730–1); Moor Park, Herts. (c. 1732); Cassiobury Park, Herts. (n.d.); attributed: The Mynd, Hereford (1724); Clandon Park, Surrey (1731–5).

For full details see G. W. Beard, *Apollo*, July, 1964.

Baily, John (early 19th cent.). Bust at Sir John Soane's Museum; Wotton House, Bucks (1821–3), *C. Life* 15th July, 1949.

Baker, Thomas (fl. 1775). Sketchley's *Bristol Directory*, 1775.

Barnes, James. *Ibid.*

Bates, W. (fl. 1710). St Paul's Cathedral, *Wren Soc.*, XV, p. 196.

Bayley, John (fl. 1769). Ditchley, Oxon. (1769). Oxford Record Office, Dil/1/p/3r.

Bayly, Abraham (fl. 1775). Sketchley, *op. cit.*

Beale, Henry (fl. 1716–17). Upper Warden (1716) and Master (1717) of the Worshipful Company of Plaisterers. London Guildhall Library, MS 6122/3.

Bernasconi, Bernato (fl. 1770–1820). An important worker in the late 18th cent. Gothic revival period. He worked at many houses such as Clandon (1770–84). *See Select Cttee. on Arts and their connection with Manufactures*, 1835–36. Evidence of C. R. Cockerell; Gunnis; *C. Life*, 7th November, 1952.

Bernasconi, Francis (fl. 1800–35). Probably son of Bernato; also worked in scagliola. Some commissions, among many to choose from: Cobham Hall, Kent (1800–9), Gunnis, p. 51; Westminster Abbey, Great Tower (1803), Abbey Archives; Shugborough, Staffs. (1803 and 1805), Hussey, *E.C.H., Mid-Georgian*, p. 85, *C. Life*, 11th March, 1954; Windsor Castle (1805), P.R.O., Works 5/93; Compton Place, Sussex (1806), Estate Office MSS; London, Grosvenor House (1807), Grosvenor Archives, Eaton Hall; Ashridge Park, Herts. (1813–15), Brownlow Archives, Belton; Ashburnham Place, Sussex (1813–19), Ashburnham Archives, East Sussex Record Office, 2809, 28, 38–41, 2847–8; Eastnor Castle, Herefs. (1816), Building Books,

House Archives. *See* also A. P. Oppé, *English Drawings at Windsor*, 1950, p. 93.

Betson, Thomas (fl. 1730–45). Compton Place, Sussex (1730–3), Estate Office MSS, P. File 2, Lord Wilmington's account book, 1st August, 1733; Wimpole Hall, Cambs. (1745), B.M. Add. MS 36228, f. 190.

Bettington, Joseph (fl. 1775). Sketchley, *op. cit.*

Bever, – (fl. *c*. 1770). Master to Clarke (q. v.). *See The Plaisterer's Bill for work done . . . at Somerset House*, Charles Clarke, 1783.

Birch, John (fl. 1720). Purley Hall, Berks. (1720), *Particulars and Inventories of the Late Directors of the South Sea Company*, II, 1721.

Blackley, S. (fl. 1708–10). St Paul's Cathedral, *Wren Soc.*, XV, pp. 169, 196.

Blincoe, Christopher and John. Carshalton, Surrey, (1719–20); Wimbledon, Surrey (1720), *Particulars and Inventories . . . op. cit.*, I, 1721.

Blomfield, Joseph (fl. 1776–95). Subscriber to George Richardson's (q.v.) book, 1776. Hartlebury Castle, Worcs. (1782), E. H. Pearce, *Hartlebury Castle*, 1926, p. 287; Shrewsbury, St Alkmund's (1794–5), *Shrewsbury Chronicle*, 7th November, 1794, 30th October, 1795; attributed: *c*. 1790 Lion Inn Assembly Room, Shrewsbury.

Blount, – (fl. 1668–9). London, St Sepulchre's, Holborn, *Wren Soc.*, XIX, p. 51.

Bodington, Edward (fl. 1775). Sketchley, *op. cit.*

Bradbury, Robert (fl. 1675–6). Sudbury Hall, Derbys., (1675–6). Worked with James Pettifer. Vernon archives; *C. Life*, 22nd and 29th June, 1935.

Brown, William Worked at Powderham Castle, Devon, 1755, *C. Life*, 11th July, 1963, p. 80.

Brownrig, G. (fl. 1710). St Paul's Cathedral (1710), *Wren Soc.*, XV, p. 196.

Bunce, John (fl. 1717–18). Upper Warden (1717) and Master (1718), Worshipful Company of Plaisterers, Guildhall Library MS 6122/3.

Burnett, John (fl. 1726). Assistant to John Hughes (q.v.). Compton Place, Sussex (1726–7), Estate Office MSS, Box P, file 5.

Burnop, William (fl. 1799). Hesleyside, Bellingham, Northumberland, supplied capitals and did plastering (1799), *History of Northumberland*, 1940, XV, p. 253.

Burton, Thomas (fl. 1678–89). Will, P.C.C. 1689; London, St Stephen, Coleman Street (1678–9), *Wren Soc.*, X, p. 53, p. 124, XII, p. 53, XIX, p. 53. Thomas Burton (? son) was contestant for the job of Plasterer to Christ's Hospital, London, in 1698.

Calderwood, – (fl. 1726–7). Worked under William Adam at Mavisbank; attributed: the Drum, Edinburgh. J. Fleming, *Robert Adam, and his Circle*, 1962.

Campelman, Ralph (fl. 1735–6). Castle Howard, Yorks., plain plastering (1735–6), House archives.

Carabellas, – (fl. *c*. 1798). Ickworth House, Suffolk (1798), Colvin, p. 218.

Carlile, Charles (fl. 1713). Apprentice to Isaac Mansfield (q.v.); Guildhall Library, Boyd's Index to Apprenticeship Registers.

Casell, R. (fl. 1710). St Paul's Cathedral, *Wren Soc.*, XV, p. 196.

Cheek, Thomas (fl. 1770–80). Guildhall Library MS 6122/4.

Chillingworth, William (fl. *c*. 1803). Aynhoe Park, Northants. (*c*. 1803), *C. Life*, 16th July, 1953, p. 205.

Chippine, Henry. Master, Worshipful Company of Plaisterers, 1652, Guildhall Library MS 6122/2.

Chislo, – (fl. 1730). Shaw Hall, Berks. (1730), Baker, *Brydges*, p. 370 fn. 2.

Clark, Thomas (18th cent.). Master Plasterer, Office of Works, 1761–82. Worked at Holkham Hall, Norfolk, Hussey, *E.C.H.*, *Early Georgian*, p. 140; Milton House, Northants., 1750, Record Office, Fitzwilliam Misc., Vol. 156; London, Horse Guards (1753), R.I.B.A., Building Accounts; Cambridge, Old University Library (1758), Registry Audit Book, 1759, Vice Chancellor's vouchers, 16th May, 1759; Ashburnham Place, Sussex (1760), *C. Life*, 23rd April, 1953; London, Somerset House (1782), R.I.B.A. MS 725, 121 (42.B).S.

Clarke, Charles (fl. 1783). Subscriber, James Paine's *Plans . . .* 1767; worked at Somerset House and possibly the Manor House, Milton, Berks, *C. Life*, 24th December, 1948. He published a long virulent pamphlet on the work at Somerset House in 1783 (copy, R.I.B.A. Library).

Clarke, Samuel (fl. 1683). St Paul's Cathedral, *Wren Soc.*, XIII, p. 168.

Clayton, Thomas (fl. 1740-76). Yard at Leith; Edinburgh, The Drum (1740), helped by Calderwood, Hamilton Archives, Lennoxlove; Holyroodhouse, Hamilton apartments (information kindly communicated by Mr John Fleming); Blair Castle, Perthshire (1747-57), House Archives 4011.D(4) 31-9; attributed: Hopetoun House, W. Lothian (*c.* 1754); Dumfries House (*c.* 1756); Glasgow, St Andrew's Church (*c.* 1756); Edinburgh, St Andrew Square. House for Sir Laurence Dundas, B.M. Add. MS 41133, f. 53. Subscribed to Thomas Chippendale's *Director*, 1754

Cole, J. (fl. 1708-10). St Paul's Cathedral, *Wren Soc.*, XV, pp. 169, 196.

Collins, F. (fl. 1765). Linley Hall, Salop, bills at house.

Collins, Thomas (1735-1830). Apprenticed, 1750, to William Wilton (q.v.). Married 17th November, 1761, Henrietta Patterson at St Mary Le Bone, Middx. Had bank account (Drummonds) with Sir William Chambers. Melbourne House (1772), B.M. Add MSS, 41133; Drapers Company Hall (1774)—worked with Joseph Rose, proposal and bill in Company's possession; subscribed to George Richardson's *A Book of Ceilings* . . . 1776. Worked with Charles Clarke at Somerset House. Was an executor and trustee to Sir William Chambers, F.S.A. (1789). Portraits: *C. F. von Breda*, Dr J. Gurney Salter Coll; *Beechey*, Marylebone Town Hall. My own researches on Collins were extensively supplemented by those of Colonel J. H. Busby, who published a typescript memoir on Collins in 1965. Further details of Collins will be given in my forthcoming *Decorative Plasterwork in Great Britain, 1530-1830* (Country Life).

Collins, William (1721-93). Provided classical casts and medallions for such houses as Harewood, Kedleston, Burton Constable. Gunnis gives a useful summary of his career.

Columbani, Placido (fl. *c.* 1744-80). Downhill, Co. Antrim (1775), *C. Life*, 6th January, 1950; Mount Clare, Roehampton, Surrey (*c.* 1780), Hussey, *E.C.H.*, *Mid-Georgian*, p. 240.

Combes, John (fl. 1681-1709). Master of the Worshipful Company of Plaisterers in 1701, and one of the Auditors in 1709. A Thomas Combs was Upper Warden (1718) and Master (1719). Worked at St Augustine, Watling Street, London, *Wren Soc.*, XII, p. 144; a 'Combs' was paid for unspecified work at Canons, Baker, *Brydges*, p. 99.

Coney, – (fl. 1771-83). Worked with Clayton in Edinburgh (1771-2); under Charles Clarke in London at Somerset House (1783). B.M. Add. MSS 41133, f. 53; Charles Clarke (q.v.), *The Plaisterer's Bill* . . . 1783. A Stephen Coney worked at Powderham Castle, Devon, in 1755, *C. Life*, 11th July, 1963, p. 80.

Cordey, John (fl. 1710-11). Upper Warden (1710) and Master (1711) Worshipful Company of Plaisterers.

Corlett, Richard (fl. 1804-13). Worked in Cheshire at Eaton Hall (1804-12) and Eccleston Church (1809-13), Grosvenor Archives, Eaton Hall.

Cortese, Joseph (fl. 1745-78). Italian at Whitby and Wakefield. Will, at York, mentions his son, Joseph, also a plasterer. Worked at Studley Royal (1745-52); Gilling Castle (1740-); Beverley Guildhall (1762); Kilnwick Hall (1772): Newburgh Priory (1764-5).
See G. W. Beard, *Apollo*, July, 1964.

Crabtree, Ely (fl. 1760-1803). Worked under John Carr at Wentworth Woodhouse, and at Everingham Roman Catholic Church. R. B. Wragg, York Georgian Soc. 1955-6, p. 60; *C. Life*, 10th October, 1957; *Arch Rev.*, September, 1957, p. 198.

Cramillion, Barthelemi (late 18th cent.). Dublin Rotunda Hospital. Worked with William Lee and Robert Hallam. C. P. Curran, *The Rotunda Hospital*, 1945, p. 40.

Crisp, William (fl. 1719-20). Purley Hall, Berks., (1719-20), *Particulars and Inventories . . . op. cit.*, II, 1721.

Cromwell, Henry (fl. 1698). Master, Worshipful Company of Plaisterers, 1698.

Crouch, John (late 17th cent. -1715). Master, Worshipful Company of Plaisterers, 1715. Worked in London, *Wren Soc.*, X, pp. 115, 124.

Cryer, Clement (fl. 1769-1800). Continued business of Joseph Rose, Junior (q.v.), Christie's Sale Catalogue, 10th April, 1799.

Danserfield, George (fl. 1674-9). Holyroodhouse, various rooms and Great Staircase (1674-9), Turner, pp. 146-8. They may have worked at Holme Lacy and Eye Manor, Herefordshire.

Daves, Charles. Master, Worshipful Company of Plaisterers, 1653.

Dawson, Robert (fl. 1742–52). London, 17, Arlington Street (1742–51), R.I.B.A. MSS 728.3(42.13)A.; 44, Berkeley Square, accounts in Sir John Soane's Museum.

Dennis, Thomas (late 18th cent.). Apprentice to Thomas Stocking, senior (q.v.). Bristol City Archives, Apprentices' Book, 1777–86, p. 369.

Denston, Abraham (fl. 1725–65). Cambridge, Senate House (1725–6), W. Millar, *Plastering, Plain and Decorative*, 1897, p. 20; Kedleston, Derbys., plain work, Curzon Archives, Book 3R, pp. 60–3 and Bills, 1759.

Dewick, Petty (fl. 1697). Sir John Moore's School, Appleby, Leics. (1697), *Wren Soc.*, XI, p. 100.

Doogood, Henry (fl. 1663–1707). Worked with John Grove, and was employed by Wren at 32 City churches. Master, Worshipful Company of Plaisterers, 1700. He also worked at Tunbridge Wells, Church of St Charles the Martyr (1682–90), M. Whiffen, *Stuart and Georgian Churches*, 1947, p. 97; Pembroke College Chapel, Cambridge (1663), *Willis and Clark* I, p. 147; Trinity College, Cambridge; Lichfield, Bishop's Palace (1689), *C. Life*, 30th December, 1954; a Ralph Doogood worked at St Paul's (1708–10), *Wren Soc.*, XV, pp. 169, 196.

Dungan, Richard (fl. 1605–9). Knole, Kent (1605–7), Record Office, U269A/1/1, Account Book, Thomas Earl of Dorset; London, Whitehall Palace (1606–9), *Arch. Jnl.*, CX, 1953, p. 151.

Dyer, Robert (fl. 1686–92). London, St Andrew, Holborn (1686–92), *Wren Soc.*, X, pp. 13, 106.

Eales, John. Contestant for job of plasterer, Christ's Hospital, 1698, *Wren Soc.*, XI, p. 70.

Earl, James (fl. 1791–2). Kingston upon Hull Directory, 1791, Civic Records, M843.

Eastbourne, Martyn (fl. 1650–2). Master, Worshipful Company of Plasterers, 1650–2.

Eaton, – (fl. 1615). Chantmarle, Dorset (1615). Dorset Record Office, Sir John Strode's Notebook, Hutchins, *History of Dorset*, 1873, IV, p. 5.

Edisbury, Kenridge (fl. 1685). St Paul's Cathedral, *Wren Soc.*, XIII, p. 201, XVI, pp. 20–1.

Edmondson, John (fl. 1694–1704). London, St Swithun, Cannon Street, *Wren Soc.*, XIX, p. 56. Master, Worshipful Company of Plaisterers, 1704.

Ellis, James (fl. 1712–20). Greenwich, St Alphege (1712–14); Deptford, St Paul (c. 1715), *Arch. Rev.*, March, 1950. Renter Warden (1715–16) and Auditor (1719) of the Worshipful Company of Plasterers. His partner, James Hands, died in 1718.

Elsey, Richard (fl. 1707–8). Upper Warden (1707) and Master of the Worshipful Company of Plaisterers (1708)

Engleheart, Francis (fl. 1770–2). Used by Sir William Chambers on plain plastering and at Kew Palace, Surrey. Worked possibly on plasterwork at 356, Kew Road, Kew, Richmond, where he once lived. B.M. Add. MS 41133, 13th May, 1770, 12th March, 1772; Paine's Bank Account, Messrs Coutts and Company.

Enzer, Joseph. A Dutch worker of whom little is known. Employed about 1726 at Arniston. M. Jourdain, 1926, p. x; J. Fleming, *Scottish Country Houses Open to the Public*, 1954.

Fenton, Joseph (early 17th cent.). Bromley-by-Bow ceiling (now Victoria and Albert Museum); may have worked at Craigievar Castle, Aberdeenshire, 1625–6, Fleming, *op. cit.*, p. 42.

Fewkes, George (fl. 1750–63). London. The Mansion House (1750), Pevsner, *Buildings of England, London*, Pt. I, 1957, p. 176, Pl. 68B. Took an apprentice, John Cook, 1763.

Fifield, David (fl. 1690). East Hattley, Cambs. 1690–made oath that work there is by Henry Margetts (q.v.); Castle Howard, Sir George Downing Accounts.

Fludyer, William (d. 1691). Will, P.C.C. 1691.

Fly, J. (fl. 1710). St Paul's Cathedral, *Wren Soc.*, XV. p. 196.

Foster, – (fl. 1737). London, Cavendish Square. Baker, *Brydges*, pp. 199, 285.

Franceys, Samuel (fl. 1760). Melbourne, Derbys., decorative work, 1760, house archives.

Franchini, Paul and Philip (1st half 18th cent.). *See* G. W. Beard, *Apollo*, July, 1964.

Garrard, George (1760–1826). Modeller in plaster and bronze. Gunnis; D. Stroud, *Henry Holland*, 1950, pp. 37, 49.

Gill, E. (fl. 1697). Petworth, Sussex (1696–7). House Archives, William Miller's Account Rolls.

Gill, Robert (fl. 1718–29). Knowsley, Lancs. (1718–29), Lancs. Co. Record Office, Knowsley MSS.

Ginks, C. (fl. 1708). St Paul's Cathedral (1710), *Wren Soc.*, XV, p. 169.

Glynn, – (fl. 1707). London, St James, *Wren Soc.*, X, p. 124, XIX, p. 22.

Godfrey, T. (fl. 1710). St Paul's Cathedral (1710), *Wren Soc.*, XV, p. 196.

Good, William (fl. 1720). Purley Hall, Berks. (1720–1); *Particulars and Inventories . . . I.* 1721.

Goodenough, Edward (fl. 1656). Master of the Worshipful Company of Plaisterers, 1656.

Goudge, Edward (late 17th and early 18th cent.). One of the most talented of late Renaissance workers, Goudge seems to have had an early connection with Hawksmoor. Vertue says that Goudge did 'frettwork ceilings' at Justice Mellust's house in Yorkshire. This was probably Samuel Mellish of Doncaster, Deputy-Lieutenant for Yorkshire, who died in 1707. Colvin, p. 272. Vertue says that Hawksmoor was 'Clerck to Justice Mellust' and it seems probable Goudge introduced him to London circles. While Goudge's main work was in late 17th-century houses, particularly those in which Captain William Winde had a hand, his work had important repercussions on style at the turn of the 18th century. He worked on the following commissions.

Northampton, Sessions House (1684–8), *Arch. Jnl.*, CX, p. 181; Hampstead Marshall, Berks. (1688); Belton House, Lincs. (1688); Combe Abbey, Warwicks. (1688), Colvin, p. 685, plans, corres., in Bodleian Library; Castle Bromwich, Warwicks. (1688–90); Swallowfield, Berks. (1690–1); Petworth, Sussex (1691–2), Petworth Archives, Richard Stiles Account Rolls, 1691–2; Chatsworth, Derbyshire (1696–7), House Archives, James Whildon's Account, 121, 3, 5, 135, F. Thompson, *History of Chatsworth*, 1949, pp. 166–8.

For a general account of Goudge's work see G. W. Beard, *C. Life*, 9th May, 1952. Goudge also did building work for Thomas Coke. (Melbourne, Derbys. Archives, Coke MSS, Parcel 98). By 1702 his business had dwindled away for lack of money with his patrons and the increase in decorative painting. He is often credited with work at Lamport (*Connoisseur*, November, 1964) and at Burghley, but the work at the last is by Edward Martin (q.v.).

Green, Charles (fl. 1723). Worcester, Guildhall (1723), City Archives, Guildhall Building Accounts, 29th April, 1723.

Greenhough, William (fl. 1768–70). Boynton Church, E.R. Yorks. (1768–70), *C. Life*, 22nd July, 1954, p. 283. A James Greenough was living in Beverley in 1791 (Battle, Hull and Beverley Directory, 1791).

Griffin, John (fl. 1742). Bristol, The Exchange (1742). City Archives, Exchange Building Book; John Wood, *A Description of the Exchange of Bristol*, 1745 (John Griffin was a subscriber).

Grilten, R. (fl. 1710). St Paul's Cathedral, *Wren Soc.*, XV, p. 196,

Grinsell, John (fl. 1712–13). Upper Warden (1712) and Master (1713) of the Worshipful Company of Plaisterers.

Grivens, R. (fl. 1708). St Paul's Cathedral, *Wren Soc.*, XV, pp. 169, 196.

Groome, Richard (fl. *c.* 1780). London, Somerset House (1780), Charles Clarke. *The Plaisterer's Bill . . .* 1783.

Grove, John (fl. 1657–1708). One of Sir Christopher Wren's master plasterers. He had an extensive practice from the Restoration onwards and was Master Plasterer to the Office of Works, 1660–1708. His son John was also a plasterer. He worked on many commissions with Henry Doogood and at the Queen's House, Greenwich (1661), *Survey of London*, XIV, p. 72; Queen's Privy Chamber, etc. (1662), P.R.O. E 351/3276; Clarendon House, Piccadilly (1664–7), R. T. Gunther, *The Architecture of Sir Roger Pratt*, 1928; Emmanuel College Chapel, Cambridge (1675), Willis and Clark, II, pp. 703–9; Royal College of Physicians, Dining Room (1678) (dem. 1879), H. W. Robinson and W. Adams, *Diary of Robert Hooke*, 1935; Windsor Castle (1681–7), W. St John Hope, *Windsor Castle*, 1911 pp. 321, 329; Badminton House, Gloucs. (1682–3), Child's Bank (Glyn Mills), Account 1st Marquess of Worcester; Trinity College, Cambridge, Library Staircase (1686–7), Willis and Clark, II, p. 540.

Hanwell, W. (fl. 1780–90). Arbury Hall, Warwicks. (1786), Saloon, assisted by G. Higham and Robert Hodgson. Newdegate MSS, Warwick. Co. Record Office; *C. Life*, 29th October, 1953.

Hayes, William (fl. 1713–14). Upper Warden (1713) and Master (1714) of the Worshipful Company of Plaisterers.

Helford, Thomas (fl. *c.* 1760). One of thirteen figures in a picture by Robert Pyle, 1760, which was destroyed by fire in 1940. *C. Life*, 30th March, 1945, p. 556; Colvin, p. 334.

Henderson, James (fl. *c.* 1755–1778). A York plasterer best known for his association with the architect John Carr. Freeman of York 1764, established near Bootham Bar, York. Took an apprentice, William Holliday of Byland, in 1765. His own son Thomas was apprenticed to him in 1764. There was probably a working relationship between Giuseppe Cortese (q.v.) and Henderson, and the latter acted as executor to Cortese's will in 1778. R. B. Wragg, *York Georgian Society*, Report, 1955–6; York Reference Library, *Register of Apprentices*, D14, 1766, ff. 73, 93. Worked at Fairfax House, Castlegate, York (1762), Yorks. Arch. Soc., Newburgh archives; Harewood House, Yorks. (1765), plain plastering; Cannon Hall, Barnsley (1766–7), Sheffield Reference Library, Spencer-Stanhope MSS; Kirkleatham Hall (1767); Temple Newsam, Leeds (1771); Gilling Castle, 'Gothick Temple' (1771), Wragg, *op. cit.*

Hillam, James (fl. *c.* 1780). London, Somerset House (1780), Charles Clarke, *The Plaisterer's Bill . . . 1783*.

Hollingshead, William (fl. 1687). His will is P.C.C. 1687 f. 49.

Hollins, William (fl. 1660). Master (1660) of the Worshipful Company of Plaisterers.

Hughes, John (fl. 1719–29). London, Burlington House, Piccadilly (1719–21), Chatsworth, Burlington House Account Book; Compton Place, Sussex (1729), Estate Office Archives, P. File 2. These documents indicate Hughes died in November, 1729.

Hurst, – (fl. early 18th cent.). London, Greenwich Hospital; corresponded with Sir James Thornhill, *Wren Soc.*, VI, pp. 67–8.

Huss, Richard (fl. 1710–20). Birmingham, St Philips Church (1710); M. Whiffen, *Thomas Archer*, 1950, p. 15; Wentworth Castle, Yorks. (1720), B.M. Add. MS 22241.

Jackson, George (1756–1840). Founded firm of plasterers in 1780 who worked for Robert Adam. Present firm of G. Jackson and Sons Ltd continues. George's son John bought the Carton-Pierre process from France, and his grandson introduced fibrous plaster.

Jemmett, T. (fl. 1710). St Paul's Cathedral, *Wren Soc.*, XV, p. 196.

Jenkins, John (fl. 1753–9). Powderham Castle, Devon (1753–9), Richard Polwhele, *History of Devonshire*, 1793, accounts published by Mark Girouard, *C. Life*, 11th July, 1963, p. 80. Jenkins had two assistants, William Brown and Stephen Coney. Howell Jenkins, possibly a relative, did other work at Powderham in 1739.

Kelly, Hugh (fl. 1750–67). Dublin, House of Commons and Lords (*c.* 1750); Dublin, Rotunda Hospital (1766–7), C. P. Curran, *The Rotunda Hospital*, 1945, p. 40.

Kibblewhite, – (fl. 1774–7). Redbourne Hall, Lincs. (1774–7), Lincs. Co. Record Office, Red (3/1/4/6/2), 34, 36, 44, 51.

Kidgell, Henry (fl. 1686). His will is P.C.C. 1686.

Kilminster, – (fl. 1772). Chirk Castle, Denbighs., Saloon (1772), *C. Life*, 12th October, 1951.

Kinsman, Joseph (fl. 1637–55). Ham House (1637–8), Victoria and Albert Museum *Guide Book* to house, 1950, p. 36. Kinsman was Master of the Worshipful Company of Plaisterers in 1655.

Kipling, John (fl. 1761). Freeman of York, 1761, *Surtees Society*, Vol. 102.

Lance, David (fl. 1691–1724). Master Plasterer, Office of Works, 1708–24. Worked for Edward Goudge (q.v.) to whom he may have been apprenticed. Petworth, Sussex, (1691), Earl of Bradford's MSS, Weston Hall, Box 76, William Winde's letter of 27th April, 1691. In his capacity as Master Plasterer, Lance submitted proposals for work at various London Crown properties, *Wren Soc.*, VI, pp. 58, 62, 63, VII, pp. 261–2, 214; *Post Boy*, 27th December, 1712; Cal., Treasury Papers XXIX, Pt. 2, p. 102.

Lee, Francis (died *c.* 1638). Mentioned in York Arch. Soc. *Jnl.*, XXVI, p. 144.

Lee, James (fl. *c.* 1611). Hatfield House, Herts. (1611), *Arch. Jnl.*, CXII, 1955, p. 121.

Lycense, Thomas. Master of the Worshipful Company of Plaisterers, 1659.

Mabbs, Robert. Upper Warden (1715) and Master (1716) of the Worshipful Company of Plaisterers.

MacClure, John. Culzean Castle, Ayrshire (c. 1777). John Fleming, *Scottish Country Houses Open to the Public*, 1954, p. 90.

McCullagh, James (fl. 1761–85). Worked in Dublin. Master of the Plasterers' and Bricklayers' Guild, 1778, *Georgian Society*, 1909, I, pp. 16–17; C. P. Curran, *The Rotunda Hospital*, 1945, p. 40.

MacGlashan, – (fl. 1770–80). Worked for Sir William Chambers, Charles Clarke, *The Plaisterer's Bill . . .* 1783.

Mansfield, Isaac (fl. before 1697–1729). Son of Samuel Mansfield, plasterer of Derby. Settled at York (Freeman 1704, Sheriff 1728–9). Also lived in Henrietta Street, near to James Gibbs, for whom he often worked. Was at Castle Howard (1710), House Building Books; five London churches, *Arch. Rev.*, March, 1950; Burlington House, Piccadilly (1720–1), Chatsworth, Burlington House Account Book; Langleys, Essex (1721), Essex Co. Record Office, Tufnell accounts, *Connoisseur*, December, 1957, p. 211; Cambridge, Senate House (1725), Little, *Gibbs*, 1955, pp. 60–1. Samuel Mansfield, Isaac's father, worked at Sudbury, Derbys., in 1672–5, *C. Life*, 22nd–29th June, 1935. Isaac subscribed to *Vitruvius Britannicus*, III, 1725, and with his son Isaac, to Gibbs's *Book of Architecture*, 1728. He took as apprentices Charles Carlile in 1713 and Samuel Smith in 1724.

Mantle, William (fl. 1726). Subscriber to Leoni's *Alberti*. Noted Vol. III, 1726. A plasterer of this surname worked at Moulsham Hall, Essex (1729), Essex Co. Record Office, D/DM/A5.

Margetts, Henry (fl. 1684–1704). East Hatley, Cambs. (1684), Castle Howard, Sir George Downing Accounts; Chatsworth, Derbys., as Master Plasterer (until 1695); F. Thompson, *Chatsworth*, 1949, pp. 36, 59, 67; Kiveton, Yorks. (c. 1700), Yorks. Arch. Soc., Duke of Leeds MSS, Box 33.

Martin, Edward (fl. 1657–99). Worshipful Company of Plaisterers, fined for arrears 1657, Beadle 1660, Master 1699. Worked in London at St Nicholas Cole Abbey, Queenhithe, *Wren Soc.*, X; Arbury, Warwicks., Chapel ceiling (1678), Warwick County Record Office, Newdegate MSS, *Wren Soc.*, X, p. 22; Burghley House, Northants. (1682), Childs Bank (Glyn Mills) Exeter Bank Account, 1st July, 1682, 14th February, 1682–3.

Martin, John (fl. 1676–82). Windsor Castle (1676–82) W. H. St John Hope, *Windsor Castle*, 1911, pp. 314, 321, 485.

Meade, Thomas (late 17th cent.). Mentioned in Robert Hooke's *Diary* (1935 edn., p. 60); London, St Lawrence Jewry (1678), *Wren Soc.*, XIX, pp. 24–6; St Mary Abchurch, *ibid.*, X, p. 124.

This man may be the 'Medde' who worked in the late 17th cent. at Hampton Court, *Wren Soc.*, IV, p. 25.

Mines, John (fl. 1726–30). Westminster School (1726), Abbey Archives 35394,*Wren Soc.*, XI, p. 45; Wolterton, Norfolk (1730), *C. Life*, 25th July, 1957, p. 168.

Moor, Robert (fl. 1745–70). Radway, Warwicks. (c. 1745), Miller account books, Warwick County Record Office (frequently mentioned); Alscot, Warwicks (1750–2), *C. Life*, 22nd May, 1958, p. 1126; Arbury, Warwicks. (1755), Hussey, *E.C.H.*, *Mid-Georgian*, p. 43; Stoneleigh Abbey, Warwicks. (c. 1760), Shakespeare's Birthplace Trust, Leigh MSS.

Morris, Daniel (died 1697–8). Plasterer to Christ's Hospital, *Wren Soc.*, XI, p. 70; London, St Edmund the King; St Michael, Wood Street. Worked on both occasions with John Sherwood, *Wren Soc.*, XII, p. 44.

Mott, Richard (fl. 1752–99). Apprenticed to Joseph Rose, senior, 1752. Worked for the family firm for over forty years. In 1799 he bought lots at Joseph Rose junior's sale, Christie's, 10th April, 1799.

Nicholson, Thomas (fl. 1754–74). Apprenticed to James Henderson (q.v.) in 1766. Freeman of York, 1774. York Reference Library, Apprenticeship Register; *Surtees Society*, Vol. 102.

Nollekens, Joseph (1737–1823). Better known as a sculptor (Gunnis). George Richardson in his *Book of Ceilings . . .* 1776, p. 3, says the bas-reliefs of the two ceilings in the Drapers' Company were 'excellently modelled by the ingenious Joseph Nollekens'.

Oliver, – (fl. 1763). Chirk Castle, Denbighs. (1763), *C. Life*, 12th October, 1951. Possibly the Thomas Oliver who worked at Tabley House, Cheshire (1762–7), Hussey, *E.C.H.*, *Mid-Georgian*, p. 58.

Page, Joseph (fl. mid 18th cent.). Freeman, Kingston-upon-Hull, 1740. Maisters House, Hull (c. 1750), Edward Ingram, *Leaves from a Family Tree*, 1951, p. 177.

Papworth, John (1750–99). Master Plasterer, Office of Works. Employed by Sir William Chambers. At his death his business was carried on by his eldest son, Thomas. Worked at Inveraray Castle (1780–2), Wyatt Papworth, *John B. Papworth*, 1893, p. 3; R.I.B.A., Library, MS 725.121 (42 B/S), 11; *C. Life*, 25th June, 1953, p. 2061; St Marylebone Rate Books, 1778–91.

Parker, William (fl. 1677–96). Mentioned in records, Worshipful Company of Plaisterers, 1677; Denham, Bucks. (1691–5), J. Harris, *Records of Bucks*, XVI, 1957–8, p. 195; West Wycombe, Bucks., Hussey, *E.C.H.*, *Early Georgian*, p. 239.

Patroli, —. Claydon, Bucks. (late 18th cent.), Lipscomb, *Buckinghamshire*, I. p. 186.

Pearce, William (fl. 1762–72). Accounts, Sir John Soane's Museum, mostly under Henry Holland's supervision. Bowood, Wilts. (1762–6), Lansdowne Archives; Claremont, Surrey (1772), *C. Life*, CVIII, p. 60, Hussey, *E.C.H.*, *Mid-Georgian*, p. 135. May have worked at Berrington Hall, Herefs.

Pedrola, —. Ormsby Hall, Lincs. (1755). Assisted Joseph Rose, senior. N. Pevsner and J. Harris *Bldgs of England*, *Lincs.*, 1964, p. 370.

Perritt, Thomas (1710–59). Probably trained under his father Jonathan, a plasterer and bricklayer. Freeman of York, 1737–8. Master of Joseph Rose, senior. Married (1) Anne Etty, 8th December, 1739, York Minster; (2) Grace Perritt, 8th July, 1748, Hampsthwaite Green. Chamberlain of York 1753. Died intestate, York Administrations, 13 December, 1759.

Worked at Nostell Priory (*c.* 1740), Temple Newsam House, Leeds (1741–7), York, Assembly Rooms (1744), Doncaster, Mansion House (1745), Kilnwick Hall (1749) and probably at many other Yorkshire houses such as Sheriff Hutton and Womersley Park. *See* p. 59 for a more detailed statement of his work.

William Perritt, perhaps the elder brother of Thomas, worked in Yorkshire at Baldersby (1724–8), Leeds Reference Library, Newby MSS; Studley Royal (1728) Estate MSS, Parcel 286; and at the Ranelagh Amphitheatre, Chelsea (1741–2), P.R.O., C/105/37/32; Farnborough, Warwicks. (1750), *C. Life*, 18th February, 1954; London, Grosvenor Square (1761–3), Compton House, Sussex, Estate Archives, Box Q; Glynde Church, Sussex (1761–8), Sussex Arch. Soc. *Collections*, Vol. 20; *C. Life*, 28th April, 1955.

Perwick, Edmund. Master of the Worshipful Company of Plaisterers, 1661–2.

Pettifer, James. Succeeded Daniel Morris as Plasterer, Christ's Hospital, 1698, *Wren Soc.*, XI, p. 70; London, St Bride's Fleet Street (1702), *ibid.*, XIX, p. 14; St James, Piccadilly, *ibid.*, X, p. 124.

Plura, – (fl. 1710–12). At Castle Howard. Assisted Giovanni Bagutti (House Buildings Books). May have been connected with Plura family of Turin and Bath, *Connoisseur*, November, 1956, Gunnis.

Pope, William. Upper Warden (1719) and Master (1720), Worshipful Company of Plaisterers.

Porter, Thomas (fl. 1683–1703). London, St Paul's Cathedral (1683), *Wren Soc.*, XIII, p. 168; Dyrham, Glos. (1694–1703), Dyrham MSS B13/2, B/15/5.

Powell, Robert (fl. 1680–1706). London, St Clement Danes (1680–8), *Wren Soc.*, X, p. 111. Master of the Worshipful Company of Plaisterers (1706).

Pritchard, William (fl. *c.* 1780). London, Northumberland House (*c.* 1780), Alnwick Castle Archives UI.11.7.

Puttenham, Richard (fl. 1749). London, house in Burlington Gardens for the Robinson family (1749), Leeds Reference Library, Newby MSS 2277/20/4.

Quarenghi (fl. 1775). Wardour Castle, Wilts. (1775), Hussey, *E.C.H.*, *Mid-Georgian*, p. 124.

Rhodes, William (fl. 1771–6). Drayton House, Northants. (1771–2), N. V. Stopford Sackville, *Drayton*, 1939, pp. 33–5; subscribed to George Richardson's *Book of Ceilings . . . 1776*.

Richardson, George (*c.* 1740–*c.* 1813). Draughtsman to the Adam brothers. Colvin lists his published works. Kedleston, Derbys. (1759), Estate Archives. Richardson published the Great Hall ceiling in his *A Book of Ornamental Ceilings, in the style of the Antique Grotesque*, 1776, dedicated to Lord Scarsdale.

Ridley, William (fl. 1661). Durham Castle (1661), *Surtees Society*, 55 (1872), 356.

Roberts, Thomas (1711–71). Oxford, Magdalen College (1738), W. G. Hiscock, *A Christ Church Miscellany*, 1946, pp. 68–71; St John's College (1742), H.M.C., *Oxford*, 1939, p. 106; Radcliffe Camera (1744), assisted Charles Stanley (q.v.), Oxford Hist. Soc., XIII, 1953–4; Ditchley (1749 and 1760), Oxford Co. Record Office,

Dillon MSS I/p/3ab/am. He may have worked at Grey's Court, *C. Life*, 30th June, 1944; All Souls, Codrington Library (1750); Christ Church, Library (1752–62), Hiscock, *op. cit.*; Bodleian Library, Tower Room (1753), *Bodleian Library Record*, October, 1956; Queen's College, Library (1756), J. R. Magrath, *Queen's College*; Hartwell, Bucks. (1764), Hussey, *E.C.H.*, *Early Georgian*, p. 201; Rousham (1764), *C. Life*, 24th May, 1946, p. 949; Heythrop Hall, undated (dest. by fire 1831), Mrs Lybbe Powys, *Diary*, 1899 edn., p. 200. He may have worked at Honington Hall, Warwicks (1753–8), Hiscock, *op. cit.*, and at Kirtlington with Charles Stanley.

A Nicholas Roberts was Master (1712) of the Worshipful Company of Plaisterers.

Robinson. John Robinson, at Castle Howard, 1724, Building Books; Peter Robinson, Thorndon Hall, Essex (1768), Essex Co. Record Office, D/DPA58.

Rose family. This group dominated English plasterwork for much of the 18th century. See p. 70 for an account of their activities.

Rothwell, – (fl. 1765–87). Harewood House, Yorks. (1765). Worked with James Henderson. York Georgian Soc., Report, 1955–6, p. 59; Brighton, Pavilion (1787), H. Roberts, *Royal Pavilion*, 1939, p. 28.

St Michele, John Baptist (fl. 1734). London, St Bartholomew's Hospital, Great Hall (1734), Little, *Gibbs*, p. 115.

Sefton, Thomas (18th cent.). Plasterer at Newcastle – 'the same man who did Mr Mills's house lately and is recommended by him as a very honest careful man'. Earl of Harrowby MSS, Nathaniel Ryder Notebooks, No 67.

Serena, Francesco Leone. In England by 1725. Worked at Ditchley, Bramham Park, and in London at Lord Bingley's house and at Cavendish Square for Lord Chandos.

See G. W. Beard, *Apollo*, July, 1964.

Shann, Robert. Master (1710), Worshipful Company of Plaisterers.

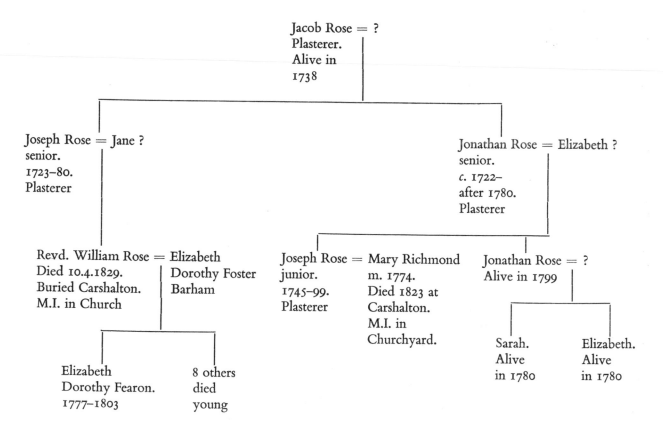

Shepherd family. Edward Shepherd, the 18th-century architect, who died in 1747, began life as a plasterer. Colvin. His brother John worked in London on a house in Hanover Square for Sir Theodore Janssen (1720), *Inventories of the South Sea Company*, II, 1721, and was employed at Shaw Hall, Berks. (1728), by Lord Chandos, Baker, *Brydges*, p. 370.

Sherwood, John (fl. late 17th cent.). Worked extensively on the Wren City churches. List in *Wren Soc.*, X. Mentioned in Robert Hooke's *Diary* on several occasions (1935 edn., pp. 14, 180, 229, 320, 338, 401). A Thomas Sherwood worked at All Hallows the Great, *Wren Soc.*, X, p. 47.

Smith, Samuel (fl. 1710–24). Apprenticed to Isaac Mansfield in 1724, aged 14. A Samuel Smith was working at Purley Hall, Berks., in 1720–1. Boyd's Index to Apprenticeship Registers, Guildhall Library; Purley Hall Building Accounts, 1720–1.

A William Smith was a contestant for the job of plaisterer, Christ's Hospital, 1698, *Wren Soc.*, XI, p. 70.

Snare, Quintin (fl. *c.* 1730). York bricklayer and plasterer, York Minster Library MS BB5; York, Assembly Rooms (1732–3), York Reference Library, Assembly Room Minute Book, 1729–58.

Snow, William (fl. 1762–6). Bowood, Wilts. (1762–6). Received £294 (Lansdowne Archives), acted as a sub-contractor for Henry Holland.

Stanley, Simon Carl (Charles), (1703–61). Born, Copenhagen, 12th December, 1703. In England by 1726–7. Returned to Denmark, 1746. Died 17th February, 1761. *See* p. 32 for an account of his work.

Stanyon, Abraham. Master (1657–8) of the Worshipful Company of Plaisterers.

Stapleton, Michael. Worked in Dublin. Died 1801. *Georgian Society*, I, 1909, p. 17; *Jnl.* Royal Soc. Antiquaries of Ireland, 1940; *C. Life*, 31st January, 1947, p. 278.

Steede, Miles. Master (1654), Worshipful Company of Plasterers.

Stocking, Thomas, senior (1722–1808). Of Bristol. May have come from Dublin. Free Burgess, 1763. His son Thomas was apprenticed to him (Bristol Apprentices Book, 1764–77, 23). He was joined about 1790 by Robert Harding who carried on the business

when Stocking retired. He died 10th September, 1808, aged 86. Felix Farley's *Bristol Journal*, 17th September, 1808. He had another apprentice, Thomas Dennis, in 1786. Stocking did the plasterwork in Bristol at Arno's Court, The Royal Fort and St Nicholas's Church. His important commission was work at Corsham Court (1763–6). Received £570. Responsible for much work in the south-west. That at Midford Castle, Somerset, may be by him (*C. Life*, 3rd–10th March, 1944). *See* W. Ison, *Georgian Buildings of Bristol*, 1952, pp. 44–5.

Symonds, Richard (fl. 1705). Hill Court, Herefs., Staircase ceiling. *C. Life*, 27th January, 1966, p. 183

Thomas, Joseph (before 1730–77). Free Burgess of Bristol, 1730. Died 6th May, 1777. Clifton Hill House Bristol (1748–50), Ison, *op. cit.*, pp. 47, 178

Toogood, Arthur. Master (1663), Worshipful Company of Plaisterers.

Toozey, John. Master (1702–3), as above.

Vassalli, Francesco (fl. 1724–63). One of the team of Italian *stuccatori*. *See* p. 29 for an account of his work, and G. W. Beard, *Apollo*, July, 1964, for a catalogue of activity with references. Vassalli's first recorded employment was at Sutton Scarsdale, Derbys., in 1724 and the last at Shugborough Hall, Staffs., in 1763.

Walker, Thomas. Master (1705), Worshipful Company of Plaisterers.

Ward, Matthew (fl. 1762). York, Fairfax House (1762). Small amount of work, Yorks. Arch. Soc., Newburgh MSS. A Ferdinand Ward worked in Dublin at the Rotunda Hospital, C. P. Curran, *op. cit.*, p. 40.

Watson, Grace (fl. 1775). London, Berkeley Square (1775), Robert Child's house, Victoria and Albert Museum, Osterley Archives.

West, Robert (died 1790). Well-known Irish plasterer and master-builder. His brother John was also a plasterer. *C. Life*, 25th October, 1946, p. 758, Georgian Society I, 1909, p. 9, *Jnl. Royal Soc. Antiquaries of Ireland*, 1940, C. P. Curran, *op. cit.*, 1945, pp. 3, 40.

Weston, Ned (fl. 1738–43). Assistant to John Woolston (q.v.), Lamport Church (1738–43), *C. Life*, 10th October, 1952, p. 1108.

Wetherill, Robert (late 17th cent.–1717). Tunbridge Wells, St Charles the Martyr (1682 and 90), worked with Henry Doogood (q.v.). M. Whiffen, *Stuart and Georgian Churches*, 1947; Greenwich Hospital, asked to be employed, *Wren Soc.*, VI, pp. 31, 56; Blenheim Palace, Oxon., D. Green, *Blenheim Palace*, 1951, pp. 60, 104, 128; Hampton Court (1717), *Wren Soc.*, VII, pp. 201–2.

White, John (fl. 1627). Winton Castle, East Lothian (1627), Received £100, Jourdain, 1926, p. 35.

White, Thomas (fl. 1764–9). Milton Manor House, Berks (1764–9), *C. Life*, 24th December, 1948.

Whitehead, John (fl. 1750–60). Edgecote, Warwicks. (1753), Jourdain, 1926, xiii; Braxted Lodge, Essex (1754–56), Essex Co. Record Office, D/DDCA13, f 118; London, Soho Square. Worked under Thomas Dade on two houses for the Robinson family (1758–9), Leeds Reference Library, Newby Hall MS 2785A.

Wilkins, Chrysostom (fl. early 18th cent.). Was in charge of many plasterers at St Paul's Cathedral. Subscribed 2nd edn., Leoni's *Palladio*. Worked for Hawksmoor at three churches, and for Gibbs at St Mary-le-Strand. Colvin; *Arch. Rev.*, March, 1950. His brother John assisted him at many works.

Wilkinson, Richard. Subscribed to James Paine's *Plans . . . of Noblemen and Gentlemen's Houses*, 1767.

Wilmott, Humphry (fl. 1750–73). London, Mansion House (*c.* 1750) with George Fewkes, (q.v.). He was Master (1773), Worshipful Company of Plaisterers. His son John was apprenticed to him in 1767.

Wilton, William (fl. 1722–65). Father of the sculptor. Stanmer, Sussex (1722), Hussey, *E.C.H.*, *Early Georgian*, p. 56; London Foundling Hospital (1740), Turner,

p. 224, pl. 299; Linley Hall, Salop (1765). Worked with F. Collins. Bills at House. Attributed: Firle Place, Sussex (Library) *c.* 1750, *C. Life*, 3rd March, 1955, pp. 621–2.

Wood, John (late 18th cent.). Northallerton, N.R. Yorks., Court House; *York Georgian Society Report*, 1955–6. A Joseph Wood was a Freeman of York, 1778, Surtees Society, Vol. 102.

Woolston, John (fl. 1738–40). Of Northampton. Alderman of the town. Lamport, Northants., Music Hall, over Staircase, Library ceiling (1738), Northants. Record Office, Isham MSS; *Arch. Jnl.*, CX, 1953, p. 205; *C. Life*, 3rd October, 1952, p. 1023; Lamport Church (1740), *ibid.* Attributed: Easton Neston, Dining Room, *Arch. Jnl.*, *op. cit.*, p. 210; Althorp (p. 58).

Worrall, George (fl. 1724–61). Master Plasterer, Office of Works, 17 March, 1724/5–1761. He succeeded David Lance in this office and was himself succeeded by Thomas Clark on 25th November, 1761.

Wright, John, and others. A John Wright was apprenticed to Joseph Rose, senior, in 1753 for seven years. Rose was then living at Doncaster. The John Wright who worked at Stanford Hall, Leics., 1743, may have been a relative. *C. Life*, 11th December, 1958, p. 1410. Syston Hall, Lincs., Lincs. Co. Record Office, Thorold MSS VI/VII/5. A 'Mr Wright' is described as 'the ornament man' at Thorndon Hall, Essex (1768), Essex Co. Record Office, D/DPA58. A Thomas Wright was working in London in 1662, mending 'ye frett ceeling in ye Queen's Chappell', P.R.O. E351/3276.

WOODCARVERS, IRON SMITHS AND OTHER CRAFTSMEN

Adair, John (fl. 1763–9). Carver. Shugborough, Staffs. (1763–9), *C. Life*, 4th March, 1954, p. 593; Syon House, Middx. (1764), *see* p. 82.

Alcock, Nicholas (fl. late 17th cent.). Carver. London, Kensington Palace. Provided mouldings, etc., *C. Life Annual*, 1955, *Wren Soc.*, VII, p. 153.

Alcott, Joseph (fl. 1796–1815). Carver and scagliola column maker. Worked at Stoke Park; Arbury; Coventry House, Piccadilly; and Goodwood, Gunnis; Shugborough (1805), Scagliola pillars for Saloon, *C. Life*, 11th March, 1954, p. 678. Subscribed to George

Richardson's *Vitruvius Britannicus*, 1802 – 'Mr Alcott, Scagliola Column maker'.

Alken, Sefferin (fl. 1744–83). Carver. Worked at Stourhead; Milton House, Peterborough; Longford Castle; Wimpole; Blenheim Palace and Somerset House. In 1763 he was living at Dufours Court, Broad Street, Golden Square. As a member of the Alken family of sporting painters he had good contacts, and worked frequently for Robert Adam. He subscribed to the architect's *Spalatro*, 1764. A Samuel Alken worked for Sir William Chambers and subscribed to his *Treatise* *on Civil Architecture.* A William Alken was apprenticed in 1757 to the Oxford joiner John Taylor. Heal; B.M. Add. MS 36228, f. 190; Northants Record Office, Private Accts, Duke of Montagu, 1754–56, Vouchers 114; Boyd's Index to Apprenticeship Registers; W. Shaw Sparrow, *British Sporting Painters*, 1922

Ansell, Robert (fl. 1767). Carver. Subscribed to James Paine's *Plans . . . of Gentlemen's House*, 1767.

Austin, Cornelius (fl. late 17th cent.). Joiner and carver. Responsible for much fine work in Cambridge, *Wren Soc.*, V, pp. 28–9, 37–8, 41–4; D. Green, *Grinling Gibbons*, 1964, pp. 80–2.

A John Austin (fl. 1700–3) also worked as joiner in Cambridge at St Catherine's College (1700), Aymer Vallance, *Greater English Church Screens*, p. 135; and Christ's College (1701–3), *C. Life*, 2nd May, 1936.

Bakewell, Robert (1685–1752). Wrought iron smith. From my own researches and those of Mr Michael Felmingham it is possible to give some previously unrecorded facts. The mention of Robert Bakewell in the rent rolls for Castle Donington, Leicestershire, at Melbourne caused us to search the Castle Donington Parish Registers. Among the thirty-five Bakewell entries or so noted that of Robert's baptism is given, with his brother Thomas, on 29th May, 1685. His father, also named Robert, was a wheelwright (his sons' baptisms are recorded as 'Proms. sons'—(?promiscuous) and in his will of 30th October, 1730, he mentions his sons Robert, Thomas and John (b. 1683), and his daughter Elizabeth (b. 1689), Leicestershire County Archives.

Bakewell had a yard in Derby, Oakes Yard off St Peter's Street (a property of the Liversage Charity, founded 1529), and it is the registers of St Peter's Church which record his burial there on 31st October, 1752. His will dated 13th October, 1752, is at Somerset House. It is quite uninformative, but describes him as 'Robert Bakewell of Derby in the County of Derby, Gatesmith'. He briefly mentions his wife Mary and 'all my children'. It was proved in March, 1753. His business was continued from new premises by his former apprentice and foreman, Benjamin Yates, who advertised to this effect on 1st December, 1752 (p. 183). No tombstone or monument survives at St Peters. M. Ayrton and A. Silcock, *Wrought Iron and its Decorative Use*, 1929; *C. Life*, 2nd May, 1952, p. 1338, 27th September, 1962.

He worked at Melbourne Hall, Derbys., 1706–11, garden arbour, etc., *see* p. 38; Staunton Harold, Leics.

(c. 1711), gates in Church, staircase balustrade in house. I do not support the theory (*C. Life*, 24th February, 1950) that this work is later than Bakewell (and we now know he lived until 1752). He worked for Lord Strafford, 1716 (£200), B.M. Add. MSS 22241, f. 7; Derby, St Werburgh's Church, Font Cover, 1718 (£12), restored 1893–4, receipt, 5th June, 1718, Radburne Hall MSS, cited in *Derbyshire Countryside*, July–September, 1951. A wrought-iron table with marble top at Radburne is attributed to Bakewell; Derby, All Saints, 1722–5, Chancel Screen and Gates, and Churchyard Gates (moved to present position, 1958), Ayrton and Silcock, *op. cit.*, M. Whiffen, *Stuart and Georgian Churches outside London*, 1947, p. 95; Derby, Lombe's Silk Mill, 1728. Gates, moved at side of Derby Public Library, 1926; Okeover, Staffs., 1736–49, Entrance gates, staircase and other work. Received £451. Assisted by his pupil Benjamin Yates. Okeover MSS, Bills, I, 3–5, *C. Life*, 23rd and 30th January, 12th and 19th March, 1964. Oxford, Radcliffe Camera, 1744–6, Seven ornamental gates, S. G. Gillam, *Building Accounts of the Radcliffe Camera*, Oxford Hist. Soc., 1958, xviii.

A considerable body of work has been attributed to Bakewell over the years. The sources are listed on p. 39. *See* also R. Lister, *Decorative Wrought Ironwork*, 1960, pp. 97–102. I visited most of the work in April, 1965. Bakewell's characteristic wavy bar within a rectangle is found on the Foremark Church, Derbys., communion rails and churchyard gates. Those at Etwall disappeared when the Hall was demolished, but, other than this, Bakewell's work in Derbyshire, as listed by N. Pevsner, *Buildings of England. Derbyshire*, 1953, p. 135, is I think a correct indication of his wide patronage.

Barlow, William (fl. 1740–54). Carver. London, 44, Berkeley Square (1745–6), Accounts in Sir John Soane's Museum; Arlington Street, Mr Pelham's house (1749). Worked with James Richards (q.v.), R.I.B.A. Library MS 728.3 (42, 13A).

Bartoli, Dominic (late 18th cent.). Scagliola worker. Later known as Richter and Bartoli. Castlecoole, N. Ireland (1795), Joseph Rose letters, Castlecoole, *Connoisseur Yearbook*, 1956.

Best, George (fl. 1715). Carpenter. Beverley, Sir Charles Hotham's house (c. 1715), *Georgian Soc., E. Yorks.*, 1956–8, p. 42.

Blakesley, Robert (fl. 1772–84). Carver. Of York, in partnership with James Officer to 1772, Freeman 1776. Wentworth Woodhouse (1784), gilding, which he would do 'as well as any man in this County', *York Georgian Society, Report*, 1955–6, p. 61.

Blockley, Thomas (1705–89). Locksmith. Of Birmingham. Appears in Birmingham Directories, 1767–88. His death is recorded in *Aris's Birmingham Gazette*, 5th January, 1789: 'One of the first locksmiths in the kingdom'. Lamport, Northants. (1734–9), Northants Record Office, I.L.3966, 4208, 4212; Kirtlington, Oxon (1746), Hoare's Bank, Dashwood Account 22.12.1746; Radcliffe Camera, Oxford (1750), *Oxford Hist., Soc.*, 1958, p. 86–7; Shardeloes, Bucks. (1763), Bucks Co. Record Office, Shardeloes MSS; London, 20, St James's Square (1766), National Library of Wales, Williams-Wynne MSS.

Bodett, – (fl. 1673). Badminton, Glos. (1673). Child's Bank, 1st Marquess of Worcester account.

Boson, John (fl. 1729–43). Carver. Partner to John How. Subscribed to Leoni's *Alberti*, 1726. Worked at East India House, Leadenhall Street, London, Gunnis; four City Churches, St Alphege, Greenwich; St George, Bloomsbury; St John, Horsleydown; St Luke, Old Street, *Arch, Rev.*, March, 1950; Westminster Abbey (1729), carved woodwork, screen and organ gallery; Canterbury Cathedral (1732), reredos, Vertue, III, pp. 88, 116; *Survey of London*, XXXII, 1963, p. 521.

Bromwich, Thomas (fl, 1740–87). As paper-hanger and decorator Bromwich had a very successful business. He supplied from The Golden Lion on Ludgate Hill, London, wallpaper to Horace Walpole, and in 1763 was appointed 'Paper Hanging Maker In Ordinary to the Great Wardrobe'. He was Master of the Paper-Stainers' Company in 1761, and died in 1787. He had an account at Drummonds Bank (noted 1767). Heal; *Strawberry Hill Accounts*, ed. Paget Toynbee, 1927, pp. 66–8; E. A. Entwistle, *The Connoisseur*, October 1952.

Broval, Thomas (fl. 1724). Joiner. Of Warwick. Sutton Scarsdale, Derbys. (1724). Name appears on lead-rising plate formerly at house, Colvin, p. 552.

Bumpstead, John (late 17th cent.). Carver. Christ's Hospital, and valued carving, St Stephen Walbrook, *Wren Soc.*, X, p. 121, XI, p. 69.

Buncker, George (fl. 1728). Wrought-iron worker. Gates at Dulwich College (1728), R. Lister, *Decorative Wrought Ironwork*, 1960, p. 119.

Caesar, Anthony (fl. 1727–8). Carver. London, Harcourt House, Cavendish Square (1727–8), Bramham Park, Yorks., Bingley letter-book.

Carpenter, Edmund (fl. 1688). Carver, Belton, Lincs. (1688), carved various chimney-pieces in Gibbons style, Gunnis; D. Green, *Grinling Gibbons*, 1964, pp. 114–15, 123. Samuel Carpenter (1660–1713) of York was a prominent stone-carver (Gunnis), and John Carpenter of York (perhaps a relative to Samuel) was a carver in partnership with Daniel Harvey.

Chalet, – (late 17th cent.). Wrought-iron worker. Signed a receipt on behalf of Jean Tijou for work at Chatsworth (1688), Chatsworth archives.

Champion, Charles (fl. late 17th cent.). Gilder. Whitehall Chapel, Gilding organ, *Wren Soc.*, VII, p. 131.

Chanarden, Lewis (fl. 1675–6). Carver. Badminton, Glos. (1675–6). Child's Bank, 1st Marquess of Worcester's Account, 11.5.1675, 9.6.1676.

Chaplin, John (late 17th cent.). Joiner. Worked at Chatsworth and Kiveton. F. Thompson, *A History of Chatsworth*, 1949; Yorks. Arch. Soc., Duke of Leeds MSS, Box 35.

Chesne, Gideon du (fl. 1703–9). Carver. Principally a stone-carver. Carved stone heads at Ditton (1703–5); Boughton, Northants., arms over stables (still owed £15 in 1709), Boughton House, Parcel D11, Part 2.

Chicheley, Richard (early 18th cent.). Carver. London, St Paul's Deptford (1710), *Arch. Rev.*, March, 1950.

Chuke, Michael (1679–1742). Carver. Of Kilkhampton. Said to have studied with Gibbons in London. Stowe, Bucks., Reredos, Organ-Screen, Pulpit (1707), Gunnis; D. Green, *Grinling Gibbons*, 1964, p. 146.

Churchill, John (fl. 1706–18). Carpenter. Master Carpenter, Office of Works, 1706–18.

Cleare (Cleere), Richard (fl. 1662–82). Carver. Coleshill, Berks. (1662), *C. Life*, 29th July, 1919, p. 116, R. T. Gunther, *The Architecture of Sir Roger Pratt*, 1928, p. 97; Great Model of St Paul's, *Wren Soc.*, XVI, p. 205; Sheldonian Theatre, Oxford, *ibid.*, XIX, pp. 94, 96–8; City Churches of St Olave, Jewry; St Stephen, Walbrook; St Swithun, Cannon Street; and St Bartholomew, Exchange, *Wren Soc.*, X, pp. 56, 121, XIX, pp. 10, 55–6.

Cleare, William (fl. 1668–1690). Joiner Badminton, Glos. (1668), Child's Bank, 1st Marquess of Worcester's Account, 20.11.1668. Cleare had an extensive City practice and also worked like Richard Cleare at Oxford, the Chelsea Hospital, and on the models for St Paul's. *Wren Soc.*, references cited, Vol. 20. East Hatley, Cambs. (1683), wainscoting at 8s. 6d. a yard. His wife Anne received payment at her husband's death in 1690, Castle Howard MSS, Sir George Downing Accounts.

William Cleare, junior, worked at St Paul's Cathedral (1695–6), *Wren Soc.*, XV, pp. 3, 6, 7.

Clerici, Charles (late 18th cent.). Scagliola worker. Wentworth Woodhouse, Yorks., Saloon floor; Thoresby, assisted plasterer, Ely Crabtree (q.v.), *C. Life*, 10th October, 1957.

Collett, Nicholas (fl. 1760–5). Carver. Friend of Thomas Gainsborough. State Coach (George III, designed Sir William Chambers), decorative carving, Gunnis.

Cousin, Peter (fl. 1702). Gilder. May have been a relative of Antonio Verrio's gilder, René Cousin. Worked, Hampton Court, *Wren Soc.*, XVIII, pp. 160–1.

Crouch, – (fl. 1767). Joiner. Subscribed to James Paine's *Plans . . . of Noblemen and Gentlemen's Seats*, 1767.

Darby, John (fl. 1723–33). Carver. London, Christchurch, Spitalfields (1723–9); St Luke, Old Street (1727–33). Thomas Derby worked at five other City Churches. *Arch. Rev.*, March, 1950.

Davies, Robert and John (fl. 1680–1748, etc). Wrought-iron workers. Sons of Hugh Davies. Worked extensively in the Wrexham and Chirk areas. *See* p. 37 for an account of their work.

Davies, Roger (fl. 1682–1709). Master joiner. Ragley, Warwicks. (1680), Hooke's Diary (1935 edn.), entries dated 26.3.1676, 11.7.1679; M'Espinasse, *Robert Hooke*, 1956, pp. 101–2, 137; Burghley House, Northants. (1682–3). A 'Mr Davies' is mentioned in the Exeter Bank Account, Child's Bank, 23rd June, 1682–3. This may be Roger Davies, or William Davies, seemingly a relative, who worked at Chatsworth, F. Thompson, *A History of Chatsworth*, 1949, p. 49; Boughton House, Northants. (1687–92) and Montagu House London. £3,606 was due to Davies for work done 1687–92. £1,546 of this was for work at Boughton, and £2,560 at Montagu House. He provided 223 yards of wainscoting and a communion table for Weekly Church (c. 1700, £452), Boughton Archives, Parcel D11, Part 2; Whitehall, Chapel (1686), Canterbury Cathedral, Choir Stalls; Chelsea Hospital; St Paul's Cathedral (with Hugh Webb), Greenwich Hospital, and several City Churches.

William Davies, as noted above, worked at Chatsworth (1692–4) with Thomas Young, Joel Lobb and Samuel Watson.

Dawson, John (fl. 1764). Carver. Of Westminster. Okeover, Staffs. (1764), House archives, Building file, Leak Okeover.

Deringer, – (fl. 1688). Carver. Recommended for employment (1688), St Paul's Cathedral. *Wren Soc.*, XVI, p. 62.

Draper, John (fl. 1690). Locksmith. Petworth, Sussex (1690), brass locks and hinges, *Sussex Arch. Collections*, XCVI, 1958.

Dryhurst, James (fl. 1727–62). Carver. Employed by James Brydges, 1st Duke of Chandos, at his London house in Cavendish Square (1727–8), Baker, *Brydges*, p. 277; London, house in Grosvenor Square for Lord Northampton (1761), Compton Place, Sussex, Estate Archives, Box Q. A Thomas Dryhurst is one of the figures in a picture by Robert Pyle painted in 1760, destroyed by fire 1940, *C. Life*, 30th March, 1945, p. 556.

Dubois, Nicholas (c. 1665–1735). Architect and carver. His architectural career is discussed by Colvin. He is said to have erected the unusual staircase at Chevening House, Kent, in 1722. Tipping, *English Homes*, V.i, p. 23.

Dugdale, Thomas (fl. 1678–1714). Carver. Of Liverpool. Chirk Castle, Denbighs. (1678), panelling, Long Gallery. Chirk Castle Archives. Gunnis notes that this is probably the Thomas Dugdale whose will was proved in 1714.

Edney, William (early 18th cent.?). Wrought-iron worker, from Bristol. St Mary Redcliffe, gates (1710). Received £110. *See* p. 40 for an account of his work.

Emmett, William (fl. 1641–1700). Carver. Probably born 1641. Sculptor to the Crown before Gibbons, succeeding his uncle, Henry Phillips. Liveryman, Joiners' Company, 1666. Kensington Palace (1690),

British Arch. Assoc. Jnl., 1951, p. 4. He worked also at Whitehall, Hampton Court, several City Churches, Chelsea Hospital, and the Temple Church. Two carved capitals by Emmett from this Church are at the Bowes Museum, Barnard Castle. *Wren Soc.*, XX, references cited, *Papers illustrative of the History of Chelsea Hospital*, 1872, pp. 169–70. Worked with William Morgan.

Essex, James (fl. *c.* 1700–1749). Carpenter-joiner. Of Cambridge. Father of the architect James Essex (1722–84). Did most of the woodwork in the University in the first half of the 18th century. *Willis and Clark*, III, pp. 540–1.

Etty family, of York, carpenter-joiners-builders. An account of the activities of this family is given on pp. 22–4.

Fisher, Richard (mid 18th cent.). Wood carver and sculptor, Gunnis. *The York Journal*, 15th July, 1746, indicates that Fisher had just moved from Ripon to the Minster yard at York 'where all sorts of Carved and Statuary Work, both in Wood, Marble and Stone, either for Household furniture, or Monumental, and Sepulchral Monuments, are performed, in the neatest manner, and at moderate Prices . . . '. Fisher had an extensive patronage and worked for the Darley family at Aldby and the Aislabie family at Studley Royal, Ripon, Borthwick Institute, York, Darley MSS; Studley Royal, Estate Office, Parcel 286.

Foljambe, Francis (early 18th cent.). Wrought-iron worker. Arbury Hall, Warwicks. (1719), estimate for gates. Warwick Co. Record Office, Newdegate Archives (p. 39).

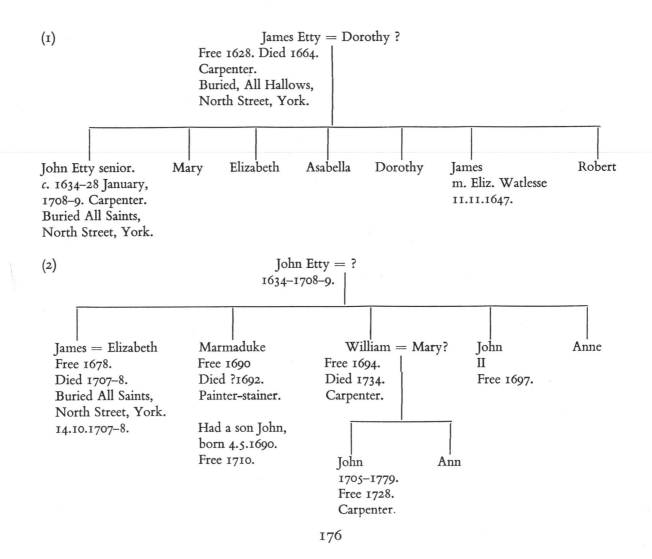

Fort, Alexander (fl. late 17th cent. – 1706). Master joiner. Master Joiner, Office of Works. Made coffin of William III. Employed at Hampton Court, Kensington Palace, Windsor Castle, Chatsworth, Farley Hospital, Monmouth House, Soho. His son Thomas applied in 1706 to succeed his father as Master Joiner, *Wren Soc.*, XX, references cited; F. Thompson, *A History of Chatsworth*, 1949, pp. 135, 137, 143, 145–6, 148–9.

Frogley, Arthur (fl. *c.* 1660–1700). Master carpenter. Master Carpenter for Sir Christopher Wren, with Richard Frogley, at Sheldonian Theatre, Oxford. Worked in several Oxford colleges, H.M.C., Oxford, *Wren Soc.*, XIX, p. 92. For Richard Frogley's work see Gunnis.

Gamble, – (fl. 1770). Carver and gilder. Kedleston, Derbys. (1770). Received £6 16s. for 'guilding the organ case', Kedleston archives; *Connoisseur Yearbook*, 1958.

Gardom, John (late 17th cent.). Wrought-iron worker. Worked at Chatsworth, Kiveton, etc. Pupil of Jean Tijou. (*See* p. 40.)

Gibbons, Grinling (1648–1721). Master carver. Born 4th April, 1648, of English parents, at Rotterdam. Came to England about 1667 and early went to York where he was with (but not apprenticed to) John Etty (1634–1708/9). Left for London. Discovered by John Evelyn. Appointed Master Carver in wood to the Crown by Charles II, a position he held until the reign of George I. For a full list of his works see D. Green, *Grinling Gibbons*, 1964.

Gilbert, John (mid 18th cent.). Carver from London. Lived in Great Queen Street. Upholder to George III. London, Mansion House (1752), *Connoisseur*, December, 1952, p. 181; *The Mansion House*, H. Clifford Smith, 1957, pp. 13, 19. He also worked for Robert Adam at Croome Court, Worcs. (1767), and Mersham-le-Hatch, Kent. Trans. Worcs. Arch. Soc., 1960; Hussey, *E.C.H.*, *Mid-Georgian*, p. 100.

Goff, Thomas (fl. 1720s). Wrought-iron worker. Senate House, Cambridge, railings to designs of James Gibbs. Received £446, University Registry, Vice-Chancellor's receipts.

Goodyear (Godier), Jonathan (died 1732). Carver. Wentworth Castle, worked under William Thornton (q.v.), *C. Life*, 25th October, 1924, quotation from diary kept by John Hobson, 1726–35.

Gosset family. Carvers, gilders. Isaac Gosset (1713–99) did wood-carving at Moulsham Hall, Essex, but is better known as a wax-modeller. Jacob Gosset was a carver and picture-frame maker. Subscribed to Leoni's *Alberti*, 1726. Gunnis.

Gravenor, James (fl. 1760–70). Carver. Stone carving at Kedleston, Derbys. Gunnis. Received £3 13s. for carving ornaments in the frieze, etc., of the Organ designed by Robert Adam and gilded by Mr Gamble. Kedleston Archives; *Connoisseur Yearbook*, 1958.

Greenway, Robert (late 17th cent.). Locksmith. Winslow Hall, Bucks. (*c.* 1700), provided locks. As the Royal Locksmith he was criticised by the architect, William Talman, *Wren Soc.*, IV, p. 60, XVII, pp. 73, 86.

Grew, John (late 17th cent.). Carver. Assistant to Edward Pearce (q.v.). Worked at Sudbury Hall, Derbys. (1670s), *C. Life*, 22nd June, 1935.

Guy, – (fl. 1719). Carver. Oxford, All Souls College, Chapel Screen, 1719 (£127). *C. Life*, 23rd June, 1928. An Edward Guy was doing wainscoting at Knowsley, Lancs., *c.* 1720. Lancs. Co. Record Office, Knowsley Archives, Accounts 1718–29.

Hallam, John (late 17th cent.). Joiner. Chatsworth, Derbys. (late 17th cent.). F. Thompson, *A History of Chatsworth*, 1949, pp. 37, 67.

Harvey (Hervey, Hervé), Daniel (1683–1733). Born in France, 1683. Worked mainly in stone, at Castle Howard and Wentworth Castle (4 capitals in wood). In partnership at Atherton Hall, Lancs. and Newby Park (Baldersby), Yorks., with John Carpenter. Settled at York. Died there 11th December, 1733. Buried at St Olave's Church, York. B.M. Add. MSS 22241, ff. 11, 20, 29; *see also* p. 50 of this book.

Hobcraft, John (mid 18th cent.). Carpenter, architect, from London. Colvin gives an account of his architectural career. He also did jobs as varied as providing the mahogany doors to the Long Gallery, Corsham Court, Wilts. (1766).

Hopson, Sir Charles (died 6th April, 1710). Master Joiner. Master (1708) of the Joiners' Company. Appointed Master Joiner, Office of Works (1706). Worked at St Paul's Cathedral, Eton College, etc. His son John (died 9th June, 1718) was Master Joiner, Office of Works, 1710–18. Colvin; *Wren Soc.*, XV, XXI, XX, pp. 104–5.

How, John (fl. 1712–30). Carver. London, St George's, Hanover Square (1712–24); St George's, Bloomsbury (1720–30), *Arch. Rev.*, March, 1950.

Howgill, John (fl. 1727). Carver. Of York. London, Harcourt House, Cavendish Square, chimney cartouche (1727). Bramham Park, Yorks., Bingley letter-book, 28th November, 1727.

Hurlbut, William (fl. 1679–83). Master carpenter. Of Starton, near Coventry. Ragley Hall, Warwicks. (1679–83), *Walpole Soc.*, XXV, p. 98.

Jones, Aaron (fl. 1757–75). Carver, gilder. Chandelier in the Bristol Moravian Chapel (1757). Listed in Sketchley's 1775 Bristol Directory at 10, Clare Street as 'Carver, Gilder, and Looking Glass Manufacturer'. Bryan Little, *City and County of Bristol*, 1954, p. 221.

Jones, Henry (1649–1721). Joiner. Lamport Hall, Northants. (1686). Music Room wainscoting. Northants. Record Office, Isham Archives; *Northants. Arch. Soc.*, 1951; Colvin.

Jones, Richard (fl. 1712–24). Carver. Of Wapping. London, St Alphege, Greenwich (1712–24), *Arch. Rev.*, March, 1950. A Robert Jones, carver, was invited to submit proposals at Greenwich Hospital (late 17th cent.), *Wren Soc.*, VI, p. 31. A Richard Jones, smith, provided a 'Large Iron Fence round the Church' (St Paul's Cathedral) 1714. M. Ayrton and A. Silcock, *Wrought Iron and its Decorative Use*, 1929, p. 98.

Kay (Key), Joseph (late 17th – early 18th cent.). Locksmith. King's Blacksmith, 1699. Worked at the Cottonian Library; Kensington Palace and Hampton Court. He provided brass locks, keys and hinges at Castle Howard, Yorks. (1709–10). *Wren Soc.*, IV, p. 60, VII, p. 128, XI, p. 53, XVIII, pp. 152–3; Castle Howard, Building Bills, 12 January, 1709/10.

Kinward, Thomas (mid 17th cent.). Carver. Master Carver, Commonwealth period. Worked at Clarendon House, various Royal works (1662), P.R.O. E/351/3276; and was presumably the 'Mr Kinwood' who, Walpole says, walked in the procession at Cromwell's funeral, 'Anecdotes of Painting', *Works*, 1798 edn. II, p. 280; R. T. Gunther, *The Architecture of Sir Roger Pratt*, 1928.

Langdale, Edward (fl. 1668). Carver. Foreman to the Carver at Sheldonian Theatre, Oxford. *Wren Soc.*, XIX, p. 92.

Lanscroon, Jean Baptiste (late 17th cent.). Carver. Not to be confused with the decorative painter Gerard Lanscroon. Chatsworth, Derbys. (1695), Limewood festoons, F. Thompson, *A History of Chatsworth*, 1949, pp. 36, 167, 169.

Lawrence, Richard (fl. 1764–83). Carver. Manor House, Milton, Berks. (1764–73), carving, including panelling and overmantel, Dining Room, *C. Life*, 24th December, 1948, p. 1333; Somerset House (wood and stone, 1780s); probably the carver of this name who worked at Strawberry Hill, Middx. Gunnis; R.I.B.A. Library; Somerset House Accounts II; Strawberry Hill Accounts, ed. Paget Toynbee, 1927, p. 157.

Le Sage, John (late 17th cent.). Carver and gilder. Worked for Earl of Bristol (1690), at Hampton Court. Heal; *Wren Soc.*, IV, p. 60.

Lightfoot, Luke (1722?–89). Carver. His most exuberant work was the carving at Claydon House, Bucks., for the Verney family, *Arch. Rev.*, 1926. *See also Jnl., Furniture History Society*, Vol. 2, 1966, for new facts.

Linnell, William (fl. 1720–63). Carver, cabinetmaker. Supplied furniture to Sir Richard Hoare, and to William Drake for Shardeloes. Lived 28, Berkeley Square, London. Oxford, Radcliffe Camera (1746–7), carved work. *Oxford Hist. Soc.*, 1958, pp. 53, 64; *Wren Soc.*, XVII, p. 82; Heal; R. Edwards and M. Jourdain, *Georgian Cabinet-Makers*, 3rd revd. edn. 1962, pp. 15–16.

John Linnell was probably his son or nephew. The architect C. H. Tatham said he was 'in the first line of his profession'. Died 27th March, 1796, and buried Paddington churchyard.

Lobb, Joel and Henry (late 17th cent.). Joiners, carvers. Joel and Henry worked at Chatsworth, and Joel at Castle Howard and Carlisle House, London. F. Thompson, *A History of Chatsworth*, 1949, pp. 36, 43, 59, 148–9; Castle Howard Archives.

Loerhuick, Anthony (late 17th cent.). Carver. Whitehall, Chapel, *Wren Soc.*, VII, p. 131.

Lord, – (late 17th cent.). Carver. Denham Place, Bucks. (1692), chapel carvings. *Records of Bucks*, XVI, Pt. 3, 1957–8, p. 195.

Lowe, Thomas (late 17th cent.). Carver. Christ Church, Newgate Street, and Temple Church, London. *Wren Soc.*, X, p. 124, pls 58, 60.

Madden, John (fl. 1745). Carver, gilder from Bath. Subscribed to John Wood the elder's *A Description of the Exchange of Bristol*, 1745.

Maine (Mayne), Jonathan (fl. 1680–1704). Carver. Maine, with Gibbons, Pearce, Young, and Davis, was one of the most important woodcarvers of the late 17th cent. Liveryman of Joiners' Company, 1694, *C. Life*, 31st December, 1948. Worked at several City churches, St Paul's Cathedral, Eton College, Christ's Hospital, *Wren Soc.*, Vol. XX, references cited; Burghley House, Northants. (with Thomas Young, 1682–4), Child's Bank, Exeter Bank Account (£402 11s. 3d, 1682–1684/5); Oxford, Trinity College Chapel (1695), *C. Life, op. cit.*; Kiveton, Yorks. (1703–4), received £103 16s. for carving in the Chapel at this house, built for the 1st Duke of Leeds. Yorks. Arch. Soc. Library, Duke of Leeds MSS, Box 33; D. Green, *Grinling Gibbons*, 1964.

Marshall, William (late 17th cent.). Wrought-iron worker. Of London. Chatsworth, Derbys. (1686), gates and palisade. F. Thompson, *A History of Chatsworth*, 1949, pp. 61, 212, 214; petitioned at St Mary's, Warwick, 1694, *C. Life*, 26th April, 1962, p. 975.

Mawson, Benjamin (early 18th cent.). Copper-smith. St Paul's Cathedral (1718–19), M. Ayrton and A. Silcock, *Wrought Iron and its Decorative Use*, 1929, p. 98.

Mew, – (fl. 1668). Locksmith. Badminton, Glos. (1668). Child's Bank, 1st Marquess of Worcester's Account, 22nd June, 1668.

Miller, James (fl. 1760). Carver. Holkham Hall, Norfolk, Chapel screen (1760). Succeeded Marsden as resident carver, *C. Life Annual*, 1954, p. 47.

Minn, – (fl. 1712–24). Joiner. Oxford, Clarendon Buildings (1712), All Souls College, Chapel Screen (1719), *C. Life*, 23rd June, 1928.

Mitchell, John (fl. 1697). Carpenter. Of London. Bristol, St Peter's (1697), reredos and re-seating. C. F. W. Dening, *The XVIIIth Century Architecture of Bristol*, 1923.

Mitley, Charles George (1705–58). Carver. Apprenticed to Daniel Harvey in 1720. Worked at Castle Howard (1736); York Minster, gothic Pulpit (1741); Studley Royal, chimney-piece in the Chinese Bedchamber (1748). Died 26th August, 1758, buried at St Cuthbert's, York. Boyd's Index to Apprenticeship Registers, Guildhall Library; Gunnis; Colvin; J. B.

Morrell, *York Monuments*, pp. 41, 59, 69, 122; will at Borthwick Institute, York; *C. Life*, 1st August, 1931, p. 133, pl. No 13; Studley Royal, Estate Archives, Parcel 286.

Moore, Thomas (fl. 1756–78). Carpet-maker. Of Chiswell Street, Moorfields, London. Trade card illustrated by Heal, pp. 119–20. Made many carpets for Adam houses and to the architect's design. These included those for Croome Court, Worcs. (1768); Syon House, Middx. (1769, signed); Osterley Park, Middx.; 20, St James's Square (c. 1774, £232 10s. 6d); one for Horace Walpole. He won the Society of Arts premium of £25 in 1757 for a carpet 'in many respects equal, and in some respects superior to those imported from Persia and Turkey'. A. F. Kendrick and C. E. C. Tattersall, *Hand-woven Carpets*, 1922, I, pp. 80–1; *Journal* of Lady Mary Coke, ed. J. A. Home, II, p. 242; *Dictionary of English Furniture*, ed. R. Edwards, 1954; Williams-Wynne MSS, National Library of Wales; *Strawberry Hill Accounts*, ed. Paget Toynbee, 1927, p. 126; 1842 Sale Catalogue of Strawberry Hill, 24th Day, Lot 16.

Murray, George (fl. 1752). Carver. London, Mr Pelham's House, Arlington Street. Great Room Chimney frame (1752), R.I.B.A. Library MS 728.3(42.13A).

Nadauld, – (early 18th cent.). Carver. Worked at Castle Howard and Chatsworth. (*See* p. 45). His descendants lived at Ashford, near Bakewell, Derbys., until recent years. F. Thompson, *A History of Chatsworth*, 1949, p. 36; Castle Howard, Building Books.

Neale, John (fl. 1730). Gilder. London, Mr Pelham's House, Arlington Street. Gilded frames and mirrors (1750); source as above.

Newman, William (fl. 1676–94). Carver. Worked at several City Churches. *Wren Soc.*, X, p. 115; XIX, p. 43.

Nutt, Edward (fl. 1730). Wrought-iron worker. Grimsthorpe Castle, Lincs., Forecourt Gates, 1730. Pevsner and Harris, *Buildings of England, Lincs*, 1964, p. 556.

Oakey (Okey), Charles (fl. 1683). Carver. Samuel Watson (q.v.) was apprenticed to him, Gunnis; Lyson's *Derbyshire*, p. 153; Badminton, Glos. (1683). Received £18. Child's Bank, Duke of Beaufort Account, 9th July, 1683.

Oram, William (fl. 1748–77). Carpenter. Master Carpenter, Office of Works, 1748–77.

Orson, John (fl. 1760). Carver. Kyre Park, Worcs. (1760). Received £70 (doors, chimney-pieces, etc.), Hussey, *E.C.H.*, *Early-Georgian*, p. 219.

Owen, Robert (late 17th cent.). Joiner from London. Worked with Henry Lobb at Chatsworth. F. Thompson, *A History of Chatsworth*, 1949, pp. 37, 67.

Palmer, James (fl. 1766). Smith and brass-founder to George III. Corsham Court, Wilts. (1766). Gilt-metal door fittings. Received £65. Hussey, *E.C.H.*, *Early-Georgian*, p. 233.

Paris family (late 17th cent.). Wrought iron workers from Warwick. Worked in that town and at Stoneleigh. *C. Life*, 26th April, 1962, p. 975; *Trans., B'ham Arch. Soc.*, LXV, 22–5, LIX, 72–3.

Partridge, William (fl. 1683). Locksmith, wrought-iron worker. East Hatley, Cambs. (1683). Locks, hinges, latches, etc., Castle Howard, Sir George Downing Accounts; Gates at Trinity College, Cambridge (1691–2), received £400, College Account Books.

Paty family (18th cent.). Carvers. Of Bristol, masons, statuaries, etc. W. Ison, *Georgian Buildings of Bristol*, 1952, pp. 39–43; Colvin; Gunnis.
    Thomas Paty (1713–89) was the main wood-carver. Bristol, Royal Exchange, 1743; Redland Chapel, Bristol, 1741–3. Subscribed to John Wood's *Description of the Exchange*, 1745. He died 4th May, 1789; Michael Knowles, Bristol School of Architecture thesis on Paty family; *Bristol Journal*, 9th May, 1789.

Pearce, Edward (c. 1635–1695). Carver. Son of the decorative painter Edward Pearce. Worked at Sudbury, Derbys. (1676–7), Great Staircase (£112 15s. 5d.), etc.; London Painter Stainers' Hall. With John Oliver designed woodwork of Emmanuel College, Cambridge, executed by Cornelius Austin (q.v.). Worked at several City Churches; Wolseley Hall, Staffs. (staircase); Royal College of Physicians; designed Bishop's Palace, Lichfield. Gunnis; Colvin; *Guildhall Miscellany* I, 1952; A. D. Englefield, *History of the Painter Stainers' Company of London*, 1923, p. 138; Willis and Clark, II, p. 707; *Wren Soc.*, Vol. XX, references cited; R. Plot, *Natural History of Staffordshire*, 1686; *C. Life*, 30th December, 1954.

Pelletier, Renée and Thomas (late 17th–early 18th cent.). Gilders. Presumably the mother and brother of John Pelletier who worked at Boughton for the Duke of Montagu and at Hampton Court. R. Edwards and M. Jourdain, *Georgian Cabinet-Makers*, 1962, p. 35. They received £2,382 13s. 6d. for gilding at Boughton and Montagu House, 1692–1708. Thomas claimed the amount in 1709 as executrix of his mother. Boughton, Lord Charles Scott's Notebooks, 19, pp. 63–4; Executors' Accounts, 1st Duke of Montagu.

Pettit, Paul (fl. 1732). Gilder. Royal Barge (1732). Gilded work. M. Jourdain, *William Kent*, 1948, p. 82 fn. 5.

Philips, – (fl. 1763). Carver. Chirk Castle, Denbighs. (1763), New Drawing Room, *C. Life*, 12th October, 1951, p. 1150.

Phillips, Henry (fl. 1662–85). Master Carver in wood to the Crown. P.R.O. E351/3276; *Wren Soc.*, IV, p. 71; Gunnis.

Phillips, John (fl. 1725–51). Carpenter. One of the most important craftsmen of this period. Worked at Radcliffe Camera, Oxford; Christ Church, Oxford; Alscot Park, and Ragley Hall, Warwicks; Wimpole, Oxon. He was one of James Gibbs's 'favourite' craftsmen and consistently appears in the architect's bank account (Drummonds). Colvin; *Oxford Hist. Soc.*, 1958; B.M. Add. MSS 36228, f. 190; 23218, entry 3.8.1759.

Phillips, Thomas (c. 1689–1736). Carpenter. Worked in London at St Martin-in-the-Fields; St Peter's, Vere Street; Tower of London; Denmark House; Whitehall, Treasury Buildings. Colvin.

Plested, Nicholas (late 17th cent.). Carver. Worked in London and at Winslow, Bucks. *Wren Soc.*, XVII, p. 74.

Pope, William (died 1678). Master Carpenter. Warden of the Carpenters' Company, 1670. Colvin.

Poulteney, Thomas (late 17th cent.). Carver. London, St Peter's, Cornhill, worked with Thomas Askew. H. Avray Tipping, *Grinling Gibbons*, 1914, p. 164.

Richards, James (fl. 1721–59). Master Sculptor and Carver in Wood, Office of Works, 1721–59. *See* p. 31 for an account of his work.

Ritson, Jonathan (c. 1780–1846). Carver from Whitehaven. Employed by Duke of Norfolk at Arundel. After Duke's death in 1815 went to Petworth. D. Green, *Grinling Gibbons*, 1964, pp. 107–8.

Robinson, – (fl. 1703). Carpenter. Assistant to Nadauld (q.v.) at Castle Howard (1703). May have been Thomas or Edward Robinson who worked with George Best (q.v.) at Sir Charles Hotham's house at Beverley (c. 1715). Castle Howard, Building Book 1700–20; Georgian Soc., E.R. Yorks., IV, 1956–8, p. 43.

Robinson, Thomas (late 17th–early 18th cent.). Wrought-iron worker, from London. Worked at St Paul's Cathedral under Tijou (1696–1714). M. Ayrton and A. Silcock, *Wrought Iron and its Decorative Use*, 1929, p. 92; the authors list many works said to be by Robinson, but for which exact documentation is lacking. Robinson provided the New College, Oxford, gateway (1711) and received £170. He is also credited with those at Trinity College. J. Harris, *English Decorative Ironwork, 1610–1836*, 1960, p. 16.

Rogers, W. G. (1792–c. 1867). Carver, Restorer. Born Dover, 1792. Restorer of Gibbons period carvings (e.g. Belton); exhibited at Great Exhibition, 1851. There are two swags signed by him at Temple Newsam House, Leeds. R.I.B.A. Proceedings, 1867, p. 180; H. Avray Tipping, *Grinling Gibbons . . .* , 1914, pp. 197–8; D. Green, *Grinling Gibbons*, 1964, pp. 84, 114, 121, 146.

Ross, Charles (fl. 1750–1). Joiner. Twickenham, Marble Hill (1750–1). Norwich Public Library, Hobart MS, 8862. A Joshua Ross of Bath subscribed to John Wood the elder's *A Description of the Exchange of Bristol*, 1745.

Ryder, Richard (fl. 1668–1683). Carpenter. Master Carpenter, Office of Works, 1668–83.

Sabyn, – (fl. 1705–6). Carpenter. Castle Howard (1706), Cornices, friezes, etc. House Archives, Masons' and Carpenters' Book, 1702–8, Building Bills, 1700–40, Folder 2. His work was measured by Hawksmoor and William Etty.

Selden, John (fl. 1688–1715). Carver. Petworth, Sussex (1688–97). Carving in Chapel and Hall of State. Died at Petworth, buried 12th January, 1715. Petworth Archives, Account Rolls of John Bowen (1696) and Richard Stiles (1692); *Sussex Arch. Collections*, XCVI, 1959; D. Green, *Grinling Gibbons*, 1964, pp. 106–8.

Shaw, – (fl. 1770). Joiner. Used by Sir William Chambers at Woburn and Ampthill, set up bookcases. B.M. Add. MSS 41133, 24.3.1770.

Smallwell, John (fl. 1700–5). Joiner. Worked in London at St Paul's Cathedral (1700); Canterbury Cathedral (1704); Master of the Joiners' Company

(1705). His son (?) was Master Joiner, Office of Works 1718–61. He, or his son, worked for the Duke of Newcastle at several properties under the direction of Sir John Vanbrugh. Colvin; B.M. Add. MSS 33442; *Wren Soc.*, XX, p. 209.

Swan, Abraham (fl. 1750–7). Carpenter and Joiner. Issued many books of architectural designs (Colvin), Edgecote House, Warwicks. (1750), received £1,990 10s., *C. Life*, 10th January, 1920; Blair Castle, Perthshire. Designed front staircase (1757), *C. Life*, 11th November, 1949; Abraham Swan, *Collection of Designs in Architecture*, 1757.

Thornton, William (1670–1721). Joiner. One of the most skilled of the York joiners. Colvin; J. B. Morrell, *York Monuments*, 1944, Pl. 46. He worked in Yorkshire at Castle Howard (1706–11), wainscoting; House Archives, Masons' and Carpenters' Book, 1702–8; Beverley Minster (1716–20), restored N. transept to vertical by means of timber framing; engraving of 1739 by F. Geldart; Roxburghe Club, 1890, F. Drake, *Eboracum*, 1736, p. 260; Beningbrough Hall, 1716, probably erected house for John Bourchier and did wood-carving (*See* p. 51); Beverley, Sir Charles Hotham's house. Received £1,116. East Riding, Yorks., Record Office, DDHO/15/4. His name appears in the Bank account of the Earl of Strafford (Child's Bank) and suggests he did the carving at Wentworth Castle (*cf.* entry under Godier).

He died on September 23, 1721, and was buried at St Olave's Church, York. The monumental inscription on the W. wall, bearing the arms of the Joiners' Company, says:

Near/This Place lies the Body of/
William Thornton, Joyner &/ Architect;
who departed this/ life Sep: 23: 1721:
Aged 51 Years/ Also/ Robert his son,
who departed/ this life Apr: 12: 1724
in the/ 21st Year of his Age.

His will (Borthwick Institute, York Wills, 1721, ff. 37–8) was made 19th September, 1721. His executors were his son and John Bagnall (q.v.), plasterer, of York and Leeds. It shows he had 4 sons and 3 daughters by his wife, Ann. *See* pp. 48–51 for an account of his work.

Thorp, John (fl. 1706–28). Marble-cutter and supplier. Of Bakewell, Derbys. Gunnis records him working at Melbourne, Derbys. (1706); Castle Howard (1711–12); Knowsley, Lancs. (1721); Bramham, Yorks. (1727). I have noted the following: Beverley, Yorks., Sir

Charles Hotham's house (1717), Georgian Soc., E.R. Yorks., IV, 1956–8; London, Harcourt House, Cavendish Square; Bramham, Yorks., Bingley Letter Book, 1727–8; York, Mansion House, marble table (1729), York Reference Library, Mansion House, Chamberlain's List.

Thrisk, Henry (fl. 1692–1729). Carver from York. Freeman 1692. Mansion House, York (1729), 'four Corinthian capitals at 15s a pair £3.' York Reference Library, Mansion House, Chamberlain's List.

Tijou, Jean (late 17th cent.–*c.* 1712). Wrought-iron smith. Worked extensively at Hampton Court, St Paul's Cathedral and at country commissions such as Ampthill, Kiveton, Chatsworth, etc. *See* p. 37 for an account of his work. M. Ayrton and A. Silcock, *Wrought Iron and its Decorative Use*, 1929; J. Harris, *English Decorative Ironwork*, 1610–1836 (1960); *Survey of London*, XXIX–XXX.

Tilston, Thomas (fl. 1760–70). Decorative smith. Worked at many Robert Adam designed houses providing staircase balustrades, etc. These included 20, St James's Square, Kedleston and Shardeloes. He is frequently mentioned in the architect's bank account (Drummonds); *Connoisseur Yearbook*, 1959; National Library of Wales, Williams-Wynne Archives; Bucks. Co. Record Office, Shardeloes Archives, 1763 (received £44 2s.).

Timbrell, Benjamin (–1754): Carpenter. Worked principally with James Gibbs, and, with Thomas Phillips, did the structural woodwork, St Martin-in-the-Fields, at a charge of £5,615. Colvin. He had a bank account at Drummonds and appears frequently in the account of James Gibbs at the same bank.

Tobin, Maurice (fl. 1762). Wrought-iron worker. York, Fairfax House (1762), railings, Yorks. Arch. Soc., Newburgh archives, 21.8.1762.

Tushaine, – (early 18th cent.). Carver. Castle Howard (1706), House Archives, Masons' and Carpenters' Book, 1702–8.

Verhuyck, – (early 18th cent.). Carver. Elizabeth Verhuyck claimed £136 in 1709, on behalf of her late husband, for work he had done at Boughton, Northants., and Montagu House, London. Boughton Archives, Executors Accounts, 1st Duke of Montagu.

Warren, John (late 17th–early 18th cent.). Wrought-iron worker. Denham Place, Bucks. (1692–4), *Records of Bucks*, XVI, Pt. 3, 1957–8, p. 196; possibly the John Warren who provided gates at Clare College, Cambridge (1713–14), R. Lister, *Decorative Wrought Ironwork*, 1960, pp. 115–20. The attributions to him in Ayrton and Silcock, *op. cit.*, are ambitious and we know that work at Arbury is by Foljambe (q.v.). J. Harris, *op. cit.*, makes the reasonable suggestion that as Warren worked under William Stanton at Denham he may have done so at Belton, Lincs., where Stanton was mason-contractor under (possibly) William Winde. Other smiths who worked with Warren at Denham were Daniel Byfield, Zach. Godmin, and Henry Truman.

Wateridge, John (fl. 1770–80). Painter and gilder. Alnwick Castle, Northumberland (*c.* 1770), gilding ornaments in Chapel. '2/9d by the square foot', and received £665 1s. 4d. Alnwick Castle MS U.I.46.

Watson, Samuel (1663–1715). Carver. Trained under Charles Okey (q.v.). His main activity was the wood-carving he carried out with others (mostly Young, Davis, Lobb) at Chatsworth. He probably worked at Melbourne (1706). His sketchbooks (apart from Chatsworth MSS) are in the Library of Derbyshire County Council (*C. Life*, 9th February, 1951) and the Bodleian Library. Notes in the latter, kindly drawn to my attention by Mr John Harris, mention his fellow craftsmen, Lobb, Davis, and indicate ('February ye 16th? 1691/2), that he may have worked with them at Burghley House, Northants. The Ferrers monument at Tamworth, Staffs., is now thought to be a work of Grinling Gibbons rather than Samuel Watson. D. Green, *Grinling Gibbons*, 1964; F. Thompson, *A History of Chatsworth*, 1949; Gunnis.

Wilcox, Jonathan (late 17th cent.). Carpenter. Worked under Sir Christopher Wren, and Captain William Winde, Combe Abbey, Castle Bromwich, Warwicks, Colvin. Weston Hall, Staffs., Box 74, Winde letters.

Wilkes, John (died 1733). Locksmith from Birmingham. Living in the Old Square (No 9) from 1713 to 1733. As one of the best known of the late 17th-century locksmiths, Wilkes provided locks with elaborate mechanisms. These may be seen at Arbury, Warwicks., Stoneleigh, Warwicks., Victoria and Albert Museum. He provided locks (now lost) at Weston Underwood, Bucks., Sutton Scarsdale, Derbys., Castle Bromwich, Warwicks., and Worcester Guildhall. Joseph Hill and R. K. Dent, *Memoirs of the Old Square, Birmingham,*

1897; *C. Life*, 1920, pp. 705–7. Worcester City Archives, Guildhall Accounts, 16.9.1725.

Woodward, Francis (fl. 1701–3). Carver. Cambridge, Christ's College (1701–3), received £145, *C. Life*, 2nd May, 1936. A Thomas Woodward did ornamental carving in the Chapel, St Catherine's College, Cambridge (dedicated 1st September, 1704). Aymer Vallance, *Greater English Church Screens*, p. 135.

Wragg, Thomas (mid 18th cent.). Wrought-iron worker. Oxford, Radcliffe Camera. Rail for Great Staircase 'of best Swedish Iron according to a drawing of the said Mr Gibbs'. *Oxford Hist. Soc.*, 1958, p. 60.

Wyatt, Edward (1757–1833). Carver and gilder. Worked at Windsor Castle and Carlton House. *c.* 1808, Gunnis.

Yates, Benjamin (*c.* 1736–59). Wrought-iron worker. Assistant to Robert Bakewell (q.v.). Okeover Hall, Staffs. (1736–49 and 1756–9). After Bakewell's death in 1752 he supplied gates and railings for which he received £69. Okeover Archives, Book of Bills, I, 3–5. Transcripts by Mrs L. E. Tanner.

In 1752 at Robert Bakewell's death Yates took over the business. He advertised in the *Derby Mercury*, 1st December, 1752:

> Benjamin Yates, Irongate Smith, who served an apprenticeship, and was after, for upwards of twenty years, Foreman to the late ingenious Mr Robert Bakewell, of the same business, in Derby, deceased, Hereby gives notice, that he intends to carry on the said business at his new built shop in the Wardwick, near St Werburg's Church in Derby, where any gentleman may have iron gates, pallisadoes, &c., for gentlemen's seats, and other public buildings; with all the several branches thereof, performed in the compleatest manner; as was done during the lifetime of his master. By their Humble Servant, B. Yates.

Young, Thomas (late 17th cent.). Carver from London. Worked with Davis, Lobb and Watson at Chatsworth. Young acted as master carver until 1692. After that date the other three signed a new agreement. F. Thompson, *A History of Chatsworth*, 1949, pp. 149-50.

Some Specimen Costs of Interior Decoration in the Eighteenth Century

There is, as yet, no general economic history of the country house which takes full account of research in libraries, record offices or bank archives. The following studies give some help for the eighteenth-century period.

Ashton, T. S., *Economic Fluctuations in England, 1700–1800*, 1959.

Clifton-Taylor, Alec., *The Pattern of English Building*, 1962.

Habbakuk, J. H., 'The building of Burley on the Hill, 1694–1708', in *Studies in Social History presented to G. M. Trevelyan*, ed. J. H. Plumb, 1955.

Jenkins, Frank, *Architect and Patron*, 1961.

Summerson, Sir John, "The Classical Country House in 18th Century England', Cantor Lectures, 1959. Royal Society of Arts, *Journal*, July, 1959, pp. 539–87.

In the early eighteenth century it was still customary either to employ a builder directly on time rates, contract with a builder to build at a fixed rate, or arrange with the craftsmen to do specified work at an agreed rate for a basic measurement, such work often being independently assessed. The architect usually agreed the bills submitted by these men. Some examples are given below.

General Costs
1694–1704

Kiveton, Yorkshire. Architect: William Talman.
Building, 1694–1704. Demolished *c.* 1812.

	£ s. d.		£ s. d.
'Plaster	167.11.11	Whitesmith	277.10. 5
Painter	72.18. 6½	Bricklayers	795. 0. 5½
Mason		Masons	207. 2. 9
[Joshua Arnold: he also worked		Carpenters	434.15. 2
at Chatsworth]	361. 4. 0	Levelings	408. 0. 4

Appendix II

	£ s. d.		£ s. d.
Masons	1330.14. 5	Draughts	784. 0. 1
Plumber	153. 7. 3	Blacksmith	193. 7. 0
Joyners	261. 3. 1		
Ropes &c.	103. 7. 1	The main craftsmen employed received nearly £5000.	
Bricks	389. 6. 9		
Timber bought	149.18. 0	Surveyor Contractor (Daniel Brand	
Slitting stone	253.10. 6	and his son Daniel)	2693.16.11
Deales & slitting	255.14. 7	House-Painting (Thomas Highmore)	144.16. 8
Leade	1092. 0.10	History Paintings (Louis Laguerre)	279. 7. 3
Paviers	133. 6. 0	Wood-Carving (Jonathan Maine)	103.16. 0
Iron	349.10.10	Plasterer (Henry Margetts)	375.16. 6
Labourers	1551. 6. 7	Ironwork (Jean Tijou)	206. 6. 0
Crown Glass	47. 1. 0	Joinery (John Chaplin)[1]	706.14. 8
Window Locks	36. 0. 0	Stone-Cutter (James Hardy)	130. 4. 6.'

Total expenditure on the house in its eight years of building amounted to £15,028 18s. 6d.

Lit.: Yorks. Arch. Soc. Library, Duke of Leeds MSS, Boxes 3, 16, 32, 33 give most of the relevant documentation. The Laguerre contract (Box 13, item 20) was published in *Burl. Mag.*, November, 1956. *See* also G. W. Beard, *Leeds Arts Calendar*, No 46–7, 1961.

EARLY 18TH CENTURY

'Prices of building att Wrest in Bedfordshire, Duke of Kent.

	£ s. d.		£ s. d.
Bricks p. 1000	0.12. 0	Bringing home p. 100.	0.15. 0
Carriage, 300 at a load	0. 1. 0	Wainscott. p. ft. 2 inch.	0. 0. 5
Lime p. quarter	0. 2. 6	Do 1 inch	0. 0. 3
Carriage of 40 Bushells	0. 1. 6	Painting p. yard	0. 0. 8
Stone for foundations p. Load	0. 1. 6	Laths p. 100	0. 1. 0
Carriage p. Load	0. 1. 6	Lath Nails p. 1000	0. 1. 8
Stone from Ketton p. ft.	0. 1. 6	Nails for boarding,	
Carriage from Bedford p. Tunn	0. 8. 0	under ye Lead ¼ of a	
Timber. p. ft.	0. 0.10	thousand to a square	0. 1. 3
Bringing home 50 foot		Nails for frameing p. square	0. 0. 4
in a Load at 1d p. foot.	0. 4. 2	Do for flooring	0. 0.10
Sand p. Load.	0. 1. 0	Do. and glue for	
Lead. p. including all Expences	12. 0. 0	wainscoting. p. yard	0. 0. 1
Running & laying p. ft.	0. 1. 8	Hair p. Bushel	0. 0.10
Deal Boards p. 100.	7. 0. 0	glazeing p. foot	0. 0.11
Do. White for panelling	4.10. 0	Stone pavement.	
Do. fine boards.	10. 0. 0	p. ft.	0. 0. 7'

Lit.: Noted *c.* 1706 by Thomas Coke of Melbourne in Derbyshire (House Archives, Garden Notebook). Both Thomas Archer and Giacomo Leoni worked for the Duke of Kent. Coke was building at Melbourne about 1708.

[1] John Chaplin's staircase is incorporated in Broomhead Hall, Penistone, Yorks., a house built in 1831. It was presumably bought at the demolition sale about 1812.

1742

Henry Pelham's house, Arlington Street, London.
Architect: William Kent.

		£	s.	d.
Bricklayer	(Ralph Crutcher)	2,228	7	4
Carpenter	(John Richardson)	481	0	0
Mason	(Joseph Pickford)	1,622	0	10
Joiner	(John Marsden)	2,798	3	9
Slater	(Richard Hughes)	106	15	2
Plumber	(John Devall)	582	6	10
Glaziers	(Richard Minns and Richard Cobbet)	140	0	0
Smiths	(Jos. Pattinson, William Alexander, Christopher Martin, Benjamin Holmes)	787	4	4¾
Plasterer	(Robert Dawson)	779	13	0
Carvers	(James Richards and William Barlow)	211	8	6
Paviors	(Edward Mist, Andrew Jackson and John Wilkins)	87	12	0
Painters	(John Jones and Thomas Abbot)			
Gilder	(James Neale)			
Measured by	Stephen Wright.			

The main building cost £13,269 5s. and £3,048 0s. 8d. was spent on an additional structure. Fitting up a kitchen and various minor works (£988 4s. 7d.) brought the total to £17,305 10s. 3d.

Lit.: R.I.B.A. Library MS 728.3 (42.13A).

c. 1765–8

Kedleston, Derbyshire. Architect: Robert Adam for remodelling of earlier plans.
Abstract of expenditure.

	£	s.	d.
Bricklayers	2,685	12	0
Masons (Joseph Hall and Francis Battersby)	6,596	1	0
Slaters (Pratt & Co.)	344	18	0
Glaziers (Joseph Taylor and William Cobbett)	477	10	11½
Copper Smith, etc., and skylight (William Kinsman)	307	0	0
Plumbers	1,354	4	6
Painter (Thomas Smith)	113	17	0
Carpenters/Joiners	5,104	8	0
Plasterers (Abraham Denston [plain] Joseph Rose and Co. [decorative])	1,520	12	0
Ironmongers & Smiths work	478	12	0
Carvers (Joshua Hall and George Moneypenny)	2,501	3	0
Chimney-pieces to 4 Rooms (Joseph Pickford and Michael Spang)	990	0	0

Sundries brought the total to £22,508 9s. 4¼d.

Lit.: Kedleston Archives, 1765, Account Book, 3R.

Appendix II

Plasterwork

1689

Castle Bromwich Hall, Warwickshire. Plasterer: Edward Goudge. Architect: Captain William Winde.
'Sʳ John Bridgeman's bill for Plasterers worke this year done by Edward Goudge'
'Octob. 21.1689.

For makeing two frett ceillings in the Parlor and Chamber over itt p. agreement	50. 00. 00
To be allowed towards travelling charges	02. 00. 00
For makeing A midle paine molding enriched in the Chamber over the Parlor and makeing braces between the spandrills, which was more than my bargaine by my Ladys orders	02. 00. 00
for makeing two Coates of Armes in ye Shields yt were in ye Parlor Ceilling which was more than my bargaine by Sʳ John's orders	01. 00. 00
for plastering ye back Stairecase and Seller Ceilling and ye Staircase by agreement	07. 00. 00
for 83 yards & 7 foot of whitenge frett worke in ye Dineing roome at 9d p. yard	03. 02. 10
for 38 yards & 6 foot of whiteing frett worke in the Staire case at 9d p. yard	01. 09. 00
for 97 yards of floating in ye great Staire case at 12d p. yard	04. 17. 02
for 134 yards of plastering in ye passage comeing into ye great Starecase & Clossett and partition in ye great Chamber and partition in ye great Chamber and partition in ye Great Parlor at 6d p. yard	03. 07. 03
for ye frett Ceilling in ye halfpiece of ye great Stares	03. 10. 00
for 48 pound of white Kidds hair at 6d p. pound	01. 04. 00
for one new sack. 2s. 6d. & another 1s. 4d.	00. 03. 10
for Wateridge & Portridge twice to fetch the white hair out of Southwark and sending it to the Carryers	00. 03. 00
for 137 yards of whitening in the Porch and Hall at 2d p. yard by agreement	01. 02. 10
	80. 19. 11
Remains due from last years accompt	2. 0. 0
June ye 29th 1691. this bill being notified comes to	82. 19. 11'

Lit.: Earl of Bradford's Archives, Weston Hall, Staffs., Box 86; G. W. Beard, *C. Life*, 12th October, 1951, p. 1157; 9th May, 1952.

187

1725

Ditchley, Oxfordshire
'The Italian Plaisterer's Account for
worke done by them in severall rooms att Ditchley
By Agreement.'
'Imp. For doing the Basso relieves in the Hall & the
Brast heads with the flowers in the four corners

of the ceiling	£26.	5.	0. [Fig. 34]
for the 9 Bustos	16.	16.	0.
for finishing the Salloon entirely	105.	0.	0.
For doing the six Images over the pediments	21.	0.	0.
For doing the four eagles in the Hall	4.	4.	0.
For the four roses in the ceiling	2.	2.	0.
For the Festoons under the Bustos	10.	10.	0.
For doing the Drawing roome ceiling	15.	15.	0.'

Lit.: Oxford County Record Office, Dillon MSS I/p/3h.

1747

Blair Atholl, Perthshire. Plasterer: Thomas Clayton. [Fig. 84]
'Estimate of prices of stucco work and plaster work to his Grace
the Duke of Athol &c. Your Grace furnishing Lime, hare, sand
and scafolds and all Carridges.

By Thos. Clayton, July 17th 1747'
'To Comon plaster at 3 pence per yard
To plane Stucco or hand finishing at 10 pence per yard
To plane Stucco or hand finishing with panells at 16 pence per yard
To plane Cornices at 6 pence per foot
To Cornices with 2 Inrichments at 14 pence per foot
To Cornices with 3 Inrichments at 18 pence per foot
To Ionick Cornices full Inriched at 3 Sh. per foot
To Corinthian Cornices full Inriched at 4 Sh. pr. foot
I furnishing Stucco for Ionick and Corinthian Cornices.'

Lit.: Blair Atholl MSS 40 II D.(4)34. There is an extensive Clayton 'archive' at this house showing that he did
work almost to the value of £2,000, 1747–56.

1766–70

Harewood House, Yorkshire. Work by Joseph Rose, senior and junior.
Rose received in all £2,829 17s. 0d. The account is signed as examined by Robert Adam and by Joseph Rose
junior 'for the use of my uncle Joseph Rose' on 7th August, 1770. It reads:

'Stucco work done for Edward Lascelles Esq. p. Jos Rose.
Jan 24th 1766 to March 10 1770 vizt.

Dining room	224. 8.	224. 8
Musick room	130. 3.	
Add to ditto extra work not in the first Estimate viz	35. 5.	
ornament panels over two doors & two ditto next Picture Frames		165. 8.

188

Appendix II

Library		221. 9	
Great Hall		333 [Fig. 102]	
Great staircase		206	
Mr Lascelles			
Dressing Room	49		
Mr Lascelles			
Bedchamber	34	163	
Lady's dressing room	42		
Occasional Dressing or			
Lodging Room	38		
Study		53	
Portico ceiling		20. 10	
Circular room exclusive of glass frames		125. 0	
State bedchamber		128	
Principal Dressing room		152	
Ceiling & Cove of Salon	158		
Entablature & sides of ditto	167	325	
Drawing room next salon		171. 10	
Second or great drawing room		235	
Great Gallery		335	
		————	
		2858. 5	
Deduct from Honeysuckles in the			
Great Drawing room		8. 8	
from the Gallery the finishing over the			
Chimney not done		20. 0	
		————	
		28. 8.	
		2829. 17.	
		————	
By cash on acct recd of		2085. 13. 0	
Mr Popplewell			
1770. July 13. By Mr			
Lascelles Draught		300.	
		————	
		2385. 13.	
	Ballance	444. 4	
		————	
		2829. 17. '	
		————	

Lit.: Harewood House, Rose sketchbook. A quotation of 1775 from the correspondence between the Jesuit, Father Thorpe, and Lord Arundell shows the use of Italians: 'They [English plasterers] certainly work very well in stucco yet they now offer a young [Italian] lad £300 p.an. and all expenses of journey diet and lodging, if he will agree to work stucco in England for five years.' I am indebted to Mr Howard Colvin for drawing my attention to this reference, and to Mr. R. J. R. Arundell for permission to publish it.

Bibliography

MANUSCRIPT SOURCES

1. BRITISH MUSEUM

Additional Manuscripts

41133–36	Sir William Chambers: Letter books, 4 vols.
23218	Conway-Walpole letters, Artari at Ragley.
18238–48	Harley-Oxford material, William Thomas's notebooks.
33442	Newcastle House, Nottingham Castle, etc., Joiner's accounts, 1715–19, etc.
22241 & 22257–62	Strafford material, relating to Wentworth Castle, Yorks.

2. PUBLIC RECORD OFFICE

C104/97	Commissioners for rebuilding town and Church at Warwick.
E190, 340–8	Kingston-upon-Hull Port Books. Useful for ascertaining goods from Holland and Scandinavia entering Yorkshire for use in building and decoration.
S.P. Foreign 99/68–69	Lord Northampton's Embassy to Venice, 1762–3. Accompanied by Richard Bagot and James Wyatt. (*See* p. 92).
Works, E351/3276; 3293–3302; 6/9–10; 6/11–13	Useful for details of expenditure on royal residences and for names of craftsmen, prices, etc.

2. BANKS

Of recent years research in bank archives (many banks have appointed archivists) has become a recognised feature of, at least, economic historians' monographs. Such material has been less used by the art and architectural historian. Dr Kenneth Garlick and Mr Alastair Smart in their respective studies of Sir Thomas Lawrence and Allan Ramsay, the late Mrs M. I. Webb in research on Henry Cheere, and Dr Percy Young on Handel, are exceptions which come readily to mind. A detailed study of the ways the archives may be used in providing information of use for such a book as this is badly needed – ideally one must be economist and art historian. I have therefore here given full notes in the hope they may assist future researchers. My selection was admittedly personal and I have long lists of untraced accounts or of those which do not start in time to record the income and expenditure when building and decoration were in hand. At best such records are a substitute, to be sparingly used, and too much must not be read into them.

For general information see: F. G. Hilton Price, *Handbook of London Bankers*, 1890; D. M. Joslin, 'London Private Bankers, 1720–85', *Economic History Review*, Vol. VII, 1954, No 2, pp. 167–86; Histories of most banks are available and are noted under each entry below. They usually only mention a few important accounts.

THE BANK OF ENGLAND

Ledgers, and indexes to account-holders, 1694 onwards. The names of payees are not recorded as regularly as in some bank records, but the income side is useful for indicating the amount in an account at a time when the patron was building. The accounts of many Directors of the South Sea Company (and that of the Company itself) are preserved. These include Sir John and Sir Francis Eyles, Sir Theodore Janssen and Sir James Bateman.

Janssen employed Colin Campbell in building at Wimbledon, Surrey, in 1720. His account on 21st May, 1720, held £117,390 6s. 8d. (ledger 45, 1718–20).

Other accounts noted included the East India Company, Lord Foley, George Frederic Handel, the Earl of Hertford, William Pitt, and a John, Robert, James and William Adam joint account, 1770–80.

Bibliography

Lit.: Sir John Clapham, *The Bank of England*, 1944; 'The Private Business of the Bank of England, 1744–1800', *Economic History Review*, Vol. XI, 1941, pp. 77–89.

BARCLAYS, GOSLINGS BRANCH

Goslings Bank was established in 1650 and amalgamated with Messrs Barclay and Co. (as it then was) in 1896. Its earliest ledger is dated 1714. There are abstract books, 1750 onwards, which provide a quick means of ascertaining what accounts were held. These include:

Thomas Anson (1750, Shugborough)
Trustees for Blandford Fire (1731–6)
Thomas Bromwich (paper-hanger and supplier, 1767)
John Carr (?the architect), 1780
Thomas Carter (sculptor, 1750)
Earl of Derby (Knowsley in an earlier account at Drummonds)
Henry Holland Snr. and Jnr. (architects, 1761–80)
Sir Justinian Isham (Lamport)
Earl of Oxford, as Executor, Duke of Leeds (Hornby Castle, 1730)
Simon Pantin (silversmith, 1721–)
Nicholas, Earl of Scarsdale (Sutton Scarsdale, *see* p. 28)
Bowater Vernon (occasional payments to John Vanderbank, the tapestry weaver)
Earl of Westmorland (contains no material relevant to the building of Mereworth, *see* p. 32 fn. 3)

MESSRS COUTTS AND CO.

Founded *c.* 1692. A Royal account since 1716, and regularly since the time of George III. Political and literary figures banked here including Chatham, William Pitt the younger, Fox, Grenville, James Boswell, Sheridan, Sir Joshua Reynolds, Sir Thomas Lawrence and Fanny Burney.

I examined the account of James Paine, senior, the architect, 1761–85. His son's account is also here.
Income

1761:	£1,192 6s. 0d.	1763:	£1,694 16s. 7d.
1765:	£1,524.	1766:	£3,442 18s. 10d.
1768:	£9,561 6s. 6d.	1769:	£8,343.
1771:	£13,890 7s. 7d.	1773:	£9,128 14s. 3d.
1775:	£3,923.	1785:	£2,646 and £4,000.

Payments are made to William Atkinson (mason); Thomas Blockley (locksmith); Thomas Bromwich (paper-hanger); Henry Cheere (sculptor); Francis Engleheart (plasterer); Henry Holland (architect, two payments, 1772); William Kinman (copper-smith); George Richardson (plasterer); Joseph Rose (plasterer); Joseph Wilton (sculptor).

GLYN MILLS AND CO., CHILD'S BRANCH

Ledgers survive from the 1660s to 1733, after which date none seems to exist until modern times. The Child's ledgers are unusually full for the late seventeenth century, the clerk on many occasions recording the occupations of payees. I examined the following accounts. That marked ★ contains no information about craftsmen.

Duke of Ancaster
Duke of Beaufort (formerly as Marquess of Worcester, Badminton, 1660–). Payments to craftsmen, including Grinling Gibbons
Duke of Bedford
Duke of Bolton
★Sir John Brownlow (Belton, 1677–86)
Duke of Buckingham (opens 12th October, 1706, with a payment of £230 to Louis Laguerre, decorative painter)
Duke of Bridgewater
Duke of Devonshire
Earl of Dorset
Marquess of Exeter (Burghley, 1678–1700). Payments to craftsmen. See Dictionary entries under Maine, Margetts, and D. Green, *Grinling Gibbons*, 1964, p. 112
Earl of Kingston
1st Duke of Leeds (Kiveton)
Leigh family (Stoneleigh, eight accounts, but not Edward, 3rd Lord, employer of Francis Smith, *see* p. 28)
1st Duke, and Sarah, Duchess of Marlborough (Blenheim)
Robert Harley, Earl of Oxford
Duke of Rutland (Belvoir)
6th Duchess of Somerset (Petworth)
Sir Rowland Winn (Nostell, 1714–32, 1749–55)

Lit.: Roger Fulford, *Glyn's 1753–1953*, 1953.

HOARE AND CO., LTD.

Founded in 1672. Ledgers survive from 1673. Modern card-index to accounts held. I noted the following accounts. Those marked ★ provide no information about craftsmen at the time of building.

Robert Benson, Lord Bingley (Bramham, *see* p. 48)
★William Blathwayt (Dyrham)
1st Duke of Bolton (another account at Child's)

James Brydges, 1st Duke of Chandos (another account at Drummonds)

Duke of Buckingham (1714)

Earl of Burlington (1717)

*3rd Earl of Carlisle (Castle Howard)

2nd and 3rd Earls of Clarendon

*Spencer Compton, Lord Wilmington (Compton Place, *see* p. 32)

Lord Conway, and Earl of Hertford (Ragley)

Sir James Dashwood (Kirtlington, 1740–50). Payments to Thomas Blockley (locksmith), Henry Cheere and Thomas Hinchcliff (sculptors), and William Smith, architect. (*See* p. 34)

*Thomas, 2nd Baron Foley (Great Witley)

Countess of Home (payments to Joseph Rose and others re 20, Portman Square)

George, 1st Lord Lyttelton (Hagley), *see* p. 64.

*Ralph, 1st Duke of Montagu (Boughton)

William Murray, 1st Earl of Mansfield (Kenwood, 1769–72). Payments to Robert Adam, John Devall (mason), William France (cabinet-maker), John Phillips (carpenter), Joseph Rose (plasterer), Antonio Zucchi (decorative painter)

Earl of Nottingham (Burley-on-the-Hill, 1697)

Francis Smith (architect, see p. 28). 1733–8. William Smith as executor £50 payment (5th February, 1734) to William Wilton, sculptor. Balance of £3,664 in 1736

6th Duke of Somerset (Petworth)

William Stanton (sculptor)

Richard Symes (? joiner)

*Thomas Vernon (Hanbury)

Sir John Wentworth (1715)

Thomas Wentworth (1698)

> *Lit.:* A list of important accounts held, 1673–1718, is given in *Hoare's Bank, A Record, 1672–1955* (1955).

MARTIN'S BANK

Early ledgers are lacking. The 1726–31 Letter Book shows that Colonel Fane, later Earl of Westmorland, for whom Colin Campbell designed Mereworth, Kent (1723–4) had money in South Sea and East India Company stock.

ROYAL BANK OF SCOTLAND, DRUMMONDS BRANCH

The founder, Andrew Drummond, carried on a business from about 1697 onwards amongst Jacobite refugees in Amsterdam. The ledgers survive from 1717.

The most important accounts to the art historian are those of:

Robert Adam (architect, 1764, checked to 1771 only)

Matthew Brettingham (architect, noted 1775)

Lancelot 'Capability' Brown (landscape gardener and architect, noted 1760. Very full account)

William Chambers and Thomas Collins in partnership. Continued by Sir William Chambers (architect)

Sir Henry Cheere (sculptor, very full account)

Thomas Chippendale (cabinet-maker, 1770, very small account)

Giovanni Battista Cipriani (decorative painter, noted 1775, small account)

John Cobb (cabinet-maker, noted 1770. Balance of £16,564 19s. 10d. Out payments mainly 'to bearer', some to William Hallett the cabinet-maker)

Nicholas Dubois (architect, noted 1725)

Henry Flitcroft (architect, noted 1742)

James Gibbs (architect, 1723–54, full account)

John Hobcraft (carpenter-builder, noted 1770–80)

Henry Keene (architect, noted 1755, full account)

Giacomo (James) Leoni (architect, noted 1738–9, small account)

John Phillips (carpenter, noted 1720, account includes payments to James Gibbs)

Joseph Rose (plasterer, 1770 only, 1765 at Hoare's)

Louis François Roubiliac (sculptor, 1752–62).

Benjamin Timbrell (carpenter, noted 1726, 1745)

Harman Verelst (painter, noted 1745, small account)

The following accounts were also examined and the first year of appearance recorded.

Duke of Atholl (noted 1725)

Richard Bagot (as executor to the Earl of Northampton, 1763–5, see p. 92)

Lord Bathurst (noted 1740, payment of £90 to Alexander Pope)

Lord Bolingbroke (noted 1750)

Sir Henry Bridgeman (noted 1770)

James Brydges, 1st Duke of Chandos (1725–, full account)

Duke of Buccleuch (noted 1750)

Earl of Chesterfield (noted 1740)

Earl of Denbigh (noted 1750)

Sir Lawrence Dundas (noted 1763–71, very full account)

Sir Joseph Eyles (noted 1728)

Foundling Hospital (noted 1760)
Earl of Halifax (noted 1740)
William Hamilton (noted 1740)
Lord William Hay (noted 1725)
Earl of Jersey (noted 1750)
John Patoun (author, friend of James Thomson, noted 1750)
Alexander Pope (noted 1731–8, small account)
Duke of Queensberry (noted 1725, but this is too late for his employment in 1721 of Giacomo Leoni)
Earl of Stafford (noted 1755)
Earl of Stamford (noted 1755)
Horace Walpole (noted 1732)
William Wyndham (noted 1725)
Bartholomew Zollicoffre (Secretary to Duke of Chandos)

I did not examine the Scottish ledgers at the Royal Bank of Scotland (they survive for the period 1727–49) and the Bank of Scotland, both in Edinburgh. The latter also possesses records of its subsidiaries, the former Perth United (and later) Perth Banking Company and (since 1795) those of Sir William Forbes, James Hunter and Co.

Lit. History in progress, 1966, by Hector Bolitho.

4. COUNTRY HOUSES, LIBRARIES AND RECORD OFFICES

The main sources of documents useful to the art and architectural historian are those preserved in country houses, libraries and county record offices. Of recent years the long established function of the larger reference libraries acting as a regional 'record office' has been continued with the establishment by most County Councils of record offices with trained archivists in charge. The deposits therein are eventually listed, and copies of the inventories are circulated, and in addition centrally filed by the National Register of Archives. Several offices have published detailed guides to their collections. I have used the following collections in assembling the material incorporated in the Dictionary of Craftsmen.

HOUSES

Boughton, Northants.	Montagu manuscripts, inventories of Montagu House, Executors' accounts of 1st Duke of Montagu.
Castle Howard, Yorks.	Building Books, and Bills, early 18th century (*see* p. 45).
Compton Place, Box P. (*see* p. 31). Sussex.	
Dyrham, Gloucs.	Blathwayt manuscripts, BB5 and BB13.
Enville, Staffs.	Stamford manuscripts.
Hagley, Worcs.	Lyttelton manuscripts.
Melbourne, Derbys.	Coke manuscripts.
Okeover, Staffs.	Leak Okeover manuscripts, 1740–50 (*see* p. 39).
Petworth, Sussex.	Late seventeenth- and early eighteenth-century account rolls.
Studley Royal, Yorks.	Aislabie manuscripts, Parcel 286, and Robinson letters.
Weston Hall, Staffs.	Bridgeman manuscripts, Letters of Captain William Winde.

LIBRARIES AND RECORD OFFICES

Ashmolean Museum, Oxford. Gibbs drawings.
Birmingham Reference Library. Gough, Hagley Hall (Lyttelton) and Hanbury Hall manuscripts.
Bodleian Library, Oxford. Gough collections.
Buckinghamshire C.R.O. (Aylesbury). Shardeloes manuscripts.
Essex C.R.O. (Chelmsford). Moulsham, Petre.
Hereford Public Library. Bateman (Shobdon) manuscripts.
Kent C.R.O. (Maidstone), Cobham, Westmorland.
Lancashire C.R.O. (Preston). Derby (Knowsley), Lilford (Atherton), Towneley (Towneley Hall).
Leeds Reference Library, Battie-Wrightson; Lane-Fox (Bramham); Newby Hall; Temple Newsam.
Leeds, Yorkshire Archaeological Society Library. Duke of Leeds, Newburgh, Thoresby manuscripts.
Lincolnshire C.R.O. (Lincoln). Monson, Redbourne, Thorold manuscripts.
London, Guildhall Library. Livery Company Records.
London, Royal Institute of British Architects. Somerset House manuscripts.
London, Society of Antiquaries. Prattinton manuscripts.
London, Victoria and Albert Museum. Hoare, Osterley manuscripts.
Middlesex C.R.O. (London). Earl of Jersey manuscripts.
Northamptonshire C.R.O. (Northants.). Isham, Fitzwilliam (Milton) manuscripts.
Oxfordshire C.R.O. (Oxford). Dillon manuscripts.
Sheffield, Reference Library, Fitzwilliam (Wentworth Woodhouse), Spencer Stanhope manuscripts.

Staffordshire C.R.O. (Stafford). Bagot, Shrewsbury (Alton Towers).

Stratford-upon-Avon, Shakespeare's Birthplace Trust. Leigh manuscripts.

Warwickshire C.R.O. (Warwick.). Hertford, Sanderson Miller, Newdegate manuscripts.

Worcestershire C.R.O. (Worcester). Berrington manuscripts.

York, Minster, Library. Manuscripts of Livery Companies (BB5).

York, Reference Library. Apprenticeship Registers, Sessions Books, Assembly Rooms Building Books, Skaife manuscripts.

Yorkshire, East Riding C.R.O. (Beverley). Chichester-Constable, Hotham.

Yorkshire, North Riding C.R.O. (Northallerton). Feversham (Duncombe Park).

PRINTED SOURCES (GENERAL)

Allsopp, Bruce, *Decoration and Furniture, The English Tradition*, 1952.

Architectural Publication Society *Dictionary of Architecture*. 6 vols. 1852–92. An important work despite its date.

Blunt, Sir Anthony, and Croft-Murray, Edward, *Venetian Drawings at Windsor Castle*, 1957. An important source for the careers of, in particular, Sebastiano and Marco Ricci, the Venetian decorative painters.

Campbell, Colin, *Vitruvius Britannicus*, Vol. 1, 1715; Vol. 2, 1717; Vol. 3, 1723. J. Woolfe and James Gandon published Vol. 4, 1767, and Vol. 5, 1771. A further two volumes by G. Richardson, with title *The new Vitruvius Britannicus* (1802–8).

Clifton-Taylor, Alec, *The Pattern of English Building*, 1962. This study analyses the use of all the traditional building materials. It is a reliable, well-documented and well-illustrated book.

Courtauld Institute of Art, University of London, *Annual bibliography of the history of British Art*. Vols. 1–6. 1934–1946–8. Classified bibliography with index at the end of each volume. Indexes some 160 periodicals.

Downes, Kerry, *English Baroque Architecture*, 1966

Dutton, Ralph, *The English Interior, 1500–1900*, 1948.

Fleming, John, *Scottish Country Houses and Gardens Open to the Public*, 1957.

Gotch, John Alfred, *The Growth of the English house from early feudal times to the close of the 18th century*. 2nd ed. revd. 1928.

Green, David, *Blenheim Palace*, 1951. The standard work on this Vanbrugh house.

Hussey, Christopher, *English Country Houses:*
    Early Georgian 1715–60, 1955.
    Mid Georgian 1760–1800, 1956.
A modern revision of *English Homes*, 1921–37. (*See* Tipping, H. A.)

Ison, W., *The Georgian Buildings of Bath*, 1948.
    The Georgian Buildings of Bristol, 1952.
Well-documented and well-illustrated studies.

Jourdain, Margaret, *English Interior Decoration, 1500–1830*, 1950.

— with Soame Jenyns, R., *Chinese Export Art in the Eighteenth Century*.

Kaufmann, E., *Architecture in the Age of Reason*, Baroque and Post-Baroque in England, Italy and France, Harvard. 1955.

Lenygon, F. (pseud.) [i.e. Jourdain, Margaret],
    The Decoration and Furniture of English Mansions during the 17th and 18th Centuries, 1909.
    Decoration in England from 1660 to 1770, 1914. 2nd edition revised 1927, covers period 1640 to 1760.

Lewis, Mrs Lesley, 'The architects of the chapel at Greenwich Hospital.' *Art Bulletin*, Dec, 1947, XXIX, pp. 260–7.

Lloyd, Nathaniel, *A history of the English house from primitive times to the Victorian period*. 2nd edn. Text divided by centuries. Illustrations arranged according to type, windows, staircases, etc.

London Topographical Record, Vol. XIII, 1923, *The Pantheon*. A study of James Wyatt's important building.

MacGibbon, David, and Ross, Thomas, *The castellated and domestic architecture of Scotland from the twelfth to the eighteenth century*. 5 vols., 1887–92.

Mulliner, H. H., *The Decorative Arts in England during the late XVIIth and XVIIIth Centuries*, 1923.

Murray's Architectural Guides, ed. Betjeman, John, and Piper, John. Volumes published are
    Buckinghamshire
    Berkshire
    Lancashire by Fleetwood-Hesketh, P.
    Oxfordshire

Musgrave, Clifford, *Royal Pavilion* [Brighton], 1959.

Nares, Gordon, *Royal Homes*, 1953. Describes and illustrates seven Royal Homes. The greater part of the work portrays Buckingham Palace and Windsor Castle.

Pain, William and James, *Decorative details of the eighteenth century . . .* reprinted with a preface by A. E. Richardson, 1946.

Richardson, Sir A. E., *An Introduction to Georgian Architecture*, 1949.

Royal Commission on Historical Monuments. Inventories: Bucks 2 v. Cambridge 2 v. Dorset 1 v. Essex 4 v. Herefs 3 v. Herts 1 v. Hunts 1 v. London 5 v. Middlesex 1 v. Oxford 1 v. Westmorland 1 v.

Sitwell, Sacheverell, *British Architects and Craftsmen 1600–1830*. 1st ed. 1945; many subsequent editions and reprints.

Smith, H. Clifford, *Buckingham Palace. Its Furniture, Decoration and History*, 1931.

Stratton, A., *The English Interior*. A Review of the Decoration of English Homes from Tudor times to the XIXth Century, 1920.

Summerson, Sir John, *Architecture in Britain 1530–1830*. (Pelican History of Art) 4th edn., 1963. Discusses all main workers and styles in authoritative terms.

Swan, Abraham, *Designs for Chimnies . . . also Variety of Arches, Doors and Windows*, 1765. Very rare. Copy in R.I.B.A. Library, London.

Thompson, Francis, *A History of Chatsworth*, 1949. The standard work, by the late Director of the Devonshire Collections, on this famous Derbyshire house.

Tipping, H. A., *English Homes*, 9 vols., 5,000 plates, numerous text illustrations, London, 1921–37.

This set consists of:
  Period I, Norman and Plantagenet, 1066–1484.
  Period II, Mediaeval and Early Tudor, 1484–1558.
  Period III, Late Tudor and Early Stuart, 1558–1649, 2 vols.
  Period IV, Late Stuart, 1649–1714, and Sir John Vanbrugh, 2 vols.
  Period V, Early Georgian, 1714–1760.
  Period VI, Late Georgian, 1760–1820.
  Period I and II, New Series, Mediaeval and Early Tudor, 1066–1558.

Waterhouse, E. K., *Painting in Britain 1530–1790* (Pelican History of Art, 1953).

Whiffen, Marcus, *Stuart and Georgian Churches outside London 1603–1837*, 1947.

Whinney, Margaret, and Millar, Oliver, *English Art, 1625–1714* (Oxford History of English Art, Vol. VIII, 1957). An invaluable and well-documented study.

Whitley, W. T.,
  Artists and their Friends in England 1700–99. 2 vols., 1928.
  Art in England, 1800–1820, 1928.
  Art in England, 1821–1837, 1930.

PRINTED SOURCES (SPECIAL TOPICS)

I. BIOGRAPHIES AND PORTRAITS

Benezit, E., *Dictionaire critique et documentaire des peintres, sculpteurs, dessinateurs et graveurs*, revd. edn. 8 vols. 1948–55.

Colvin, H. M., *A Biographical Dictionary of English Architects 1660–1840*, 1954.

Gunnis, Rupert, *Dictionary of British Sculptors, 1660–1851*, 1953.

Heal, Sir Ambrose, *The London Furniture Makers, 1660–1840*, 1953. A record of 2,500 cabinet-makers, upholsterers, carvers and gilders with their addresses and working dates.

Strickland, W. G., *A Dictionary of Irish Artists*, 2 vols., 1913. Includes 'every artist of any note who has worked in Ireland and those of Irish birth . . . who have followed their profession in England.'

Thieme, Ulrich, and Becker, Felix, *Allgemeines Lexikon der Bildenden Künstler von der Antike bis zur Gegenwart . . .* 37 vols., 1907–50. Supplement by Hans Vollmer, 6 vols., 1953–62. Good biographical dictionary of artists, decorators, etc.

Robert Adam (1728–92). Architect.
  Bolton, A. T., *The Architecture of Robert and James Adam*, 2 vols., 1922.
  Fleming, John, *Robert Adam and his Circle*, 1962.
  Lees-Milne, James, *The Age of Adam*, 1947.
  All three books are valuable. Bolton's contains hundreds of illustrations and contains a catalogue of the drawings in Sir John Soane's Museum. Fleming's book is the first volume of a careful study based on new information. Mr Lees-Milne provides a reliable overall study in convenient form. For portraits see *Architectural Review*, XCI, 1942.

Thomas Archer (?1668–1743). Baroque architect,
  Whiffen, Marcus, *Thomas Archer*, 1950.

Richard Boyle, 3rd Earl of Burlington (1694–1753). Architect.
  Harris, John, and Fraser, Prunella. A Catalogue of the Drawings of Inigo Jones, John Webb and Richard Boyle, 3rd Earl of Burlington, in the Burlington-Devonshire Collection. (R.I.B.A. Library, 1960)

Lees-Milne, James, *Earls of Creation*, Chapter 3, 1962.

Wittkower, R., 'Lord Burlington and William Kent'. *Archaeological Journal*, cii, 1945.

Portrait by George Knapton in the Devonshire Collections at Chatsworth.

Brydges, James, 1st Duke of Chandos. Patron.

Baker, C. H. Collins and M. I., *The Life and Circumstances of James Brydges, first Duke of Chandos*, 1949.

Colin Campbell (?–1729). Architect.

Stutchbury, H. E., unpublished Ph.D. thesis, University of Manchester, 1964.

Grinling Gibbons (1648–1720). Carver-sculptor.

Portraits: (a) By Sir Godfrey Kneller. Original at the Hermitage, ex Walpole Collection. Versions at National Portrait Gallery, Serlby Hall, Notts., Fairlawne, Kent. Engraved by J. T. Smith.

(b) By Sir John Medina. In red chalk (The British Museum). *Repr.:* Green, *op. cit.*, frontispiece.

(c) Grinling Gibbons and his wife, *c.* 1691. A 'lost' Closterman. Engraving survives.

Lit.: Baker, C. H. Collins, *Lely and the Stuart Portrait Painters*, vol. 2, p. 48.

'Gibbons's maternal ancestry,' *Notes and Queries*, September, 1943, p. 343.

Green, David, *Grinling Gibbons*, 1964. A well-illustrated study, with full bibliography and references. Two earlier books (1914), are Tipping, H. A., *Grinling Gibbons and the Woodwork of his Age*, and Bullock, A. E., *Grinling Gibbons and his Compeers*.

Whinney, Margaret, *Grinling Gibbons in Cambridge*, 1948.

James Gibbs (1682–1754). Architect.

Little, Bryan, *The Life and Works of James Gibbs*, 1955.

Portraits and busts: *see* Colvin, *op. cit.*, p. 230, and Little, *op. cit.*, frontispiece and p. 167.

Nicholas Hawksmoor (1661–1736). Architect.

Downes, Kerry, *Hawksmoor*, 1960. The standard work which lists other studies, and publishes all letters not given in *Walpole Society*, XIX, 1930–1.

Angelica Kauffmann (1741–1807). Decorative painter.

de Rossi, G. G., *Angelica Kauffmann* (Florence, 1810).

Hartcup, Adeline, *Angelica*, 1954.

Manners, Lady Victoria, and Williamson, G. C., *Angelica Kauffmann*, 1924.

Portrait: reproduced in this book, Fig. 110. By Nathaniel Dance. Oil on canvas, 30 × 25 in. Painted in Rome in 1764 when Dance was in love with Angelica.

Coll.: The Most Hon. The Marquess of Exeter. Exh: R.A., Winter, 1959–60 (126).

William Kent (1685/6–1748). Architect, decorative painter, landscape gardener.

Jourdain, Margaret, *The Work of William Kent*, 1948. Portrait by Luti at Chatsworth.

James Paine (*c.* 1716–89). Architect.

His own *Plans, Elevations and Sections of Noblemen and Gentlemen's Houses . . . executed in the counties of Derby, Durham, Middlesex, Northumberland, Nottingham and York*, 2 vols., 1767, 1783 (vol. 2).

Unpublished thesis on *James Paine the elder* by C. D. Ogden, University of London, 1951.

For portraits see the list in Colvin, pp. 430–1.

Joseph Rose, junior (1745–99). Plasterer. For an account of his career *see* p. 70.

Beard, G. W., 'A Family's 50-year Supremacy', *C. Life*, 8th December, 1960, pp. 1428–9.

'The Rose Family of Plasterers', *Leeds Arts Calendar*, No 54, 1964, pp. 6–16.

Portrait: self-portrait in crayons, 24 × 18 in., at Sledmere House, E.R. Yorks. Engraved, 1799, by Bartolozzi. The engraving is inscribed 'Joseph Rose Esqʳ/06 Feb. 11. 1799 AEtatis Suae 53./ From a Drawing in Crayons by himself/ In the Possession of Sir C. Sykes, Barᵗ'.

Sir John Vanbrugh (1664–1726). Architect.

Tipping, H. A., and Hussey, Christopher, *English Homes*, Period IV, Vol. 2. *The Works of Sir John Vanbrugh and his School, 1699–1736*, 1928.

Whistler, Laurence, *Sir John Vanbrugh*, 1938.

The Imagination of Vanbrugh and his fellow artists, 1954.

Nonesuch Press, *The Complete Works of Sir John Vanbrugh*. Vol. IV, the *Letters*, ed. Webb, Geoffrey, 1928.

Portraits: by Kneller and Closterman (National Portrait Gallery); by Jonathan Richardson (College of Arms).

2. SPECIAL TOPICS. METALWORK

Ayrton, Maxwell, and Silcock, Arnold, *Wrought Iron and its decorative use*, 1929. A comprehensive, well-illustrated book. Inevitably some of the attributions therein are now out of date.

Edwards, Ifor, 'A Midland Family of Gatesmiths' (the Paris family of Warwick), *C. Life*, 26th April, 1962.

'Robert Davies of Croes Foel', *Trans. Denbighs. Historical Soc.*, 6, 1957.

'Art in Iron', *ibid.*, 12, 1963.

'Robert Bakewell', *C. Life*, 27th September, 1962.

Ffoulkes, C. J., *Decorative Ironwork from the 11th to the 18th Centuries*, 1913. Lists smiths and ironworkers, pp. 141–4.

Gardner, John Starkie, *English ironwork of the XVIIth and XVIIIth Centuries*, 1911. Lists smiths and designers, pp. 321–23.

Gloag, John, and Bridgwater, Derek, *A History of Cast Iron in Architecture*, 1948.

Harris, John, *English Decorative Ironwork, 1610–1836*. A Collection of Drawings and Pattern Books, including A new Booke of Drawings by John Tijou 1693; A new Book of Iron Work by J. Jores 1756; The Smith's Right Hand by W. and J. Welldon 1765; A Book of Designs by J. Bottomley 1793; Ornamental Iron Work by I. and J. Taylor, *c.* 1795; etc. (1960).

In this work the author has assembled all the pattern books similar to Jean Tijou's work, all very rare today, to which he has added engravings from various other works and some original drawings. A comprehensive source-book to the subject.

Hoever, O., *Handbook of Wrought Ironwork from the Middle Ages to the end of the 18th Century*, 1962. Lavishly illustrated.

Lister, Raymond, *Decorative Wrought Ironwork in Great Britain*, 1960. Mr Lister is head of a specialist firm of smiths who have restored many fine gates. He writes with a good technical knowledge of the problems.
Decorative Cast Ironwork in Great Britain, 1963.

Weaver, Sir L., *English Leadwork, its Art and History*, 1909. Deals with external leadwork such as rain water heads, cisterns, etc., as well as Domes, Lanterns, Portrait Statues and Figures, Vases, Sepulchral Leadwork, etc.

3. SPECIAL TOPICS. PLASTERWORK

Ayscough, A., Jourdain, M., and Sitwell, S., *Country House Baroque*, 1940. Excellent detail photographs by Ayscough, an introduction by Sitwell and notes on the plates by Jourdain.

Bankart, G. P., *The Art of the Plasterer*, 1908.

Beard, Geoffrey,
'Italian Masters of Stucco', *C. Life*, 24th November, 1960.
'A family's 50 year supremacy' (the Rose family of Plasterers), *C. Life*, 8th December 1960.
'The Rose Family of Plasterers, with a catalogue of Yorkshire work', *Leeds Arts Calendar*, No 54, 1964.
'The Rose Family, with a catalogue of their work' *Apollo*, November, 1966.
'Italian Stuccoists in England' with a catalogue of their work', *Apollo*, July, 1964.

Curran, C. P., 'Dublin Plasterwork' in *Jnl. of the Royal Society of Antiquaries of Ireland*, Vol. LXX, Part 1, 1940.

Grandjean, B. L., 'L'Activité des Stucateurs Italiens, et Tessinois en Danemark, 1670–1770', *Arte e Artisti dei Laghi Lombardi*, II, 1964. A useful study showing work which would be known to Charles Stanley (*see* p. 32).

Jourdain, Margaret, *English Decorative Plasterwork of the Late Renaissance*, 1926.

Millar, W., *Plastering, Plain and Decorative*, 1897.

Murray, Peter, *Architettura Inglese e Stuccatori Italiani*, *Arte e Artisti dei Laghi Lombardi*, II, 1964.

Richardson, George, *A Book of Ceilings composed in the Style of the Antique Grotesque*, 1776.

Stebbing, W. P. D., 'The Adam brothers and their plaster', *R.I.B.A.*, *Journal*, 12th September, 1938, p. 991.

Thurston (A. P.), 'Parker's Roman Cement', *Trans. Newcomen Society*, XIX, 1938, pp. 193–206.

Turner, Laurence, *English Decorative Plasterwork*, 1927. Well illustrated, but the text has too many generalisations.

4. SPECIAL TOPICS. WOODWORK

Beard, Geoffrey, 'Georgian Woodcarvers', *C. Life Christmas Annual*, 1965.

Edwards, Ralph, and Jourdain, Margaret, *Georgian Cabinet-Makers* (1962 reprint of 3rd edn.).

For studies of *Grinling Gibbons* see section 1, p. 199.

Harris, Eileen, *The Furniture of Robert Adam*, 1963. Useful for the understanding of Adam's dealings with cabinet-makers.

Hayward, Helena, *Thomas Johnson and English Rococo*, 1964.

Joy, E. T., *The English Furniture Trade in the 18th century* (University of London M.A. thesis), 1955.

Jupp, E. B., *Historical Account of the Worshipful Company of Carpenters*, 1887.

Macquoid, P., and Edwards, Ralph, *Dictionary of English Furniture*, 3 vols. 1st edn., 1924. 2nd revd. edn., by Edwards, 1954. Shorter one-volume edn., 1965.

Morrell, J. B., *York Woodwork*.

Pinto, E. H., *The Craftsmen in Wood*, 1962.

Strange, T. A., *English Furniture, Decoration, Woodwork and Allied Arts*, 1950 reprint of 1910 edition, 3,500 illustrations.

Thorpe, W. A., 'The Sea and the Jungle in English Furniture', *Chartered Auctioneers and Estate Agents' Journal*, April, 1951. Contains useful information about the introduction and use of mahogany.

Victoria and Albert Museum, Catalogues of English Furniture and Woodwork, Vol. IV. Georgian.

Ward-Jackson, Peter, *English Furniture Designs of the Eighteenth Century*, 1958. An important, well-illustrated catalogue of drawings and pattern-books at the Victoria and Albert Museum.

5. SPECIAL TOPICS. OTHER FORMS OF INTERIOR DECORATION

Decorative Painting

Croft-Murray, Edward, *Decorative Painting in England, 1537–1837*. Vol. I, Early Tudor to Sir James Thornhill, 1962.

Vol. 2 (forthcoming) will deal with the Venetian painters in England, English artists throughout the 18th century and conclude at the nineteenth-century decoration of the Houses of Parliament.

The standard work, lavishly illustrated, with detailed catalogue of works.

Wallpaper

Entwistle, E. A., *A Literary History of Wallpaper*, 1960.

Jourdain, Margaret, 'Chinese paper-hangings', *C. Life*, 1st October, 1948, pp. 684–5.

Sugden, A. V., and Edmondson, J., *A History of English Wallpaper, 1509–1914*, 1925.

Miscellaneous

Godfrey, W. H., *The English Staircase*, 1911. An historical account of its characteristic types to the end of the eighteenth century.

Milton, T., Crunden, J., and Columbani, P., *The Chimney-Piece Maker's Daily Assistant, or a Treasury of New Designs for Chimney-Pieces*, 1766.

Richardson, George, *A new collection of Chimney-Pieces . . . 1781*.

Sekler, E. F., *The development of the British staircase*, University of London, Courtauld Inst., unpublished thesis, Misc/5.

'Shell Houses and Grottoes', *Notes and Queries*, 1942, various dates; *C. Life*, 11th February, 3rd March, 1944.

Wragg, R. B., 'Scagliola', *C. Life*, 10th October, 1957. An account of the use of the coloured plaster which imitates marble.

Index

Figures in parentheses relate to footnotes. Figures in bold type relate to plate numbers.

Index

Index

Index